Community Based Research in Sport, Exercise and Health Science

Community-based research has recently gained attention within the sport and exercise sciences. When seeking to understand community based research methodologies, one finds a diversity of approaches spanning a breadth of ontological views and equally diverse methodological approaches. Though little is known about community-based sport, exercise and physical activity research, these foci are beginning to gain scholarly attention, in part through the emerging sport for development and peace literature. This book features a conceptual introduction and eight pioneering examples of community-based research from North American, European, and Oceanic scholars. The topic matter reveals scholarship undertaken in relation to health, physical activity, youth sport, and elite sport, exemplifying work with mainstream and marginalized populations. This book, perhaps the first compilation of community-based research relating to sport, exercise and health, will be of interest to sociologists of sport, sport and exercise psychology scholars, sport management scholars, qualitative researchers, health scholars and practitioners, sport for development organizations, and research ready communities seeking to engage in localized research projects.

This book was previously published as a special issue of *Qualitative Research in Sport, Exercise and Health*.

Robert J. Schinke is the Canada Research Chair in Multicultural Sport and Physical Activity. Robert's research spans community based participatory action research with indigenous and immigrant athlete populations and elite amateur and professional sport contexts. Robert's research is funded by the Social Sciences and Humanities Research Council of Canada and the Canadian Foundation for Innovation. Robert is the Associate Editor of the *Journal of Sport and Social Issues* and *Qualitative Research in Sport, Exercise and Health*, and an editorial board member for the *Journal of Clinical Sport Psychology*.

Kerry R. McGannon is a world renowned cultural sport psychology scholar, recognized for her innovative use of qualitative research methodologies and research with minority populations and diverse cultural identities. She has been on research teams, serving as the methodologist, in externally funded projects supported by the Coaching Association of Canada, the Ministry of Tourism, Culture and Sport, the Canadian Institutes for Health Research, and the Social Sciences and Humanities Research Council of Canada. Kerry is also an editorial board member of *Psychology of Sport and Exercise* and serves on the advisory board of *Qualitative Research in Sport, Exercise and Health*. She is also the Associate Editor for *Athletic Insight*.

Brett Smith works in the Peter Harrison Centre for Disability Sport within the School of Sport, Exercise and Health Sciences at Loughborough University. His research interests include the psycho-social dimensions of disability and wellbeing, and narrative inquiry. He is an Associate Editor of the journal *Qualitative Research in Sport, Exercise and Health*.

Community Based Research in Sport, Exercise and Health Science

Edited by
Robert J. Schinke, Kerry R. McGannon and Brett Smith

LONDON AND NEW YORK

First published 2015
by Routledge
2 Park Square, Milton Park, Abingdon, Oxon, OX14 4RN, UK

and by Routledge
711 Third Avenue, New York, NY 10017, USA

Routledge is an imprint of the Taylor & Francis Group, an informa business

British Library Cataloguing in Publication Data
A catalogue record for this book is available from the British Library

ISBN 13: 978-1-138-78757-5

Typeset in Times New Roman
by Taylor & Francis Books

Publisher's Note
The publisher accepts responsibility for any inconsistencies that may have arisen during the conversion of this book from journal articles to book chapters, namely the possible inclusion of journal terminology.

Disclaimer
Every effort has been made to contact copyright holders for their permission to reprint material in this book. The publishers would be grateful to hear from any copyright holder who is not here acknowledged and will undertake to rectify any errors or omissions in future editions of this book.

Contents

CONTENTS

Citation Information

The chapters in this book were originally published in *Qualitative Research in Sport, Exercise and Health*, volume 5, issue 3 (November 2013). When citing this material, please use the original page numbering for each article, as follows:

Chapter 1
Expanding the sport and physical activity research landscape through community scholarship: introduction
Robert J. Schinke, Kerry R. McGannon and Brett Smith
Qualitative Research in Sport, Exercise and Health, volume 5, issue 3 (November 2013) pp. 287–290

Chapter 2
An exploration of the meanings of sport to urban Aboriginal youth: a photovoice approach
Tara-Leigh F. McHugh, Angela M. Coppola and Susan Sinclair
Qualitative Research in Sport, Exercise and Health, volume 5, issue 3 (November 2013) pp. 291–311

Chapter 3
Moving beyond words: exploring the use of an arts-based method in Aboriginal community sport research
Amy T. Blodgett, Diana A. Coholic, Robert J. Schinke, Kerry R. McGannon, Duke Peltier and Chris Pheasant
Qualitative Research in Sport, Exercise and Health, volume 5, issue 3 (November 2013) pp. 312–331

Chapter 4
Developing sport-based after-school programmes using a participatory action research approach
Nicholas L. Holt, Tara-Leigh F. McHugh, Lisa N. Tink, Bethan C. Kingsley, Angela M. Coppola, Kacey C. Neely and Ryan McDonald
Qualitative Research in Sport, Exercise and Health, volume 5, issue 3 (November 2013) pp. 332–355

Please direct any queries you may have about the citations to clsuk.permissions@cengage.com

Expanding the sport and physical activity research landscape through community scholarship: introduction

Robert J. Schinke, Kerry R. McGannon and Brett Smith

School of Human Kinetics, Laurentian University, Ben Avery Building, 935 Ramsey Lake Road, Sudbury, Ontario, P3E2C6, Canada

Introduction

We welcome the readership to this special instalment of *Qualitative Research in Sport, Exercise and Health*, focused upon community scholarship. When we embarked on this special call it was apparent that there would be more than a few understandings and possibilities of how 'community' would be conceptualised, constituted and researched (see also Fawcett 1991, Israel *et al.* 1998, Baker *et al.* 1999). Our experiences have been informed by a series of critical approaches. Robert's experience has been garnered through an immersed 10-year research partnership with a Canadian Aboriginal community, and evidenced through a localised decolonising methodology (Schinke *et al.* 2009). Kerry's experiences have been eclectic, including a project with a rural community in the state of Iowa broadly positioned within a social-ecological framework, and interpreted specifically using social constructionism, to gender and age as social constructions that impact physical activity perceptions and behaviour (McGannon *et al.* in press). Brett engages in narrative research with disabled people, especially those with spinal cord injuries, a community unto itself (Smith 2013). Our topics and methodological approaches only begin to tease at the diverse research that community scholars engage in, the varied methodological approaches adopted, and the differing ways in how a community might be conceptualised. Such diversity can be found not only in the work that follows, but also in the breadth of research by scholars from the sport and physical activity disciplines who are actively engaged in derivatives of community scholarship (e.g. Frisby *et al.* 2005, Forsyth and Heine 2010, Blodgett *et al.* 2011, Frisby 2011, Giles and Lynch 2012).

Despite this diversity, what might be meant by 'community scholarship'? This question is particularly important to respond to since without an understanding confusion can reign and, as we aim to readdress in the final paper in this issue, judging what counts as 'good' and 'bad' community work can become even more difficult. Accounting for the diverse meanings of community that have not been fully accounted for in sport and physical activity research (Forneris *et al.* 2013), one useful response we have found lies in the words of Cutworth (2013): 'Community-engaged scholarship is scholarly work undertaken in partnership with communities, draws on multiple sources of knowledge, crosses disciplinary lines and is reciprocal and mutually beneficial' (p. 14). Cutworth expands that community-engaged scholarship stands apart from conventional academic scholarship because by its very nature such work focuses on practical challenges and the lived realities of people residing in their communities, be these geographic or otherwise, and evidenced through what is visible (e.g. race, ability or disability) and/or invisible to the eye (e.g. sexual orientation, professional discipline). Community-focused scholarship can offer a redistribution of power among research project members as compared to non-community projects (more power to community members, less to academics), locally derived research questions and research methods, and opportunities for community betterment, during and as a result of a project (Minkler 2005). In addition, such work can ground and sometimes reorient academic scholars and their scholarship through practical contexts and challenges experienced in a society (Jensen *et al.* 1999).

In addition to the need for a clearer understanding of what is meant by community scholarship, from what we have learned thus far in both our own reading of existing community scholarship and scholarship within the current special instalment, several questions have surfaced about this scholarship. Does being considered as a community require geographic location? Is it a requirement that community research be undertaken with an underserviced or underprivileged group? Do scholars need to step outside of academic contexts and ingrained, often taken for granted assumptions about what constitutes rigorous research, in order to experience community and embark on community research? Should community members lead the conceptualisation of pertinent research approaches? Must there be applied practice derived from community projects? The possible answers to these questions opens up a fascinating, and what we believe is a productive dialogue in terms of how many among us are embarking on community research (more than one might have guessed), where community research happens, why such research happens and for whose benefit, and what sorts of experiences or outcomes – for researchers and community participants – might flow from such work.

The papers found within this special issue reveal that there can be a multiplicity of understandings in terms of what would constitute and belong in an emerging area such as community scholarship. We propose that at play within this dialogue should be academic connoisseurship (Sparkes and Smith 2013), whereby scholars might appreciate diversity and engage in subtle, complex and informed decisions. Some scholars within this issue have approached community research projects with the community members conceptualising research questions, leading data collection and analysis, and deciding upon deliverable outcomes. Others have conceptualised and then led research projects, and sought consultation during the research process, suggesting that the research projects and findings were derived from within academe from the outset. Still others have undertaken work within geographic and sport communities where the focus was placed on a community, though without direct involvement by community members. We have not identified scholars for each of the aforementioned three groups, because who belongs in each of the aforementioned categories is open to the reader's interpretation. However, these three general categories of community research are relatively common and known among scholars (see Baker *et al.* 1999). We encourage the readership not to quibble in advance about whether a given piece fulfils preset views and criterion of what community research should be, is or is not; we return to this point in our conclusion where we offer possible qualities for the readership to consider. For now, we propose that the reader consider the papers and contemplate how each authorship approached community research, why it is that the paper has been included, what it might tell us about this emerging topic area, and what might remain contentious and/or open for further research. In addition, the contributing authors and co-editors seek to engage in this dialogue as a community of scholars with you, the reader. We are looking to exchange ideas through a diversity of perspectives, always keeping in mind that whether we choose to agree or disagree on what belongs, that there is a place for discussion and negotiation within this emerging and developing area of community-based research.

Notes on contributors

Robert J. Schinke is the Canada Research Chair in Multicultural Sport and Physical Activity located at Laurentian University.

Kerry R. McGannon is a critical cultural sport psychology scholar located at Laurentian University.

Brett Smith is the managing editor of Qualitative Research in Sport, Exercise and Health and a faculty member at Loughborough University.

References

Baker, E.A., Homan, S., Schonhoff, R. and Kreuter, M., 1999. Principles of practice for academic/practice/community research partnerships. *American journal of preventative medicine*, 16 (3), 86–93.

Blodgett, A.T., Schinke, R.J., Smith, B., Peltier, D. and Corbiere, R., 2011. In indigenous words: the use of vignettes as a narrative strategy for capturing Aboriginal community members' research reflections. *Qualitative inquiry*, 17 (6), 522–533.

Cutworth, N., 2013. The journey of a community engaged scholar: an autoethnography. *Quest*, 65 (1), 14–30.

Fawcett, S.B., 1991. Some values guiding community research and action. *Journal of applied behavior analysis*, 24 (4), 621–636.

Forneris, T., Whitley, M.A. and Barker, B., 2013. The reality of implementing community based sport and physical activity programs to enhance the development of underserved youth: challenges and potential strategies. *Quest*, 65 (3), 313–331.

Forsyth, J. and Heine, M., 2010. Indigenous research and decolonizing methodologies. *In*: T.V. Ryba, R.J. Schinke and G. Tenenbaum, eds. *The cultural turn in sport psychology*. Morgantown, WV: Fitness Information Technology, 181–202.

Frisby, W., 2011. Learning from the local: promising physical activity inclusion practices for Chinese immigrant women in Vancouver, Canada. *Quest*, 63 (1), 135–147.

Frisby, W., Reid, C.J., Millar, S. and Hoeber, L., 2005. Putting "participatory" into participatory forms of action research. *Journal of sport management*, 19 (4), 367–386.

Giles, A.R. and Lynch, M., 2012. Postcolonial and feminist critiques of sport for development. *In*: R.J. Schinke and S.J. Hanrahan, eds. *Sport for development, peace, and social justice*. Morgantown, WV: Fitness Information Technology, 89–104.

Israel, B.A., Schulz, A.J., Parker, E.A. and Becker, E.A., 1998. Review of community-based research: assessing partnership approaches to improve public health. *Annual review of public health*, 19, 173–202.

Jensen, P.A., Hoagwood, M. and Trickett, E.J., 1999. Ivory towers or earthen trenches? Community collaborations to foster real-world research. *Applied developmental science*, 3 (4), 206–212.

McGannon, K.R., Busanich, R., Witcher, C.S.G. and Schinke, R.J., in press. A social ecological exploration of physical activity influences among rural men and women across life stages. *Qualitative research in sport, exercise and health*. Available from: http://dx.doi.org/10.1080/2159676X.2013.819374.

Minkler, M., 2005. Community-based research partnerships: challenges and opportunities. *Journal of urban health: bulletin of the New York academy of medicine*, 82 (2 Supplement 2, ii), 3–12.

Schinke, R.J., Peltier, D., Hanrahan, S.J., Eys, M.A., Yungblut, H., Ritchie, S., et al., 2009. The progressive move toward indigenous strategies among a Canadian multicultural research team [Special issue]. *International journal of sport and exercise psychology*, 7, 309–322.

Smith, B., 2013. Disability, sport, and men's narratives of health: a qualitative study. *Health psychology*, 32 (1), 110–119.

Sparkes, A.C. and Smith, B., 2013. *Qualitative research methods in sport, exercise & health. From process to product*. London: Routledge.

An exploration of the meanings of sport to urban Aboriginal youth: a photovoice approach

Tara-Leigh F. McHugh[a], Angela M. Coppola[a] and Susan Sinclair[b]

[a]Faculty of Physical Education & Recreation, University of Alberta, E-488 Van Vliet Centre, Edmonton, Alberta, T6G2H9, Canada; [b]Sinclair Consulting, Edmonton, Alberta, Canada

The meaning of sport to Aboriginal youth is not well understood, and this lack of understanding limits the potential to enhance their sport opportunities. Thus, the purpose of this study was to explore the meanings of sport to Aboriginal youth living in Edmonton, Alberta. Photovoice was employed as it is recognised as a decolonising and participatory research approach. Fifteen Aboriginal youth, between 12 and 15 years, participated in a sport sampler event, whereby they were provided with disposable cameras and asked to photograph objects, events, places, or people that represent their meaning of sport. Participants spoke about their photographs in talking circles, which took place two weeks after the sport sampler event. Two talking circles (one with eight and one with seven participants) were facilitated. Cultural practices (e.g. offering of tobacco to traditional knowledge keeper) were integrated into the talking circles. Talking circles were audio recorded, transcribed verbatim, and transcripts were analysed using a general 6-step qualitative analysis approach described by Creswell Four themes were developed; participants described sport as: (1) activities I've grown up playing, (2) having fun, (3) being with nature and others, and (4) believing in yourself. The information-rich pictures and related stories shared by participants provide insight into their meanings of sport. This research is a practical example of how Aboriginal youth can be actively engaged in sport research through participatory approaches.

There is a large body of literature that highlights the many physical, psychosocial, emotional and developmental benefits of sport participation for youth (e.g. Eccles *et al.* 2003, Marsh and Kleitman 2003, Holt 2008). An emerging body of literature also describes how sport and physical activity participation may positively impact the physical, mental, spiritual and emotional health of Aboriginal[1] youth (Chalifoux and Johnson 2003, Lavallée 2007, Hanna 2009). Recognising the various benefits of sport participation we, a team of researchers and a community partner, have been working with Aboriginal youth to better understand and enhance their sport experiences. Through our ongoing work with Aboriginal youth, we realise that the term sport likely holds various meanings. Having encountered similar challenges in her research of Aboriginal peoples' leisure, Fox (2007) argued that words within

Euro-North American language are often viewed as self-evident and the complex histories that accompany such words are often unclear and unexamined.

Aboriginal peoples' participation in sport in Canada has been extensive (Forsyth and Giles 2013). There is a growing body of literature that documents Aboriginal peoples' participation and achievements in national and international competitions, such as the Arctic Winter Games, North American Indigenous Games and the Olympics (e.g. Paraschak 1997, Forsyth and Wamsley 2006, Hall 2013, Heine 2013). Research has also documented the history of Aboriginal peoples' participation in sport. In her seminal work that examined the process in which the *Indian Act* shaped (and continues to shape) sporting opportunities for Aboriginal peoples in Canada, Forsyth (2007) highlighted the need for scholars to acknowledge significant historical benchmarks. She described how federal policies such as the Indian Act 'helped to legitimize and naturalize Euro-Canadian sports and games as the most appropriate forms of physical expression' (p. 109). Similarly, in some of her more recent work, Forsyth (2013) shared powerful stories of a man who attended a residential school in Northern Ontario and she described how residential schools and institutional authorities used sport and games to exert power and control over Aboriginal peoples.

The creation (and later termination) of the Native Sport and Recreation programme in Canada was another historical benchmark that shaped Aboriginal peoples participation in sport. Throughout the duration of the programme (1972–1981), Native peoples[2] in Canada resisted the reproduction of Euro-Canadian sport and when the programme was terminated, Native peoples were denied an opportunity to 'challenge the dominant interpretation of 'legitimate' sport' (Paraschak 1995, p. 13). Aboriginal peoples' definitions of sporting practices and physical activities have been shaped by their complex histories (Paraschak 1998). Eurocentric worldviews have continually challenged the knowledge of Aboriginal peoples (Battiste 2002), and it is critical for sport researchers to recognise that such worldviews continue to shape the sport participation of Aboriginal peoples.

Contemporary sport participation by Aboriginal peoples is also garnering more attention in the sport research literature. Forsyth and Giles (2013) recently released a much-needed edited book on Aboriginal sport in Canada, which includes various chapters by leading scholars on the contemporary issues associated with Aboriginal sport in Canada. One such chapter by Paraschak (2013) focused on *Sport Canada's Policy on Aboriginal Peoples' Participation in Sport* that was released by the federal government in 2005. This policy was developed in an effort to ensure the inclusiveness of the *Canadian Sport Policy* and to enhance the experience and access of sport for Aboriginal peoples in Canada (Canadian Heritage 2005). The policy clearly describes how many Aboriginal peoples do not support a distinction between the terms sport, recreation and physical activity, yet Paraschak (2013) described how government officials did not work with Aboriginal peoples to define sport, nor did they negotiate the meaning of sport with Aboriginal peoples to be included in the policy. A definition of sport was not included in the policy and by omission Sport Canada retained the right over Aboriginal peoples to define sport (Paraschak 2013).

There is a need for in-depth research that supports the exploration of Aboriginal youths' definition of sport (Findlay and Kohen 2007), as westernised definitions of sport may limit research with Aboriginal children and youth (Smith *et al.* 2010). It is challenging to move forward with sport research when the very definitions of sport for Aboriginal youth are not well understood. Findlay and Kohen (2007) used the Aboriginal Peoples Survey from 2001 to examine sport participation rates of over 33,000 Aboriginal children in Canada, and they argued that the survey may not have captured all of the distinct activities in which Aboriginal youth participate. It is possible that Aboriginal youth have an encompassing view of sport, which includes more traditional activities (e.g. hunting, trapping; First Nations Information Governance Centre 2012). Recent research by McHugh (2011) that explored the physical activity experiences of Aboriginal youth suggested that the terms sport and physical activity are often used interchangeably. Despite the study's focus on broader physical activity experiences, specific sport experiences were most often shared in the one-on-one interviews. Based on their review of Indigenous Australian physical activity research, Nelson et al. (2010) argued that little is known about what physical activity means to Indigenous[3] young people. Similarly, the argument can be made that little is known about what sport means to Aboriginal youth.

Aboriginal peoples must have control in shaping meanings of sport (Paraschak 2013). A better understanding of the meanings of sport to Aboriginal youth could enhance sport research with Aboriginal peoples and the participation of Aboriginal peoples in sport. The purpose of this research was to better understand the meanings of sport to Aboriginal youth living in Edmonton, Alberta.

Ethical considerations and participants

Upon receiving ethical approval from the authors' university research ethics board and Edmonton Public School Board, the authors began creating relationships and collaborations with students, teachers and elders at a secondary school in Edmonton, Alberta. As well, we adhered to various ethical guidelines for engaging in research with Aboriginal peoples, including Chapter 9 of the Tri-Council Policy Statement: Ethical Conduct for Research Involving Humans (TCPS2; Canadian Institutes of Health Research, Natural Sciences and Engineering Research Council of Canada and Social Sciences and Humanities Research Council of Canada 2010). A critique of the earlier (1998) version of the TCPS was provided by Brown (2005). She argued that the document is accompanied by a number of shortcomings, including an authoritarian tone that may prevent meaningful interpretation by community members. There are also critics of TCPS2 but Brant Castellano and Reading (2010) provided a detailed overview of the manner in which Aboriginal leaders were engaged in dialogue to revise the policy. We recognise the potential limitations of the TCPS2 but our team (including our community partner) drew upon the strengths of this policy to guide our research. A thorough description of the various ethical practices employed within this research is beyond the scope of this manuscript. Nevertheless, the commitment to the participatory research approach and the establishment and maintenance of research partnerships highlights some of our efforts to ensure this research was respectful.

Building legitimate relationships with community members is a critical first step in the development of research partnerships with Aboriginal communities (Fletcher 2003, Lavallée 2009). This project is part of the first author's (Tara-Leigh) ongoing programme of research that is focused on the physical activity and sport of Aboriginal youth. As an English Canadian researcher who is committed to working with Aboriginal youth, she recognises and respects the need to develop and maintain mutually beneficial research partnerships with Aboriginal youth and community partners. She has documented the importance of such relationship building in the research literature (see McHugh and Kowalski 2009). The question driving this research (i.e. what are the meanings of sport to Aboriginal youth?) was derived from some of her recent research with Aboriginal community partners in Edmonton. Sixty Aboriginal adult and youth partners participated in talking circles that sought to identify a relevant and respectful research question that addresses the sport of Aboriginal youth. Experiences shared within these talking circles suggested that it is necessary to better understand the meanings of sport to Aboriginal youth.

To address the question suggested by community partners, Tara-Leigh worked to develop additional relationships with Aboriginal youth by connecting with a secondary school in Edmonton that serves Aboriginal youth. After establishing relationships with school administrators, and over the duration of a school year (i.e. September–June), the first two authors met with school administrators, engaged in informal meetings and conversations with schoolteachers and staff, and they attended various school celebrations (e.g. school feasts) in an effort to establish and maintain relationships with various school members. Consistent to findings from Castleden *et al.*'s (2012), study of community-based participatory researchers, extensive time and commitment was needed within this study to build relationships with members of the community. As a result of the extensive time she spent in the school, the second author, Angela (a self-identified Caucasian American graduate research assistant and school volunteer) and third author, Susan (a self-identified co-researcher) established a partnership that served as a strong foundation for addressing our research question. Susan is a Cree and Michif speaker and teacher; she conducts on-land traditional teachings and is a sport coach, certified traditional games instructor, mentor, language and literacy consultant and mother. Susan helped shape the research question, and she supported the first two authors in the recruitment of participants, co-facilitated talking circles, supported data analysis and interpretation and provided feedback on this manuscript.

Photovoice: a participatory research approach

A participatory research approach is recommended when engaging in research with Aboriginal communities (e.g. Smith 1999, Battiste 2002). Participatory approaches enhance the relevance of research, and such approaches are founded on the assumption that community members are experts of their own experiences and are able to develop their own relevant research agendas (Israel *et al.* 1998). In response to a request from the youth and partners within the school, a photovoice approach was employed in an effort to address the research question. Findings from initial talking circles that Tara-Leigh held with Aboriginal community partners suggested that Aboriginal youth should be provided with opportunities to share their meanings of sport through talking circles. Despite these original suggestions, as relationships were established within the school it was critical to be responsive to the photovoice suggestion and opportunity offered by the school.

Photovoice is recognised as a participatory research approach that is typically employed in an effort to build trust and balance power between researchers and communities (Castleden *et al.* 2008). This research approach encourages participants to use photographs and personal narratives to share knowledge (Wang and Burris 1997), and supports the involvement of participants in the research process (Carlson *et al.* 2006). As argued by Poudrier and Mac-Lean (2009), photovoice is aimed at 'shifting research participants from their role in previous research as "the other" or "passive victims" studied by outsiders, to empowered activists within their own communities' (p. 309). As described in detail below, the participants' level of engagement within this research was somewhat limited and therefore we are not convinced that our photovoice approach was reflective of the decolonising research approach that has been described by Castleden *et al.* (2008). The photovoice approach did, however, provide a unique opportunity for Aboriginal youth to share their meanings of sport. As suggested by Smith and Caddick (2012), photographs provide participants with a different form for sharing their layered meanings.

The use of visual methods (including photovoice) have not been well documented within sport and exercise research, but Phoenix (2010) described the potential of such methods to emphasise the multiple meanings that are embedded within our culture. The use of visual methods are relatively novel in sport research (Smith and Caddick 2012), but photovoice has been used in research on physical activity (e.g. D'Alonzo and Sharma 2010), sport (e.g. Pope 2010, Mills and Hoeber 2013) and research with Aboriginal youth (e.g. Shea *et al.* 2011). Given the documented success of these studies to engage youth in the research process, photovoice has been extended to this sport research with Aboriginal youth.

Participants

Participants were 15 Aboriginal youth (8 females and 7 males) in grades seven and eight (ages 12–15 years) who attend a secondary school in Edmonton, Alberta. Compared to other cities in Canada, Edmonton has the second largest Aboriginal population (Winnipeg has the largest; Statistics Canada 2006). This Edmonton Public school, which serves approximately 99% Aboriginal youth, uses cultural enrichment to help promote learning and retention. Of the 15 participants, eight youth self-identified with specific Aboriginal communities[4] in rural Alberta and Saskatchewan, and seven students stated that they are from the greater Edmonton area.

As part of the relationship building process, Angela spent approximately two hours a week supporting activities (e.g. beading in art class) in the grades seven and eight classes. She developed relationships with students by supporting their everyday school activities, and 15 of the students she interacted with on a weekly basis voiced interest in participating in this research. Participants were any students who voiced interest and had returned signed consent forms.

Data generation

Each participant was given one disposable camera at a sport sampler event, which was hosted by a non-profit sport organisation. The sport sampler event was a one-day event in which students were provided with an opportunity to engage in a variety of activities (e.g. volleyball, kickball, hoop and arrow, run and scream) outside of school hours and off school property. The participants were asked to photograph objects, events, places or people that represent their meanings of sport. Following the sport sampler event, the participants returned cameras and photographs were developed. Participants were invited to talk about their photographs in talking circles, which were scheduled for two weeks after the sport sampler event.

Talking circles were used for sharing photographs and stories among participants and researchers. Talking circles have been used in previous sport research with

Aboriginal peoples (e.g. Blodgett *et al.* 2010, Schinke *et al.* 2010) and are similar to sharing circles, which have been used in other photovoice research with Aboriginal youth (e.g. Shea *et al.* 2011). Sharing circles or talking circles are similar to focus groups in that participants share experiences and stories in a group setting, yet Lavallée (2009) argued that sharing circles are quite different from focus groups in that they have sacred meaning for many Indigenous cultures. It is important to acknowledge that talking circles were used in an effort to support and promote the cultural protocols that are encouraged by the school.

Upon giving verbal and written consent, each participant took part in a talking circle; two talking circles were conducted. One talking circle consisted of seven participants and the other talking circle had eight participants, for a total of 15 participants. Susan led, and Angela supported, the facilitation of each talking circle. Both talking circles were audio recorded and lasted approximately one hour. Before the beginning of each talking circle, Angela presented Susan with a package of tobacco in an effort to acknowledge and support cultural tradition and protocols promoted within the school. As well, the tobacco served as an offering of peace and thanks to Susan for contributing her knowledge to the research and facilitating the talking circles. Within the talking circles, Susan shared her own experiences as a young body growing up in a small community in Saskatchewan and the barriers she and her community faced. At the beginning of a circle session, she stated, 'my job here today is to share with you a little bit about my experience as a Phys Ed teacher, as a coach, as well as an Aboriginal person who went through the system of sports'. Furthermore, a feast of meats, cheeses, bread, fruits and vegetables was offered to participants to support cultural protocols and practices within the school and to thank participants for sharing their knowledge.

Participants were given copies of their pictures when they arrived at the talking circle. In an effort to set the context for the discussion, participants were asked to choose two or three photographs that best represent their meanings of sport.

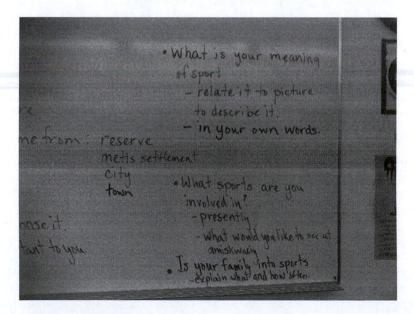

Figure 1.   Talking circle sessions.

Participants' background, photographs, meaning of sport and sport involvement were discussed in four circle sessions, which were outlined on a whiteboard (see Figure 1 for a description of specific questions addressed in the circle sessions). Participants shared their name, age and reserve, settlement or city in the first session. The second session included participants' explanation of their photographs and why they chose the photographs. In the third session, participants discussed their meanings of sport using the picture or their own experiences. During the final session of each talking circle, the participants described the sports they are involved in and sports they would like to be involved in at the school.

Data analysis

Data was analysed by all authors using a general 6-step qualitative data analysis process outlined by Creswell (2007). This approach is similar to the multistep process outlined by Blodgett *et al.* (2010) in their sport research with an Aboriginal community. First, the transcripts from the talking circles were prepared and organised. Second, the transcripts were read and re-read in an effort to gain a general sense of the participants' experiences. Third, the transcripts were coded using a process outlined by Rossman and Rallis (1998). Coding involved organising material into chunks, segmenting text into subthemes and themes and then labelling themes with a term. More specifically, Indigenous coding, a process suggested by Patton (2002), took place in that the words and terminology of the participants were used in the coding process. Fourth, theme descriptions, which are comprised of the words of the participants, were developed. The fifth step involved the development of theme labels by the authors. The final sixth step was the interpretation of the data, which is presented in the Discussion.

Consistent with D'Alonzo and Sharma (2010), who engaged in member-checking as part of their photovoice research, a knowledge sharing activity was employed in this research in an effort to discuss proposed themes with participants. The participants' reflections were sought in an effort to facilitate dialogue about the appropriateness of the researchers' initial analysis and interpretations (Smith and Caddick 2012). All participants were provided with the opportunity to engage in a group discussion regarding the findings, but only one participant attended the event. Given that the event was held at the end of the school year, it was challenging to draw students to organised activity outside of class. We managed to connect with approximately half of the participants during informal discussions and they provided feedback on the findings. Themes were not altered as a result of these discussions, but possible explanations of findings are incorporated in the Discussion.

Results

The purpose of this research was to better understand the meanings of sport to Aboriginal youth living in Edmonton, Alberta. Data analysis resulted in ten subthemes, which were subsequently grouped together into four themes that are represented by the words of the participants (see Table 1). Participants described how sport means: (1) activities I have grown up playing, (2) having fun, (3) being with nature and others and (4) believing in yourself. The themes are presented separately for purposes of clarity, but they are not mutually exclusive and the interconnectedness of themes is apparent in the theme descriptions. Each theme is

Table 1. Subthemes and themes.

Subthemes	Themes
Gender Challenging to define Contemporary activities	Activities I've grown up playing
Getting fit Travel	Having fun
Getting outside Good time with friends	Being with nature and others
Confidence Maturity and discipline Smarter	Believing in yourself

represented by direct quotes and pictures from the participants, but due to challenges associated with confidentiality and consent the last theme is not represented by a specific picture. Pseudonyms have been used to protect the anonymity of participants.

Activities I have grown up playing

Participants described sports as activities that they were introduced to as children and those that they have 'grown up playing'. Although some of the participants found it challenging to try to define sport, the majority of the activities described are those that are deemed more contemporary activities (e.g. basketball, soccer and football). Within this theme it was also apparent that some of the young women view certain sports as male dominated.

When describing her favourite sport Sara said, 'My favourite sport is soccer because I've always grown up playing soccer. And there's really no sports to play at my grandma's besides that. And that's pretty much it'. Marie described how her sport experiences have been shaped by opportunities provided by the schools she has attended. She said,

> My meanings of sport is practically very difficult because I don't get out very often. The only sport I've ever participated in is pretty much the one we got on our field trip with an elementary school and the archery classes. Those are the only sports I ever participated in.

Regardless of the experiences that shaped their meanings of sport, the participants generally described sport as a variety of contemporary sports. Emily chose a picture of a bag of volleyballs to represent her meaning of sport (see Figure 2). She said, 'I have a bag of volleyballs because I like volleyball'. Similarly, Sean said, 'My favourite sport is volleyball and I don't know why I like it'.

Embedded within this theme is the notion by some of the young women that sports are male dominated. Maya described how she likes to play a variety of sports but she recognises that there are not many girls or Aboriginal youth involved in her favourite sports. She said:

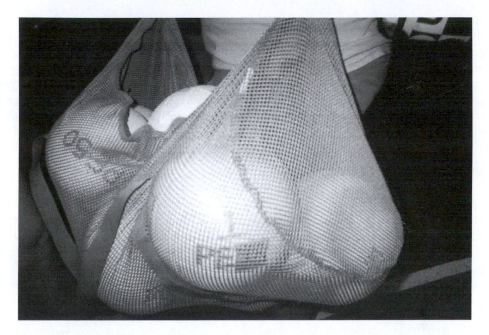

Figure 2.   Volleyballs.

> I was playing for two softball teams and I actually quit the other one and right now I'm on the softball team and we have tournaments coming and then I play sports at a youth centre I go to and when I usually play sports I'm usually the one girl playing … I'm usually the only girl playing floor hockey and I play ice hockey at my dad's ice rink and I'm usually the only girl playing too. I don't see lots of Native, Aboriginal people playing sports when I play outside of school, like there's only like one girl or two girls on the team and the rest are boys and yeah, I like sports.

Violet shared similar experiences of being involved and liking sports that are often male dominated. She said, 'In grade 4 I had a best friend but I had best friends that were all guys, they're all my cousins. They were trying to teach me hockey'. She further described how she enjoyed playing hockey but she did not feel like she was heard or understood by her male cousins when she had questions about how to play the sport. For these young women, their meanings of sport are contemporary sports, which are often male dominated.

Within this theme, it was also apparent that there is some uncertainty by participants as to what actually constitutes sport. For example, when asked about his favourite sport John said, 'My favourite sport is boxing and wrestling. Oh and football. Is swimming sport?' Andrew also expressed uncertainty as to what is, and is not, sport. When asked about his favourite sport he said, 'Is cadets a sport? Like military stuff?' It was apparent that to some of the participants in the study, sport is a relatively challenging word to define.

In an effort to try to better understand their meanings of sport, participants were asked to identify sports that they would like to see offered in their school. Martin said, 'Right now I'm in floor hockey on Friday and I would want to be in football'. Lily said, 'I'd like to see something like gymnastics … cause it would be kind of fun to learn how to do a front flip off stuff or back flips'. Other activities that participants requested were cheerleading, fastball and mixed martial arts. Eric said, 'Right now I'm training to go into boxing at my house so in the summertime I gotta skip for 20 min. And I used to be in Tae Kwon Do'. In addition to the sports in which he currently participates, Eric also described how he would also like to try martial arts. Although contemporary team sports (e.g. basketball and fastball) were identified in participants' meanings of sport, participants' meanings of sport were also comprised of less conventional sports and activities (e.g. military activities and mixed martial arts).

Having fun

Having fun was also central to participants' meanings of sport, and having fun consisted of getting fit and having opportunities to travel. Eric chose to represent his meaning of sport by showing his friends having fun (see Figure 3). When asked how his picture represents his meaning of sport he said, 'Sport to me means to have fun'. Also, defining sport in terms of being fun, Tina said, 'What sport means to me is to have fun with my friends and to get out for a while and just play and learn new stuff as you go'. Building upon the notion of fun, Jennifer defined sport in terms of its ability to promote positive emotions. She said, 'My meaning of sport is just to have fun and it makes me happy'. Emily also described the fun aspect of sport. She said, 'Sports means to me is like having fun and being active, just having fun being active and just feeling good on the inside'. When asked her meaning of sport Marie said, 'My meaning of sport, it's better than staying home

Figure 3.   Having fun with friends.

watching TV and it keeps you fit and it's fun'. The words of these participants are representative of the various experiences shared by other participants.

Participants also described how sport provides opportunities to travel, which they perceived as fun. Violet said, 'I like sports because you stay fit and you get to go different places and travel and be part of something'. Jennifer described how her 'Meaning of sport is to … travel and do things'. Even when travel is within their own city, travel is perceived as a fun aspect of sport. Tina said, 'My meaning of sport is just to have fun and it makes me happy and you can meet new people and travel to different schools'. When describing his participation in skateboarding Patrick said that sport means he can 'Travel in Edmonton to skate parks'. The various words of the participants demonstrate how these youth define sport as having fun, which includes getting fit and travelling.

Being with nature and others

As each theme is described, the interconnectedness of the themes becomes increasingly apparent. For instance, in the previous theme friends were described as an important aspect of having fun in sport. Similarly, within this theme, participants described how sport means being with nature and others. Despite the interconnectedness of themes, the words of the participants suggest a separate theme was needed in an effort to more accurately represent the participants' meanings of sport. Participants described how sport means 'being outside' and engaging in a 'good time with friends'. For example, when asked what sport means to her, Maya said:

> You can meet new people and to learn new things so you can show your friends whoever doesn't know how to play that sport you can teach them that sport … I'm doing something with people that I like to be around.

To this participant, sport means engaging with others in a variety of ways, whether it be meeting others, learning from others or teaching others. Similarly, Lily described sport as an opportunity for engaging with others in numerous ways. In describing why she likes sport she said, 'It's like having a good time with friends in a sport, travel and meet new people and win, it's fun'. Team sports were specifically identified by participants as opportunities to engage with others. Nick said, 'I was on teams last year and I liked going different places and being on a team and stuff'. Similarly, Tina described sport simply as an opportunity to be with friends. She said, 'It gives you something to do and you can see your friends and stuff like that'.

Being outside appeared to be a critical component in participants' meanings of sport. In an effort to demonstrate her meaning of sport, Sara described her picture of a tree and nature (see Figure 4). She said, 'I picked this one, the trees; I picked it 'cause nature … and the squirrel and the bird'. To this young woman, sport means engaging in the various aspects of nature. Similarly, when asked what sport means to him Nick said, 'OK, sport means being outside, having fun, and being active'. Specific sports were also described as opportunities to engage in nature or be outside. In describing why skateboarding is his favourite sport, Patrick said, 'You get to be outside every day'. Also recognising the manner in which sports can promote opportunities to be outside, Marie said, 'I would like to learn archery … and sports that aren't really in school, like outdoors and stuff. Like more interactive stuff'. As demonstrated by the various quotes, engaging with nature is part of many of the participant's meaning of sport.

Although being with nature and others was often described in separate stories, there were also stories that represent engaging with nature and others at the same time. For example, in describing a sporting event Sara said, 'I'm in there with some of my good friends … and it was like being at a farm with a bonfire'. To this participant, being with good friends and being outside at a bonfire were equally important in terms of her meaning of this sporting event.

Believing in yourself

This particular theme became obvious in the later stages of data analysis. Virtually all of the participants described how sport contributes to their personal development, such as 'believing in yourself'. Participants described how sport builds confidence and makes a person smarter, more disciplined and mature. This theme was not clear in the early stages of the data analysis, because the authors were unsure as to how to group together this relatively broad range of stories. As the analysis progressed and the transcripts were read and reread, it became clear that all of the stories could be represented as the development of various character traits. When asked his meaning of sport Eric said 'You're like becoming more mature and disciplined to fight for a war and be smarter'. To this young man, sport

Figure 4.   Nature.

means developing a number of personal traits. In facilitating the talking circles, Susan shared her experiences of playing volleyball. She said, 'I learned more than actually learning how to set. I learned how to get along with other people. I also learned how to be part of a team'. Susan described the development of specific volleyball skills as tangential to the development of various character traits.

Participants also explained how sport 'builds confidence'. For example, Lily said, 'I like volleyball because its fun and it just builds confidence, and it's fun'. Again, fun is described in this participant's meaning of sport, but building confidence is also a key component to sport. Participants cited sport as building confidence and other related terms, such as strength. For example, Jennifer said, 'The meaning of sport is like getting strong and believing in yourself'. Sara also explained, 'What sport means to me is to push you further, more competition, to get fit, make friends, have fun'. This participant's meaning of sport seems like an appropriate way to tie together the results section. Sport is defined by this participant as a means to 'push you further', and it also described as fun, and a means for getting fit and making friends. Thus, this final quote provides support for this particular theme and for the interconnectedness of all themes.

Discussion

This research is a practical example of how Aboriginal youth can and should be actively involved in sport research, and findings contribute to our programme of research that seeks to enhance sport opportunities for Aboriginal youth. Research has suggested a need to better understand the meanings of sport to Aboriginal peoples (Findlay and Kohen 2007, Paraschak 2013) and, to the youth in this study, sport was generally defined as contemporary sports. Previous literature (e.g. First Nations Information Governance Centre 2012) suggests that Aboriginal youth may have an encompassing view of sport, which includes more traditional activities. The youth in this study did not seem to have an encompassing view as their descriptions of sport were typically described as contemporary sports (e.g. volleyball, hockey and basketball) in which they have played or been exposed to in school. The participants did not describe more traditional activities, but they did provide some examples of sport that are somewhat less conventional (e.g. 'military stuff'). Findings from this research also suggest that some urban Aboriginal youth may not have a clear understanding or may not differentiate between the terms sport, physical activity and recreation (Canadian Heritage 2005). During the talking circles some of the participants even asked the facilitators if certain activities (e.g. swimming) are sports. Findings suggest that participants are unsure of specific meanings, and potentially distinction, between terms.

It is possible that the participants' conceptualisations of the term 'sport' are the result of the westernised sport messages that they receive in the urban environments that they live and call home. As argued by Forsyth (2007), various Dene and Inuit games are included in sport programmes in northern Canadian events (e.g. Arctic Winter Games) but in southern Canadian events (e.g. Canada Games), Inuit and Dene games are typically included as cultural activities. She suggested that by framing such games as cultural activities, a message is being perpetuated as to 'what constitutes legitimate "sport"' (Forsyth 2007, p. 161). The Edmonton data from the Urban Aboriginal Peoples Study (Environics Institute 2010) found that most Aboriginal peoples consider Edmonton to be home even though they may have close links to their communities of origin. It is likely that participants' meanings of sport are influenced by the dominant western sport messages and opportunities that are prevalent in the city they may call home.

During the member-checking one participant confirmed that youth do tend to see contemporary sports and traditional activities as distinct. She suggested the distinction between the two terms could potentially be attributed to the fact that there are more opportunities to engage in contemporary sport. Susan argued that there are different activities that can be introduced to students in school settings, which likely depends on individual instructors. Instructors ultimately decide on the level of inclusion of cultural teachings, in this case, traditional activities. She argued that it is possible that the participants' meanings of sport are influenced by the dominant discourse regarding what is and is not sport. Regardless of the reason as to why participants envision sport as contemporary sports, these findings may have important implications for sport researchers and practitioners. Specifically, for sport research and programming to be relevant and appropriate, it is necessary to understand the meanings of sport to Aboriginal youth. The experiences highlighted in this study cannot be generalised to all Aboriginal youth in Canada, but the richness of the experiences and pictures shared provide a glimpse into the manner in which some urban Aboriginal youth in Canada view sport.

Traditional Aboriginal sports or activities were not described by participants in their meanings of sport, despite the inclusion of various traditional activities (e.g. kickball) at the sport sampler event in which the youth took pictures for the study. Nevertheless, the findings suggest that their meanings of sport may be shaped by their traditional or Indigenous knowledge. Recognising that traditional or Indigenous knowledge is diverse and not a uniform concept, The Royal Commission on Aboriginal Peoples (1996) described traditional knowledge as a body of knowledge regarding the relationship of living beings with the environment and others. Similarly, Steinhauer (2002) argued that Indigenous knowledge is relational knowledge in that it recognises that all things in creation are interrelated. Participants also described how sport means engaging with nature and others, suggesting their meanings are influenced by their traditional knowledge. In contributing to the interpretation of results, Susan described this finding as 'nehiyaw pimatisiwin', which is living the Cree (or traditional) way of life. The meanings of sport that were shared appear to reflect the foundation of traditional knowledge in that sport was described in terms of its relational and collective meanings.

The participants' meanings of sport were also described in terms of the various holistic benefits associated with sport. Sport was described as a means to get fit, suggesting that the participants recognise the physical benefits of sport. Participants also described how sport makes them happy, disciplined, confident and mature, which suggests that participants are cognisant of the various emotional and mental benefits. Spirituality was not specifically stated in the meanings of sport described by participants, but this is not to say that they do not acknowledge the spiritual nature of sport. Sport participation can impact Aboriginal youth's physical, mental, spiritual and emotional health (e.g. Hanna 2009) and Aboriginal youth's perceived holistic benefits of participating in sport have been described in previous research (e.g. Cargo *et al.* 2007). When interpreting the findings, Susan argued that children may benefit in different ways and at different times from sport participation. She highlighted the importance of recognising individual differences, as learning may be multi-encompassing and interrelated in different ways for each person. Findings from this research suggest that the various benefits of sport are well understood by participants, even to the extent that their meanings of sport are described in terms of the holistic benefits.

The participants seem to have a very positive conceptualisation of sport as demonstrated by the stories and pictures they shared. Previous research (e.g. Schinke *et al.* 2010) has highlighted various challenges (e.g. racism and discrimination) that Aboriginal youth may face when participating in mainstream sport contexts. It cannot be assumed that the Aboriginal youth in this study have only had positive experiences in sport, but it is particularly noteworthy that when provided with an opportunity to articulate their meanings of sport the youth chose to share positive stories and experiences. Even when some of the young women described the potential challenges of participating in sports that they deemed male dominated, the stories shared were relatively neutral and they did not articulate negative experiences with the sport. This finding does not negate the significant works of various researchers (e.g. Forsyth and Giles 2007, Hall 2013) who have documented the challenges that Aboriginal women have experienced in sport. An interpretation of the manner in which gender influences participants' meanings of sport is well beyond the scope of this paper. There is a need for more research that provides opportunities for Aboriginal sportswomen to share their stories (Hall 2013).

Sport programmers or promoters may benefit by knowing that the youth in this study defined sport in terms of its positive and holistic benefits. When trying to promote sport or engage Aboriginal youth in sport it may not be necessary to highlight the benefits of sport, as such benefits seem to be well understood by youth. As suggested in previous research with Aboriginal youth (i.e. McHugh 2011) it may be more beneficial for programmers or promoters to focus their efforts on identifying strategies for overcoming potential barriers to physical activity or sport participation rather than focusing on benefits of engaging in sport. Findings from this research also shed light on aspects of sport that some urban Aboriginal youth may find meaningful (e.g. opportunities to travel and being with nature). Although these findings may serve as a useful foundation for programmers, it is important to ensure that Aboriginal peoples and communities are engaged in the development of sport or physical activity programming (Kirby *et al.* 2007, Lavallée and Lévesque 2013).

This research employed a community-based participatory approach, but it was accompanied by some challenges. Our research question was developed by Aboriginal community partners (including Aboriginal youth) and at the request of the school partners and participants we utilised a photovoice approach to address the research question. Susan was also actively involved in data collection, and she contributed to data analysis and this manuscript. A challenge in this research was trying to engage the youth in the data analysis and interpretation after they had been involved in shaping the research question and data generation. The roles and responsibilities of community partners and researchers may shift over the duration of the participatory research (Macauley *et al.* 1999), and as our research progressed towards the analysis and interpretation, we realised that this shift had occurred. When we approached this research as a team that included two non-Aboriginal researchers, we were particularly aware of, what Haig-Brown (2001) described as, our responsibility to ensure that Aboriginal peoples speak first *and* last in research. We made a strong attempt to verify findings with participants but, in retrospect, we should have put more effort into involving participants in the initial analysis and interpretation.

Our team supports Battiste's (2002) contention that researchers may be able to support Aboriginal peoples in articulating their experiences, but speaking for them is only denying them self-determination. Upon reflection, it is likely that we were negatively influenced by some of our previous experiences in which we were relatively unsuccessful in our attempts to engage Aboriginal youth in collaborative analysis processes (see McHugh and Kowalski 2009). Although we trust that our intentions as a team were transparent and respectful, we also understand the importance of critically examining who is in control of the text (Borland 2004). As we move forward in our research we will be sure to put more emphasis on engaging in dialogue with participants about their crucial role in the analysis and interpretation. Through such dialogue it may also be possible to negotiate reasonable expectations about participants' engagement in such processes, which are respectful of the time that participants are willing to commit to such research. By ensuring that Aboriginal peoples are involved in the entire research process it is possible to avoid a type of discourse (Eurocentric discourse) that Smith (1999) described as never innocent.

The participants' engagement in the various research processes did shift over time, but this did not shift our perceptions that participants were equal contributors to this research. The value assigned to different stages of the research process may vary by participant and participatory research may be burdensome to some participants (Wang *et al.* 1998). We viewed participants as equal partners who are experts in 'the matters of his or her everyday life' (Boog 2003, p. 435). As such, participants were more engaged in some aspects of the research than in others, but they were still considered equal partners in this community-based participatory research.

Our data collection was also limited in that it was a one-time, non-iterative process, whereby participants took pictures on a single day and then shared their experiences in a talking circle. This data collection procedure is consistent with previous photovoice by Shea *et al.* (2011), whereby Aboriginal youth took photographs during a one day event. We recognise the limitations associated with this procedure, including the possibility that they were not provided the opportunity at the event to take pictures that might have better represented their meanings of sport (e.g. pictures in their own home or yard). This potential limitation was acknowledged during the planning of the photovoice approach, but as a team we made the conscious decision to proceed and to respect the requests of the participants to use photovoice during this event. It would have also been beneficial to engage each participant in more than one talking circle, as previous photovoice research with Aboriginal women (i.e. Poudrier and Mac-Lean 2009) highlighted the benefits of engaging in more iterative processes. Upon reflection, we realise that the four circle sessions that comprised each talking circle might not have provided enough opportunity for participants to share specific, contextual details of their meanings of sport. By asking participants to address specific questions via each circle session, the facilitators were able to ensure that all participants had an opportunity to talk. However, the circle sessions prompted relatively brief single sentence answers, which were rarely probed by facilitators as such probing was not necessarily consistent with the talking circle format. By engaging each participant in more than one talking circle, it may have been possible to generate more rich data.

It was important to respect the schedules of the participants that were defined by the school and these specific data collection processes (i.e. single talking circle) were developed. Having said this, it is important to note that strong research relationships were established prior to the data collection and, as a result, the authors are confident that the participants were comfortable expressing their meanings of sport. Cultural protocols that were integrated into the talking circles also likely contributed to participants' engagement in the research process. This research highlights the importance of respecting and including traditional protocols, and establishing research relationships with community members, elders and Aboriginal partners.

The research is also limited in that various photographs could not be published or shared because of lack of consent. Some pictures taken by participants included individuals who were not participants in the study and, as such, there was no consent to use these pictures. The ethical challenges associated with photovoice, and processes of consent in particular, have also been acknowledged in detail by Wang and Redwood-Jones (2001). The issues associated with consent to use photographs were also coupled with challenges associated with obtaining not only participant consent but also the consent of their guardians. Our previous research with Aboriginal youth (e.g. McHugh and Kowalski 2009) described similar challenges associated with the consent process. The authors' experiences within this research support Smith's (1999) contention that informed consent is a significant process that requires constant dialogue.

Despite the limitations associated with the photovoice approach, the benefits far outweigh the challenges. The photovoice approach provided an opportunity for Aboriginal youth to share their knowledge regarding their meanings of sport. As such, this research makes a contribution to the sport literature in that the often overlooked expertise of Aboriginal youth has been highlighted. This research also makes a methodological contribution to the sport literature in that it provides a practical example of how youth can be actively engaged in research through participatory approaches. Not only did the youth optimise on an opportunity to share their knowledge but, possibly more importantly, they requested and enjoyed the photovoice approach. At the conclusion of the study the participants reiterated their enjoyment of the research approach and asked when they would be provided with another opportunity to participate in photovoice. The words of the participants support the work of Smith (2005), who argued that for many Aboriginal peoples, research processes are more important than the outcomes. As researchers committed to working with Aboriginal youth in participatory research settings, we strive to engage in mutually beneficial projects. Photovoice supported us in achieving this goal.

Acknowledgements

We would like to thank the participants for sharing their knowledge and contributing to the sport literature. This research was supported by a grant from the Social Sciences and Humanities Research Council of Canada.

Notes

1. The term Aboriginal refers to those individuals who identify as First Nations, Inuit or Métis (Statistics Canada 2006). These original peoples of Canada are distinct groups that have unique languages, histories and cultural practices.

2. The term Native peoples is used in an effort to be consistent with the terminology utilised by Paraschak (1995).
3. The term Indigenous refers to Aboriginal people internationally (National Aboriginal Health Organisation, n.d.).
4. Participants identified the names of their specific Aboriginal community, but in an effort to protect the anonymity of the participants, the community names are not shared in this manuscript.

Notes on contributors

Tara-Leigh F. McHugh is an assistant professor in the Faculty of Physical Education and Recreation at the University of Alberta. She is currently the lead academic on the University of Alberta's Certificate in Aboriginal Sport and Recreation that is jointly offered by the Faculties of Native Studies and Physical Education & Recreation. Her programme of research is focused on working with urban Aboriginal youth to shed light on the often overlooked topics of Aboriginal peoples' physical activity, sport and body image experiences.

Angela M. Coppola is a graduate research assistant and doctoral student in the Faculty of Physical Education & Recreation at the University of Alberta. Her primary programme of research is focused on working with Aboriginal youth and parents, and school communities to explore and co-create components of physical activity and sport programming. She is committed to building relationships with communities and engaging communities in the process of research and programme development. She is also committed to exploring how researchers, schools and communities can work ethically and collaboratively with Aboriginal youth to increase sport and physical activity participation.

Susan Sinclair is originally from Green Lake, Saskatchewan. She is a band member of the Canoe Lake First Nations in Saskatchewan. Presently, she is working on her MEd in the areas of Language and Literacy. She is a language keeper, a traditional knowledge keeper and a facilitator, who provides workshops to various organizations. She is developing a series of teaching resources in the Cree language which are intended for use in programmes offering Plains Cree Michif language instruction. At present, she is working with the Edmonton Public School Board as a consultant and teacher. She has worked extensively with First Nations, Metis and Inner City schools for more than 21 years. She has taught all grade levels and worked as a coordinator and consultant in the area of cultural infusion. She has learned early on the value of storytelling to pass on values, knowledge and culture of the Aboriginal people. She is firmly committed to passing on this passion to future generations through practical application and traditional storytelling methods.

References

Battiste, M., 2002. Decolonizing university research: ethical guidelines for research involving Indigenous populations. *In*: G. Alfredsson and M. Stavropoulou, eds. *Justice pending: Indigenous peoples and other good causes*. The Hague: Martinus Nijhoff, 33–44.

Blodgett, A.T., Schinke, R.J., Fisher, L.A., Yungblut, H.E., Recollet-Salkkonen, D., Peltier, D., *et al.*, 2010. Praxis and community-level sport programming strategies in a Canadian Aboriginal reserve. *International journal of sport and exercise psychology*, 8 (3), 262–283.

Boog, B.W.M., 2003. The emancipatory character of action research, its history and the present state of the art. *Journal of community & applied social psychology*, 13 (6), 426–438.

Borland, K., 2004. 'That's not what I said': interpretive conflict in oral narrative research. *In*: S.N. Hesse-Biber and P. Leavy, eds. *Approaches to qualitative research: a reader on theory and practice*. New York: Oxford University Press, 522–534.

Brant Castellano, M. and Reading, J., 2010. Policy writing as dialogue: drafting an Aboriginal chapter for Canada's tri-council policy statement: ethical conduct for research involving humans. *The international Indigenous policy journal*, 1 (2), 1–18.

Brown, M., 2005. Research, respect and responsibility: a critical review of the tri-council policy statement in Aboriginal community-based research. *Pimatisiwin*, 3 (2), 79–100.

Canadian Heritage, 2005. Sport Canada's policy on Aboriginal peoples' participation in sport. *Minister of public works and government services Canada, catalogue no.: CH24-10/2005* [online]. Available from: http://www.pch.gc.ca/pgm/sc/pol/aboriginal/2005/aboriginal-eng.pdf [Accessed 10 April 2013].

Canadian Institutes of Health Research, Natural Sciences and Engineering Research Council of Canada, and Social Sciences and Humanities Research Council of Canada, 2010. *TCPS 2-tri-council policy statement: ethical conduct for research involving humans* [online]. Available from: http://www.pre.ethics.gc.ca/pdf/eng/tcps2/TCPS_2_FINAL_-Web.pdf [Accessed 10 April 2013].

Cargo, M., Peterson, L., Lévesque, L., and Macaulay, A.C., 2007. Perceived wholistic health and physical activity in Kanien'kehá:ka youth. *Pimatisiwin*, 5 (1), 87–109.

Carlson, E., Engebretson, J., and Chamberlain, R.M., 2006. Photovoice as a social process of critical consciousness. *Qualitative health research*, 16 (6), 836–852.

Castleden, H., Garvin, T., and Huu-ay-aht First Nation, 2008. Modifying photovoice for community-based participatory Indigenous research. *Social science & medicine*, 66 (6), 1393–1405.

Castleden, H., Morgan, V.S., and Lamb, C., 2012. 'I spent the first year drinking tea': exploring Canadian university researchers' perspectives on community-based participatory research involving Indigenous peoples. *The Canadian geographer*, 56 (2), 160–179.

Chalifoux, T. and Johnson, J.G., 2003. *Urban Aboriginal youth: an action plan for change* (Senate report) [online]. Ottawa: The Standing Senate Committee on Aboriginal Peoples. Available from: http://www.parl.gc.ca/Content/SEN/Committee/372/abor/rep/repfinoct03-e.pdf [Accessed 10 April 2013].

Creswell, J.W., 2007. *Qualitative inquiry and research design: choosing among five traditions*. 2nd ed Thousand Oaks, CA: Sage.

D'Alonzo, K.T. and Sharma, M., 2010. The influence of *marianismo* beliefs on physical activity of mid-life immigrant Latinas: a photovoice study. *Qualitative research in sport and exercise*, 2 (2), 229–249.

Eccles, J.S., Barber, B.L., Stone, M., and Hunt, J., 2003. Extracurricular activities and adolescent development. *Journal of social issues*, 59 (4), 865–889.

Environics Institute, 2010. *Urban Aboriginal peoples study: Edmonton report* [online]. Toronto. Available from: http://uaps.ca/wp-content/uploads/2010/02/UAPS-Edmonton-report1.pdf [Accessed 20 April 2013].

Findlay, L.C. and Kohen, D.E., 2007. Aboriginal children's sport participation in Canada. *Pimatisiwin: a journal of Aboriginal and Indigenous community health*, 5 (1), 185–206.

First Nations Information Governance Centre, 2012. *First Nations regional health survey (RHS) 2008/2010: national report on adults, youth and children living in First Nations communities* [online]. Ottawa: FNIGC. Available from: http://www.rhs-ers.ca/sites/default/files/First_Nations_Regional_Health_Survey_2008-10_National_Report.pdf [Accessed 10 April 2013].

Fletcher, C., 2003. Community-based participatory research relationships with Aboriginal communities in Canada: an overview of context and process. *Pimatisiwin: a journal of Aboriginal and Indigenous community health*, 1 (1), 27–62.

Forsyth, J., 2007. Aboriginal leisure in Canada. *In*: R. McCarville and K. MacKay, eds. *Leisure for Canadians*. State College, PA: Venture, 157–163.

Forsyth, J., 2013. Bodies of meaning: sports and games at Canadian residential schools. *In*: J. Forsyth and A.R. Giles, eds. *Aboriginal peoples & sport in Canada: historical foundations and contemporary issues*. Vancouver: UBC Press, 15–34.

Forsyth, J. and Giles, A.R., 2007. To my sisters in the field. *Pimatisiwin: a journal of Indigenous and Aboriginal and community health*, 5 (1), 155–168.

Forsyth, J. and Giles, A.R., 2013. Introduction. *In*: J. Forsyth and A.R. Giles, eds. *Aboriginal peoples & sport in Canada: historical foundations and contemporary issues*. Vancouver: UBC Press, 1–11.

Forsyth, J. and Wamsley, K.B., 2006. 'Native to Native … we'll recapture our spirits': the world Indigenous Nations games and North American games as cultural resistance. *The international journal of the history of sport*, 23 (2), 294–314.

Fox, K.M., 2007. Aboriginal peoples in North American and euro-north American leisure. *Leisure/loisir*, 31 (1), 217–243.

Haig-Brown, C., 2001. Continuing collaborative knowledge production: knowing when, where, how and why. *Journal of intercultural studies*, 22 (1), 19–32.

Hall, M.A., 2013. Toward a history of Aboriginal women in Canadian sport. *In*: J. Forsyth and A.R. Giles, eds. *Aboriginal peoples & sport in Canada: historical foundations and contemporary issues*. Vancouver: UBC Press, 64–91.

Hanna, R., 2009. *Promoting, developing, and sustaining sports, recreation, and physical activity in British Columbia for Aboriginal youth*. Document created for First Nations Health Society [online]. Available from: http://www.fnhc.ca/pdf/Sports_Recreation_and_Physical_Activity_BC__Aboriginal_Youth.pdf [Accessed 15 April 2013].

Heine, M., 2013. Performance indicators: Aboriginal games at the Arctic Winter games. *In*: J. Forsyth and A.R. Giles, eds. *Aboriginal peoples & sport in Canada: historical foundations and contemporary issues*. Vancouver: UBC Press, 160–181.

Holt, N.L., 2008. *Positive youth development through sport*. London: Routledge.

Israel, B.A., Schulz, A.J., Parker, E.A., and Becker, A.B., 1998. Review of community-based research: assessing partnership approaches to improve public health. *Annual review of public health*, 19 (1), 173–202.

Kirby, A.M., Levesque, L., and Wabano, V., 2007. A qualitative investigation of physical activity challenges and opportunities in a northern-rural, Aboriginal community: voices from within. *Pimatisiwin: a journal of Aboriginal and Indigenous community health*, 5 (1), 5–24.

Lavallée, L.F., 2007. Physical activity and healing through the medicine wheel. *Pimatisiwin: a journal of Aboriginal and Indigenous community health*, 5 (1), 127–153.

Lavallée, L.F., 2009. Practical application of an Indigenous research framework and two qualitative Indigenous research methods: sharing circles and Anishnaabe symbol-based reflection. *International journal of qualitative methods*, 8 (1), 21–40.

Lavallée, L. and Lévesque, L., 2013. Two-eyed seeing: physical activity, sport, and recreation promotion in Indigenous communities. *In*: J. Forsyth and A.R. Giles, eds. *Aboriginal peoples & sport in Canada: historical foundations and contemporary issues*. Vancouver: UBC Press, 206–228.

Macauley, A.C., Commanda, L.E., Freeman, W.L., Gibson, N., McCabe, M.L., Robbins, C. M., *et al.*, 1999. Participatory research maximizes community and lay involvement. *British medical journal*, 319 (7212), 774–778.

Marsh, H.W. and Kleitman, S., 2003. School athletic participation: mostly gain with little pain. *Journal of sport & exercise psychology*, 25 (2), 205–228.

McHugh, T.-L.F., 2011. Physical activity experiences of Aboriginal youth. *Native studies review*, 20 (1), 7–26.

McHugh, T.-L.F. and Kowalski, K., 2009. Lessons learned: participatory action research with young Aboriginal women. *Pimatisiwin: a journal of Aboriginal and Indigenous community health*, 7 (1), 117–131.

Mills, C. and Hoeber, L., 2013. Using photo-elicitation to examine artefacts in a sport club: logistical considerations and strategies throughout the research process. *Qualitative research in sport, exercise and health*, 5 (1), 1–20.

National Aboriginal Health Organization, n.d. *Publications: terminology* [online]. Available from: http://www.naho.ca/publications/topics/terminology/ [Accessed 10 April 2013].

Nelson, A., Abbott, R., and Macdonald, D., 2010. Indigenous Australians and physical activity: using a social-ecological model to review the literature. *Health education research*, 25 (3), 498–509.

Paraschak, V., 1995. The native sport and recreation program 1972–1981: patterns of resistance, patterns of reproduction. *Canadian journal of history of sport*, 26 (2), 1–18.

Paraschak, V., 1997. Variations in race relations: sporting events for native peoples in Canada. *Sociology of sport journal*, 14 (1), 1–21.

Paraschak, V., 1998. 'Reasonable amusements': connecting the strands of physical culture in Native lives. *Sport history review*, 29 (1), 121–131.

Paraschak, V., 2013. Aboriginal peoples and the construction of Canadian sport policy. *In*: J. Forsyth and A.R. Giles, eds. *Aboriginal peoples & sport in Canada: historical foundations and contemporary issues*. Vancouver: UBC Press, 95–123.

Patton, M.Q., 2002. *Qualitative research & evaluation methods*. 3rd ed Thousand Oaks, CA: Sage.

Phoenix, C., 2010. Seeing the world of physical culture: the potential of visual methods for qualitative research in sport and exercise. *Qualitative research in sport and exercise*, 2 (2), 93–108.

Pope, C.C., 2010. Got the picture? Exploring student sport experiences. Using photography as voice. *In*: M. O'Sullivan and A. MacPhail, eds. *Young people's voices in physical education and youth sport*. London: Routledge, 186–206.

Poudrier, J. and Mac-Lean, R.T., 2009. 'We've fallen into the cracks': Aboriginal women's experiences with breast cancer through photovoice. *Nursing inquiry*, 16 (4), 306–317.

Rossman, G.B. and Rallis, S.F., 1998. *Learning in the field*. Thousand Oaks, CA: Sage.

Royal Commission on Aboriginal Peoples, 1996. *Report of the Royal Commission on Aboriginal Peoples*. Ottawa: Government of Canada.

Schinke, R.J., Blodgett, A.T., Yungblut, H.E., Eys, M.A., Battochio, R.C., Wabano, M.J., et al., 2010. The adaptation challenges and strategies of adolescent Aboriginal athletes competing off reserve. *Journal of sport and social issues*, 34 (4), 438–456.

Shea, J.M., Poudrier, J., Chad, K., and Atcheynum, J.R., 2011. Understanding the healthy body from the perspective of First Nations girls in the Battlefords Tribal Council region: a photovoice project. *Native studies review*, 20 (1), 27–57.

Smith, L.T., 1999. *Decolonizing methodologies: research and Indigenous peoples*. London: Zed Books.

Smith, L.T., 2005. On tricky ground: researching the Native in the age of uncertainty. *In*: N. K. Denzin and Y.S. Lincoln, eds. *The Sage handbook of qualitative research*. 3rd ed Thousand Oaks, CA: Sage, 85–107.

Smith, B. and Caddick, N., 2012. Qualitative methods in sport: a concise overview for guiding social scientific sport research. *Asia Pacific journal of sport and social science*, 1 (1), 60–73.

Smith, K., Findlay, L., and Crompton, S., 2010. Participation in sports and cultural activities among Aboriginal children and youth. *Canadian social trends, statistics Canada, catalogue no. 11-008* [online]. Available from: http://www.statcan.gc.ca/pub/11-008-x/2010002/article/11286-eng.htm [Accessed 10 April 2013].

Statistics Canada, 2006. *Aboriginal peoples highlight tables, 2006 census* [online]. Available from: http://www12.statcan.ca/census-recensement/2006/dp-pd/hlt/97-558/index.cfm?Lang=E [Accessed 13 April 2013].

Steinhauer, E., 2002. Thoughts on an Indigenous research methodology. *Canadian journal of Native education*, 26 (2), 69–81.

Wang, C. and Burris, M., 1997. Photovoice: concept, methodology, and use for participatory needs assessment. *Health education & behavior*, 24 (3), 369–387.

Wang, C.C., Yi, W.K., Tao, Z.W., and Carovano, K., 1998. Photovoice as a participatory health promotion strategy. *Health promotion international*, 13 (1), 75–86.

Wang, C.C. and Redwood-Jones, Y.A., 2001. Photovoice ethics: perspectives from flint photovoice. *Health education & behavior*, 28 (5), 560–572.

Moving beyond words: exploring the use of an arts-based method in Aboriginal community sport research

Amy T. Blodgett[a], Diana A. Coholic[b], Robert J. Schinke[c], Kerry R. McGannon[c], Duke Peltier[d] and Chris Pheasant[d]

[a]Human Studies, Laurentian University, 935 Ramsey Lake Road, Sudbury, Ontario P3E 2C6, Canada; [b]School of Social Work, Laurentian University, 935 Ramsey Lake Road, Sudbury, Ontario P3E 2C6, Canada; [c]School of Human Kinetics, Laurentian University, 935 Ramsey Lake Road, Sudbury, Ontario P3E 2C6, Canada; [d]Wikwemikong Unceded Indian Reserve, Wikwemikong, Ontario, Canada

In recognising the limitations of verbally based research methods for understanding and capturing the multidimensionality of lived experience, arts-based methods have been gaining ground within the social sciences. These methods embrace emotional, sensory, embodied and imaginative ways of knowing that lend to richer knowledge production and communication processes. Yet, these methods are rarely used in sport research. The purpose of the current project was to explore an arts-based method as a tool to facilitate participatory action research (PAR) and generate locally resonant knowledge about the sport experiences of Aboriginal community members in north-eastern Ontario, Canada. Mandala drawings were used to embrace an Indigenous epistemology and open up a culturally affirming space for Aboriginal athletes to share their experiences of sport relocation. Conversational interviews were then used to facilitate deeper understandings of the athletes' mandalas. The images contributed towards community action on two levels: (1) they affirmed a need for athletes to feel connected to their cultural community during relocation, therein reinforcing local efforts to support relocated athletes; and (2) they served as a resource for educating and inspiring other aspiring young athletes. The strengths and challenges of arts-based methods are discussed in relation to PAR. It is concluded that arts-based methods offer potential for community-based sport research, as these methods open up a diversity of art forms which can be adopted to reflect localised PAR processes and ways of knowing.

Introduction

'Arts-based methods' refer to the use of art in qualitative research in order to generate, interpret and/or communicate knowledge (Boydell *et al.* 2012). Although these methods are often derived from art therapy techniques, they are differentiated from 'art therapy' in that the latter is usually performed by graduate trained professionals who hold a degree in art therapy (Coholic 2010). Alternatively, arts-based methods have been used by a wide variety of researchers and professionals to assist people in expressing feelings and thoughts that otherwise might remain repressed or unconscious, or that are difficult to articulate in words. These methods include, but are not limited to, collages, paintings, drawings, carvings, photography, videography, theatre/drama, dance, music, poetry and stories (Boydell *et al.* 2012). Herein, 'arts-based methods' can be understood as an umbrella term that encompasses a broad range of visual, performative and narrative art forms in research.

Arts-based methods have been gaining ground in social science inquiry in light of increasing dissatisfaction with the way verbally based research methods have been used to emphasise intellectual knowing over other ways of knowing (Guillemin 2004, Gillies *et al.* 2005, Bagnoli 2009, Mason and Davies 2009). Most traditional research methods rely on language as the sole medium for the creation and communication of knowledge. This can become a problem when researchers use language in ways that produce logical scientific views of reality and privilege intellectual forms of knowledge (Sparkes 2002, Bagnoli 2009), producing knowledge that is 'oddly abstracted and distanced from the sensory, embodied and lived conditions of existence that it seeks to explain' (Mason and Davies 2009, p. 600). People and their lives become 'flattened' into one-dimensional forms that are often unrecognisable at the community level and accordingly, research fails to resonate with the people and communities it involves (Cole and Knowles 2008). Alternatively, arts-based methods embrace emotional, sensory, embodied and imaginative ways of knowing that extend beyond verbal and intellectual modes of thinking (Finley 2008). These research methods have been taken up as tools for gaining access to different dimensions of experience, which would otherwise remain neglected or ineffable (Bagnoli 2009, Liebenberg 2009), as well as developing knowledge that is more connected to the lives of participants (Cole and Knowles 2008).

Despite gaining recognition as a fruitful approach for social science inquiry (Boydell *et al.* 2012), arts-based methods are rarely used in sport research (Gravestock 2010). That being said, a few researchers have advocated for narrative (e.g. Sparkes and Douglas 2007, Carless and Douglas 2009, Douglas and Carless 2009, 2010, Gilbourne 2010) and performative (e.g. Llewellyn and Gilbourne 2011) art forms to be integrated into sport research as an alternative to the scientific/realist texts that have long dominated the sport sciences. In addition, the 2010 special edition of *Qualitative Research in Sport and Exercise* on 'Visual Methods in Physical Cultures' (volume 2, issue 2) made the case for visual methods (which utilise various technologies and the images they produce, namely photography and film) to be employed within sport and exercise research as a means of rendering the world in visual terms. However, beyond photography and film, visual arts-based methods, which are differentiated by the actual making of artistic creations, have remained relatively unexplored within the sport realm. Gravestock's (2010) use of drawings to achieve embodied understandings in figure skating provides one of the only examples of a visual arts-based method in sport.

The purpose of this paper is to explore mandala drawings as an arts-based method for facilitating participatory action research (PAR) and generating locally-resonant knowledge about the sport experiences of marginalised community members. The arts-based process is articulated within a local sport initiative aimed at understanding the relocation experiences of young Aboriginal athletes who move off reserves in north-eastern Ontario, Canada to pursue sport opportunities. Through this contextual example, the strengths and challenges of arts-based methods in relation to PAR are brought forward and recommendations for engaging these methods are provided. The paper builds on the aforementioned examples of arts-based research in disrupting the assumption that language (particularly in scientific/realist form) is what constitutes 'good' sport scholarship (see Phoenix 2010). This paper further contributes a new understanding of how the expressive modalities of arts-based methods can enhance community-based sport research.

Arts-based methods and Aboriginal cultures

As indicated in the Indigenous research literature (e.g. Smith 1999, Bartlett *et al.* 2007, Swadener and Mutua 2008), there is a pertinent need to develop research approaches that are methodologically and epistemologically aligned with Aboriginal cultures and designed to embrace local ways of knowing. Sport research has largely been dominated by Westernised research approaches that are fundamentally at odds with Aboriginal ways of thinking and being, and have therefore failed to contribute meaningful knowledge to Aboriginal communities (Smith 1999, Ryba and Schinke 2009, Schinke *et al.* 2009). Given this inadequacy, an arts-based method was engaged in the current project as a culturally relevant, localised form of inquiry that would more deeply resonate with Aboriginal community members and lend to decolonising knowledge-production processes that centralise Indigenous ways of knowing (Finley 2008, Swadener and Mutua 2008).

For one, arts-based activities support holistic Indigenous ways of knowing and being that emphasise the interconnectedness of the physical, mental, emotional and spiritual dimensions within an individual, as well as with the life around an individual (Coholic *et al.* in press, Archibald and Dewar 2010). Illustrating this point, Cueva (2011) found that the use of moving, drawing and sculpting in cancer education workshops with Alaska Natives 'nurtured heart, head, and body ways of knowing' (p. 14) that ultimately opened up deeper insights and expanded perspectives from the participants. Thus, in the current project mandala drawings were used to help participants share the multiple, interconnected layers of their sport relocation experiences and explore how those experiences related to their larger life journeys. Furthermore, when arts activities are linked to cultural components, they help Aboriginal participants reconnect to their culture and feel a resonance with their traditional way of life (Archibald and Dewar 2010). Given the cultural erosion that has been experienced by Aboriginal people under a legacy of colonisation and assimilation, Archibald and Dewar noted that the act of rediscovering cultural elements through art can be a powerful and healing experience. Accordingly, mandala drawings were engaged as a culturally relevant art form in the current project in order to support cultural links within participants' stories of relocation and foster a more meaningful research experience. A number of traditional Aboriginal motifs are rooted in the mandala (e.g. the Medicine Wheel and dream-catcher) and its circular form is a sacred cultural theme that affirms the values of wholeness, interconnectedness and collectivism (Dufrene 1990, Little Bear 2000). The arts-based research process was herein designed to support a circular research process that would centralise Aboriginal ways of knowing.

PAR and arts-based methods

Visual methods have long been used in anthropology (see Pink 2003) and sociology (see Packard 2008) as a means of carrying out PAR, and more recently have been used within the health sciences as a participatory approach to Aboriginal community research (e.g. Castleden and Garvin 2008, Adams *et al.* 2012). These links between visual methods and PAR stem from coinciding concerns with minimising the power differentials between the researcher and the researched and facilitating more democratised processes (Packard 2008). Based on the same premises, arts-based methods converge with PAR in multiple ways. For one, the creative process provides participants with a sense of agency in that they are able to share their experiences and thoughts in ways that are personally meaningful, therein allowing individuals to engage as the experts of their own lived experiences (Packard 2008, Bagnoli 2009). Participants may feel more in control of the research interview when they are given the opportunity to create and discuss an image on their own accord, rather than having to respond to a series of questions that are developed along the researcher's lines of thinking. In this manner, arts-based methods can be used to enrich the interview process as a more participatory experience. Similarly, the process of coming to understand the meaning that an image holds for a participant helps to reformulate the relationship between the researcher and participant, lending to a more equitable distribution of power (Liebenberg 2009). Researchers must rely on the insights of participants to better understand the various meanings being conveyed, and accordingly the research process becomes a 'mutual initiative as opposed to a hierarchical, one-way flow of information' (Liebenberg 2009, p. 445). Furthermore, in engaging creative meaning-making processes that draw upon multiple ways of knowing, arts-based methods have the power to evoke emotion, thought and action in participants and audiences in ways that cannot always be achieved through words (Cole and Knowles 2008). In this manner, when discussing the potential of visual methods in sport and physical culture research, Phoenix explained that images can make arguments more vivid and evoke deep responses from those who come into contact with them, aligning with the action component of PAR.

Given these convergences with PAR, arts-based methods have been touted as relevant conduits for understanding the experiences of marginalised, non-Western cultural groups (Swadener and Mutua 2008, Huss 2009). However, we appreciate Packard's (2008, p. 75) argument that the implicit assumption that visual (in this case, arts-based) methods inherently reduce power imbalances and situate participants as co-collaborators 'are off the mark'. Indeed, while our rationale to utilise an arts-based method is rooted in the desire to reduce traditional power imbalances and facilitate a more meaningful process for participants, we understand that PAR is not achieved through any single research method in and of itself, but rather through an ongoing process of reconfiguring power and orienting research within a local community (Kidd and Kral 2005, Brydon-Miller *et al.* 2011). An arts-based method has herein been integrated into an overarching PAR initiative with an Aboriginal community in order to better understand how arts-based methods can be used to *facilitate* PAR rather than *be* PAR.

Situating the project

The community

The community partner for this project is Wikwemikong Unceded Indian Reserve, which is located on Manitoulin Island in Ontario, Canada. Wikwemikong is one of the 10 largest First Nation communities in Canada. Approximately 3000 band members live on the reserve, with an additional 3600 band members living off the reserve (Wikwemikong Unceded Indian Reserve 2012). The community is officially recognised as Canada's only Unceded Reserve, meaning that title of its land has not been relinquished to the government of Canada.

The Wikwemikong community has engaged in a number of locally-driven sport research initiatives, stemming back as far as 2006. Recent efforts, for example, have been aimed at identifying culturally relevant strategies for increasing local sport programming capacity and athlete support (e.g. Blodgett *et al.* 2010, Schinke *et al.* 2010) and exploring Indigenous research recommendations and methodologies within sport psychology (e.g. Blodgett, Schinke, Peltier *et al.* 2011, Blodgett, Schinke, Smith *et al.* 2011). Through these initiatives, community research capacity has been centralised within academic scholarship. Local people are continuing to initiate projects from within the community, using their knowledge and skills to lead Indigenous research processes forward, as evidenced in the current project.

The research team

The research team consists of three Aboriginal community researchers from Wikwemikong and four academic researchers from Laurentian University, most of who have worked together on community-based sport projects over the past 10 years. The Aboriginal researchers include the current Chief of Wikwemikong, the manager of the Wikwemikong Youth Centre (the hub where local sport and rec-reation programmes are housed), as well as a retired vice principal. These three Aboriginal researchers contributed experiential and cultural knowledge to the pro-ject, guiding forward an Indigenous methodology that was rooted in local protocols, values, traditions and ways of knowing. The university research team members contributed their understandings of participatory research and experience with arts-based methods in ways that supported the applied contributions of the Wikwemi-kong researchers. The research team members worked together at all stages of the project in order ensure that efforts were both culturally appropriate and methodolog-ically sound. The Aboriginal researchers, however, were the local experts, and thus their insights have been the core driving force behind the research.

The project

The current project is the latest in a series of culturally-driven sport research ven-tures that have been developed by members of the research team between 2006 and 2012. In an earlier initiative, Schinke *et al.* (2006) found that elite Aboriginal ath-letes (competing nationally or higher) faced a number of culture-specific adaptation challenges as they attempted to compete within mainstream contexts, including dealing with unfamiliar cultural practices and feeling stereotyped. Building on these findings from a grassroots perspective, the Aboriginal research team members indi-cated that many young community athletes face similar challenges, as they have to relocate off-reserve and integrate into mainstream contexts in order to pursue sport opportunities which are unavailable locally. The current project was thus conceptua-lised to explore the relocation experiences of young aspiring athletes who moved off reserves in north-eastern Ontario to pursue sport opportunities within main-stream contexts. The Aboriginal researchers proposed that this project be carried out in order to identify pathways through which athletes can be better supported in pursuing their sport dreams outside of the community. At the methodological level, the project was also developed to explore the potential of an arts-based method (i.e. mandala drawings) to facilitate PAR and generate knowledge that is more deeply connected to the lives of Aboriginal community members. It is this methodological exploration that is the focus of the present paper.

The participants

Participants consisted of Aboriginal athletes who had moved off a reserve in north-eastern Ontario to pursue sport opportunities that were unavailable in their local community. Twenty-one athletes participated in the study, ranging in age from 14 to 26 years (mean age = 19.3 years), with one participant outside of this range at 41 years old. Ten of the 21 participants were male and 11 were female. The participants came from seven different reserves and they most commonly relocated within Ontario, though a few moved across provinces and into the United States. The participants consisted of ice hockey players ($n = 17$), an archer ($n = 1$), a volleyball player ($n = 1$), a pow-wow dancer ($n = 1$) and a boxer ($n = 1$). Though the researchers tried to target a variety of sport disciplines, the high proportion of hockey players reflects the prominence of hockey within north-eastern Ontario.

Methods

Training and development

The first and third authors were trained in the use of arts-based methods by the second author, who is an experienced clinical social worker as well as a researcher in this area. The second author, who was familiar with mandalas as a culturally relevant art form for Indigenous peoples, proposed that the team consider this particular arts-based method because it embraced the cultural context of the research and was also feasible and practical to carry out. Training included an experiential activity wherein the first and third authors created mandala drawings and engaged in discussions about the meaning of their creations, with the aim of gleaning a better understanding of the arts-based process and the skills required to facilitate it as a meaningful conduit for sharing lived experiences. As Huss (2009) pointed out, arts-based research necessitates skills in working simultaneously with both visual and verbal elements, which may not be familiar to researchers who are new to these methods. For instance, once a drawing is created, it is important to know how to utilise open-ended questions and statements to assist the person who created the drawing to reflect on its colours, shapes, action, position on the page and so on. It is imperative that the researcher does not make assumptions about the drawing or impose academic interpretations of it, but help the participant to share the meanings and interpretations that she/he attributes to it. Due to the ability of arts-based methods to elicit deep (sometimes unexpected) feelings about experiences, researchers must also be aware of the emotional potential of this approach and be prepared to support participants, should they experience any distress. Accordingly, an effective way to learn how to use arts-based methods is to experientially engage with these methods, under the guidance of an expert.

Following training, the first and third authors met with the three Aboriginal community-appointed research team members to discuss the relevance of the arts-based approach within the Aboriginal context and to explore its potential as a method of data collection. We acknowledge that given the PAR agenda, it could have been more ideal for the university and Aboriginal research team members to have collaborated on the initial brainstorming of arts-based approaches. As an alternative step, the community meeting was held to facilitate an open team dialogue about the mandala drawing activity (and any other potential methods), as well as to strike a consensus as to how the project could best be carried out. The first and third author led the three Aboriginal researchers through a mandala drawing activity in which they were asked to depict their experiences as community researchers and then discuss the meanings behind their images. The Aboriginal researchers affirmed the pertinence of the mandala activity when they reflected upon their creations, as they described how they each instinctively linked the circular image to core cultural themes that influenced their lives. One researcher described how he used the Medicine Wheel to depict four different stages of his research journey; another researcher used the symbol of water to depict his journey as a flowing process that rippled with various life lessons; and the third researcher identified the Seven Grandfather Teachings as guiding his vision of research. The Aboriginal researchers were excited with how the mandala process elicited their stories and they suggested that this cultural link would improve the meaningfulness of the research for the athlete participants and help them share their stories more holistically. Though other culturally-relevant art forms could have been used, such as beading, quilting or drumming, the research team concluded that these methods were much less feasible than the mandala drawings, particularly in that they required art-specific skills and expertise that the team members did not have. In confirming the use of mandala drawings, the Aboriginal researchers recommended that the art process be carried out in a space that was most comfortable for each participant (e.g. in their own home or at the community Youth Centre) so that they could feel at ease and allow their stories to be shared more openly and authentically. The Aboriginal researchers suggested that to do otherwise, by utilising an academic space such as a research lab, would be to create an intimidating research context that favours the researcher over the participants.

Mandala drawings

Following the insights of the Aboriginal researchers, a mandala drawing activity was engaged as a means of eliciting the relocation experiences of Aboriginal athletes. Mandala is a Sanskrit word meaning 'circle' or 'centre' and it refers to an art form or image that is created within a circular context (Slegelis 1987, Henderson *et al.* 2007). Jung (1973), who was the first psychotherapist to make use of the mandala as a therapeutic tool, believed it to be a visual symbol of the psyche and the quest for wholeness. Jung suggested that the act of drawing mandalas facilitated psychological healing and personal meaning in life, as the creative process helped individuals to visualise and make sense of complex experiences and emotions, while the circular form helped to promote psychic integration and a sense of inner harmony (Jung 1973, Slegelis 1987). Today, mandalas are used in a variety of ways including helping people to heal from trauma (Backos and Pagon 1999, Henderson *et al.* 2007), facilitating self-expression (Cox and Cohen 2000, Elkis-Abuhoff *et al.* 2009) and reducing anxiety (van der Vennet and Serice 2012).

In the current project, mandalas were engaged as a means of facilitating self-expression among the participants, enabling a deeper understanding of their relocation experiences to be shared. They were also selected as a culturally relevant art form, given that the circle is a highly visible and sacred theme in the Aboriginal community (Dufrene 1990, Little Bear 2000). To Aboriginal peoples, circles represent the natural life cycle of the world, including the human journey through life, and they signify ongoing transformation and movement (Little Bear 2000). Thus, they are a pertinent motif for eliciting and understanding the relocation experiences of Aboriginal athletes within a larger life journey (holistically), as well as for passing these stories on within the community in a way that emphasises the continuous and transformative movement of experiential knowledge (e.g. one athlete's relocation story can inform and inspire a future athlete's journey).

Participants were given a piece of white paper and a set of coloured pastels and instructed to begin by drawing a circle. They were then told to reflect on their experiences relocating for sport and draw anything that comes to mind. The participants held creative licence to do whatever form of circular expression made sense to them, therein engaging them in a more participatory process (Bagnoli 2009). Participants were told not to over-think the process and to let their instincts guide them. When created spontaneously in this manner, it is purported that the symbolic nature of the mandala will not only reveal conscious insights from its creator, but also provide access to deeper levels of the individual's unconscious, expressed through the use of colours, shapes, lines, numbers and motifs (Slegelis 1987, Elkis-Abuhoff *et al.* 2009).

Conversational interviews

A number of researchers who have used drawings as part of an arts-based method have proposed that this strategy be integrated with an interview (Guillemin 2004, Bagnoli 2009, White *et al.* 2010, Boydell *et al.* 2012). Guillemin (2004) utilised drawings of illness and explained how interviews are essential in eliciting from participants the nature of their drawings, including why they choose to draw particular images and the reasons for choice of colour and spatial organisation. Both the drawing and the description comprise the data, and the researcher is thus able to utilise the participants' interpretations of their drawings in the analysis rather than assume her/his own interpretation. Moreover, when drawings are followed up with an interview, they can enhance participants' reflexivity and garner a more holistic picture of the experience under investigation (Bagnoli 2009). Accordingly, in the current project, each participant's mandala was used to facilitate a conversational interview.

The conversational interview (see Patton 2002) was selected because it aligns with a community-driven Indigenous methodology in multiple ways. First, it honours the cultural tradition of storytelling as a means of transmitting knowledge, beliefs and values (Smith 1999, Little Bear 2000, Kovach 2010). In contrast to the short question-response exchanges of structured or semi-structured interviews, the open-ended and unstructured nature of the conversational interview invites participants to share stories that convey the complexity and depth of their experiences. Second, a more informal dialogical context is facilitated wherein participants are able to share their stories from an emic perspective and exert greater control over the direction of the conversation, as they prioritise pertinent themes within their stories (Patton 2002). This facilitates a reduction in power imbalances, which, like the mandala art process, invites participants to position themselves as the experts of their experiences. Third, the conversational strategy promotes a decolonising agenda in that the researcher poses contextually informed questions in situ rather than being bound to a set of pre-determined questions rooted in a priori academic assumptions (Ryba and Schinke 2009, Kovach 2010). This challenges traditional interview approaches, where a rigid set of questions are derived from the assumptions of the mainstream researcher and posed to participants in a manner that may define (or colonise) the information that is revealed and how it is expressed.

Each interview began with the following broad question: 'Can you tell me about what you have drawn in your mandala?' All pursuant questions were posed during the interviews in relation to the themes brought up by the participants and points of interest in the mandalas. The questions were aimed at encouraging the participants to reflect on the relationship between what they drew and what they experienced as a relocated athlete, therein connecting the visual data to more contextual narrative information.

Results for action

Knowledge generation in PAR is inextricably linked to action. As explained by Kidd and Kral (2005), community members are not likely to be interested in simply knowing about lived experience, but rather want to generate community-developed action that is aimed at improving people's lives. Thus, the arts-based approach in the current project was used to support actionable outcomes, which would positively contribute to the Aboriginal community.

First, although each mandala produced was highly unique, many participants constructed their mandalas with reference to cultural and community themes. For example, one participant described his mandala (Figure 1) in the following manner: 'I've got the eagle feathers hanging here, and that represents my culture, something that I stick too, something very strong that I'm very proud of … I always want to represent my culture'. Eagle feathers are sacred to Aboriginal peoples, as the eagle

Figure 1.   Mandala created by a 20-year-old male hockey player.

soars higher and sees farther than any other creature on earth, and is believed to be a messenger to the Creator. The feathers are used to symbolise honour, strength, courage, wisdom, power and freedom and are given to people who exhibit valour and bravery. In this manner, the participant's depiction of eagle feathers on hockey sticks serves to link his relocation journey with notions of bravery and honouring of the Creator. Another participant described how her mandala (Figure 2) was out-lined by the colours of the Medicine Wheel, which reminded her of the cultural teachings she was brought up with and how those teachings aided her through her sport journey. She also added 'I put a heart for home, my home in [reserve]. Wher-ever I go I'll always come back and be proud of where I'm from'. This participant describes how her heart remains in her community, no matter where she moves and indicates that she is connected to her community at a fundamental level. Through the image of a heart, her community is positioned as a core lifeline in her relocation journey, while the Medicine Wheel outline reveals the cultural frame of her life. Similarly, another participant used the symbol of a tree with roots (Figure 3) to describe how she was linked to her home community and her culture and how this connection gave her the strength to pursue her sport dreams:

> I felt tied to my roots. It was really racist and that made me more proud of who I was … I wouldn't let go of my roots. In that sense the roots helped me to see that I can go out and I can do this, I can prove that I'm not going to be another negative stereotype.

Just as tree roots are connected to Mother Earth and serve to nourish the tree, this participant developed roots in her home community and her culture, which served as sources of strength and pride during her relocation and helped her to persist after her dreams.

Figure 2.   Mandala created by an 18-year-old female hockey player.

Figure 3.   Mandala created by a 22-year-old female hockey player.

These examples demonstrate how the mandala drawing process resonated with the participants and helped them to share their experiences more holistically through a circular (Indigenous) worldview that is encompassing rather than compartmentalising. The images, and the narratives around them, reveal the participants' connectedness to their home communities and their culture, indicating that these individuals see their relocation experiences as tied to the collective rather than being solitary, individual journeys. In this manner, the arts-based research process has affirmed the need for culturally-driven, community-level efforts to continue being made to support athletes who move into mainstream contexts.

Figure 4 tells the story of an athlete who was challenged by racism, but who used that as an opportunity to learn more about her culture and to build strength through knowledge. Her mandala is encased by rays of light with the word 'life'

Figure 4.   Mandala created by a 19-year-old female hockey player.

inside to show how her relocation journey helped her develop pride in her Aboriginal identity and inspired her to make something of her life in order to give back to her cultural community. In this manner, her image highlights a growing sense of community responsibility that is aligned with an Aboriginal collectivist worldview. In Figure 5, an athlete shares how his father gave him and his siblings the opportunity to reach their full potential by enabling them to relocate for sport opportunities. By drawing his family inside the mandala and writing shared values around the perimeter, the athlete affirms the centrality of family processes within Aboriginal culture, explicating how his relocation journey stemmed from his family's emphasis on supporting one another. Figure 6 tells the story of a young athlete whose mind was flooded with questions about her decision to relocate for sport hockey and how it would affect her and her family. Though the image of a rain cloud shows how she struggled with being away from her family, a sun is used to symbolise how she persisted through the hard times in order to realise her sport dreams and make her loved ones proud. These seasonal images centralise an Aboriginal worldview that recognises the life process as being in a constant state of flux; as one season falls upon another, hardships pass and life changes in ways that bring new perspectives. Through the contrasting use of bright and dark colours alongside the image of a road, Figure 7 reveals the overwhelming emotions that one athlete experienced, ranging from fear and sadness to excitement and happiness, as she moved away from home for the first time and set out to pursue her sport dreams. Her road leads into a burst of light to show how she overcame the initial challenges of relocation and is now filled with excitement at the thought of what the future holds. The image reveals the emotional aspects of relocation which are intertwined with the physical and mental aspects of the journey, reinforcing a holistic (Indigenous) way of knowing and being in the world.

Overall, the arts-based method produced knowledge (in visual form) that is much more accessible and relevant at the community-level than traditional forms of data presentation (Cole and Knowles 2008). Each of the aforementioned mandalas tells a story in a way that may resonate more deeply and lucidly with local people than a written research report. The Aboriginal researchers demonstrated this when

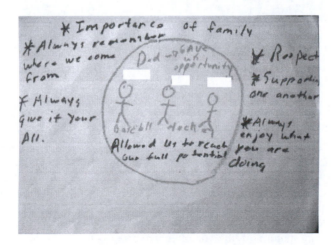

Figure 5.   Mandala created by a 23-year-old male hockey player.

Figure 6.   Mandala created by a 14-year-old female hockey player.

Figure 7.   Mandala created by a 15-year-old female hockey player.

they suggested that the images be printed on a community blanket and displayed publicly at the Wikwemikong Youth Centre. They explained how the individual mandalas fit together to reflect a more collective narrative about young Aboriginal people who are pursuing their dreams and trying to make something of themselves and how the images offered valuable teachings for local youth. Through this community display, the mandalas are now being used by sport and recreation staff to educate youth about what it is like to relocate off-reserve for sport opportunities, as well as to inspire those with dreams of their own to go out and pursue them. This reflects the circular nature of the mandala art process in terms of connecting the individual to the collective whole and emphasising the interconnectedness of lived experiences. Additionally, in using the blanket to share the mandalas with younger generations of community athletes, knowledge dissemination has taken on a circular form, cycling information from one generation to another. The arts-based method in the current project, thus, served a community-driven PAR agenda by producing knowledge that is directly amenable to local action and that sustains Aboriginal (i.e. circular) ways of thinking and being in the world.

Discussion

Although visual methods (i.e. photography and film), as well as performative and narrative art forms, have been promoted within qualitative sport and exercise research as alternatives (or supplements) to verbal modes of knowledge production, visual arts-based methods that involve the actual making of artistic creations (i.e. drawings) have rarely been used. This is disappointing, given that researchers in other social science disciplines have increasingly attested to the value of these arts-based methods for facilitating richer understandings of the emotional, sensory, embodied and imaginative dimensions of experience (Guillemin 2004, Gillies *et al.* 2005, Finley 2008, Bagnoli 2009, Mason and Davies 2009), as well as for engaging more meaningful research processes with marginalised, non-Western cultural groups (Huss 2009, Liebenberg 2009). The purpose of the current initiative was to explore and show how one arts-based method (i.e. mandala drawings) can be used in sport research to facilitate PAR and generate knowledge that resonates more deeply with marginalised (e.g. Aboriginal) community members. Towards this end, a discussion of the strengths and challenges of arts-based methods within PAR is provided, as learned through the current project.

Strengths of arts-based methods in PAR

One of the advantages of arts-based methods is that these methods are strengths-based (Huss 2009), stressing what people do well in their lives, and are therefore enjoyable for people to participate in. This may be particularly relevant for margina-lised or oppressed peoples who often have problem-saturated narratives about their lives (Coholic 2011, Coholic *et al.* 2012). For example, it is well documented how research has traditionally been conducted on Aboriginal peoples in ways that emphasise their problems and deficiencies rather than their strengths and capacities (Smith 1999). In order to support any positive change within these communities, it is imperative that a strength-based approach to be adopted that recognises and builds upon the assets of local people (Bartlett *et al.* 2007). In the current project, upon creating a mandala and completing an interview, one young woman exclaimed, 'I think it's so cool that you are doing this and asking about this stuff. It kind of reminds you that you're actually doing something really big and amazing to people'. This participant truly enjoyed sharing her story through both the art-making and interview processes, and together these processes seemed to build a sense of pride in her as she reflected on her accomplishments as a relocated athlete. Many of the participants further articulated their intent to use their stories to encourage other Aboriginal youth to pursue their dreams and make positive life choices. For example, one young woman stated,

> I want to be kind of like a role model for other people on the reserve to get out there and do what they want ... because I know a lot of people who still haven't graduated

high school. Or they graduated and they're just staying [on reserve] and not doing anything with their diploma. So just go after what you want because you can be whatever you want to be if you just work for it.

It is evident that after exploring their experiences in a positive light in the current project, some participants have been inspired to give back to their community by supporting others and acting as role models. This reflects a full-circle process in that the community engaged in this research to identify pathways for supporting local athletes, while reciprocally athletes have been inspired through their participation to give back to the local community.

A second strength of arts-based methods is that they offer expressive alternatives (or supplements) to words and talk, which may be more appealing for people not used to discussing things along Western (logical-scientific) lines of abstraction (Huss 2009). In this regard, arts-based methods hold much promise for carrying out decolonising research with Indigenous and other non-Western cultural groups (Swadener and Mutua 2008, Huss 2009), as community participants are able to engage in research through their own preferred modalities of expression (Bagnoli 2009, Liebenberg 2009). Furthermore, as explained by Kaomea (2003), art serves a decolonising agenda through a process of defamiliarisation or 'making strange', wherein we (researchers) are forced to slow down our perceptions, attend to the images and narratives in front of us, and take notice of the meaning that is beyond initial surface impressions. Defamiliarisation is important when working with a marginalised community because it helps researchers become more reflexively aware of the need to move away from our own preconceptions and ways of thinking so that meanings and perspectives that have long been silenced can be uncovered (Kaomea 2003). The mandalas in the current project, thus, helped the researchers to ask more meaningful questions about the athletes' relocation experiences in order to elicit more holistic and circular understandings of their experiences, and ultimately produce knowledge more aligned with their lives. As one example, the first researcher's thinking in the project began shifting once she realised that many of the participants' mandalas contained images of goals, aspirations and opportunities that related to larger life journeys outside of sport (such as the word 'life' and the image of a graduation cap in Figure 4 or the burst of light symbolised at the end of a highway in Figure 7). In asking participants about these elements, the researcher became aware of the fact that their relocation journeys did not always centre on their sport-related experiences and were more often focused around experiences of personal growth and the opening up of their futures. Accordingly, the researcher realised that she needed to broaden her scope of thinking and remain open to non-sport-related experiences as meaningful components of the athletes' relocation journeys.

A third and fourth advantage of arts-based methods is that the informal, creative process can help alleviate much of the tension and apprehension that participants may feel coming into the research context (Bagnoli 2009) and facilitate a less hierarchical relationship between the researcher and the participant (Spaniol 2005). For instance, in the current project the researcher conversed with the participants about school, work, family and sports, while they both created mandalas, using the activity to establish a sense of rapport and comfort, while also reducing power differentials. Many of the participants were noticeably nervous when they first came to the meeting. Rather than immediately jumping into a formal, researcher-led interview process, the art-making activity seemed to help the participants relax and engage more candidly with the researcher. These methods also facilitated participants' understanding of the arts activity as an opportunity to share their story on their own terms. When working with participants from marginalised communities who have often been made vulnerable through research, it is especially important to facilitate a research process within which participants feel safe and the participant–researcher exchange is less hierarchical. In so doing, participants are enabled to share their experiences more comfortably and openly and engage in a more collaborative process with the researcher.

Finally, arts-based methods are conducive to the action-oriented outcomes that are fundamental to PAR. As indicated by Cole and Knowles (2008, p. 62), art is not produced for art's sake, but rather to involve community members 'in an active process of meaning making that is likely to have transformative potential'. Through creative processes that embrace the multidimensionality and complexity of lived experience, arts-based methods can generate knowledge that more deeply resonates with local people, and therefore has the power to inform and provoke action (Cole and Knowles 2008, Phoenix 2010). As previously explained, the mandalas in the current project contributed to community action in reaffirming the need for local efforts to be directed at supporting athletes through the relocation process, as well as in engaging the mandalas as educational and inspirational resources for aspiring young athletes.

Challenges of arts-based methods in PAR

While arts-based methods are intended to be enjoyable and strengths-based, not all community participants will embrace these activities or feel comfortable engaging in them (Bagnoli 2009). Some participants may experience anxiety at the thought of having to draw something, while others may fear negative judgments of their creation, or even think that the activity is 'childish'. In the current project, four participants noticeably struggled with the idea of drawing a mandala and exhibited some initial resistance to the process. One participant expressed his anxiety when he stated 'I'm bad at art, I failed art class'. In these situations, it is important to reiterate that the arts-based method is a vehicle for self-expression and not an art activity per se. In addition to verbal support, warm-up exercises such as having participants doodle on a page without looking could be used to create some comfort with the process of working with arts-based materials. We acknowledge, however, that some individuals may remain resistant to the art-making process and, as experienced by Bagnoli (2009), even decline participation.

As previously indicated, researchers need to be trained in the use of arts-based methods before engaging with them, as certain skills are required to work simultaneously with both visual and verbal elements (Huss 2009). This requires the guidance of a practiced expert who can experientially lead the researcher through the art process and help him/her become comfortable with it. This takes time and may be somewhat of a challenge for researchers unaccustomed to working with non-verbal-based methods. However, it is important to note that one does not have to be an artist in order to use these methods, as the researcher does not teach art techniques (but rather, facilitates self-expression), and does not analyse/interpret the art creations (participants provide their own interpretations through the use of an interview). With time and training any researcher, including graduate students, can learn to use arts-based methods as vehicles for community-based PAR.

Conclusions

Researchers from a variety of social science disciplines have attested to the value of incorporating arts-based methods into research examining people's lived experiences, suggesting that these methods generate more in-depth understandings that better reflect the perspectives of participants (Guillemin 2004, Bagnoli 2009, Liebenberg 2009, White *et al*. 2010). As further shown in the current paper, arts-based methods can be used to facilitate PAR processes with marginalised community members, as well as to produce locally-resonant knowledge that lends to community enhancement. For instance, the circular form of the mandala drawings in this project centralised Indigenous ways of thinking, and thus contributed to a knowledge production process that reflected circular links between individuals and their community, as well as research and action. What we would like to articulate through this article is that these methods offer enormous potential for generating more meaningful and innovative community-based sport research, as they are open to a diverse range of art forms (such as drawings, paintings, collages, carvings, theatre performances, music, poetry, and stories) which can be adapted in different ways to reflect local community contexts. We recognise that the current project exemplifies just one of an infinite number of possibilities for incorporating arts-based methods within community sport research. Moving forward, other sport researchers working with Aboriginal communities (as well as other non-Western communities) may consider building on the work of the current project by exploring alternative ways of engaging arts-based methods.

It is important to note that in the current project, both the drawings and the interviews comprised the data. Rather than relying on the visual data to 'speak for itself', we used the mandala drawings as a tool to facilitate deeper discussions with the participants and generate a more in-depth, holistic understanding of their experiences. The visual data was understood as being complementary to the narrative data in terms of opening up different ways of knowing that were more aligned with the culture and lives of the Aboriginal participants. While there will be instances when researchers want visual data to stand on its own and elicit emotions and thoughts from an audience, such as a photographic display used to increase awareness of a health issue, in cases such as the current project it is necessary to have the participants translate (through words) the meanings and experiences behind their images in order for others to gain an appreciation of them (e.g. Guillemin 2004, Bagnoli 2009, White *et al*. 2010).

In whatever way an arts-based method is approached within community research, the important point is that it needs to be developed with community members in order to resonate at the local level. What works in one community will not necessarily work in another. As evidenced in the current project, it is critical to engage the local knowledge of community researchers in order to understand how an arts-based method can best be employed to serve the aspirations of PAR, as understood from a community perspective. Accordingly, academic researchers must be willing to learn *from* local community members rather than *about* them.

Acknowledgements

The authors would like to thank the Indigenous Health Research Development Program for funding this community-based research initiative. Funding was received by the third author and the Wikwemikong community researchers.

Notes on contributors

Amy T. Blodgett is a PhD student in the interdisciplinary Human Studies programme at Laurentian University. Her research interests pertain to culturally reflexive methodologies and social justice issues with marginalised sport populations.

Diana A. Coholic is an associate professor in the School of Social Work at Laurentian University. Her research investigates the effectiveness of arts-based methods for improving resilience with vulnerable children and youth.

Robert J. Schinke is a professor in the field of Sport and Exercise Psychology at Laurentian University and the Canada Research Chair in Multicultural Sport and Physical Activity. He and the Wikwemikong community members are also the grant holders of the funding that made this manuscript possible.

Kerry R. McGannon is an assistant professor in Sport and Exercise Psychology in the School of Human Kinetics at Laurentian University. Her research focuses on critical interpretations of physical activity and self-identity using cultural studies approaches and 'alternative' qualitative methodologies (e.g. narrative, discourse analysis). Such research contributes to the field of cultural sport psychology.

Duke Peltier is the current chief of Wikwemikong and the former Sport and Recreation Director. He has been the community lead on multiple research grants examining the experiences of elite Aboriginal athletes and enhancing sport programming support for local youth.

Chris Pheasant is a retired secondary school vice principal in Wikwemikong. He has extensive knowledge of Aboriginal history and cultural traditions, which he has shared in his role as a community researcher engaged in local sport psychology projects.

References

Adams, K., Burns, C., Liebzeit, A., Ryschka, J., Thorpe, S., and Browne, J., 2012. Use of participatory research and photo-voice to support urban aboriginal healthy eating. *Health and social care in the community*, 20 (5), 497–505.

Archibald, L. and Dewar, J., 2010. Creative arts, culture, and healing: building an evidence base. *Pimatisiwin: a journal of aboriginal and indigenous, community health*, 8 (1), 1–25.

Backos, A.K. and Pagon, B.E., 1999. Finding a voice: art therapy with female adolescent sexual abuse survivors. *Art therapy: journal of the American art therapy association*, 16 (3), 126–132.

Bagnoli, A., 2009. Beyond the standard interview: the use of graphic elicitation and arts-based methods. *Qualitative research*, 9 (5), 547–570.

Bartlett, J.G., Iwasaki, Y., Gottlieb, B., Hall, D., and Mannell, R., 2007. Framework for aboriginal-guided decolonizing research involving Métis and first nations persons with diabetes. *Social science and medicine*, 65 (11), 2371–2382.

Blodgett, A.T., Schinke, R.J., Fisher, L.A., Yungblut, H.E., Recollet-Saikkonen, D., Peltier, D., *et al*., 2010. Praxis and community-level sport programming strategies in a Canadian aboriginal reserve. *International journal of sport and exercise psychology*, 8 (3), 262–283.

Blodgett, A.T., Schinke, R.J., Peltier, D., Fisher, L.A., Watson, J., and Wabano, M.J., 2011. May the circle be unbroken: the research recommendations of aboriginal community members engaged in participatory action research with university academics. *Journal of sport and social issues*, 35 (3), 264–283.

Blodgett, A.T., Schinke, R.J., Smith, B., Peltier, D., and Pheasant, C., 2011. In indigenous words: exploring vignettes as a narrative strategy for presenting the research voices of aboriginal community members. *Qualitative inquiry*, 17 (6), 522–533.

Boydell, K.M., Gladstone, B.M., Volpe, T., Allemang, B., and Stasiulis, E., 2012. The production and dissemination of knowledge: a scoping review of arts-based health research. *Forum qualitative sozialforchung/forum: qualitative social research*, 13 (1), Art. 32.

Brydon-Miller, M., Kral, M., Maguire, P., Noffke, S., and Sabhlok, A., 2011. Jazz and the banyan tree: roots and riffs on participatory action research. *In*: N.K. Denzin and Y.S. Lincoln, eds. *The Sage handbook of qualitative research*. Thousand Oaks, CA: Sage, 387–400.

Carless, D. and Douglas, K., 2009. Opening doors: poetic representation of the sport experiences of men with severe mental health difficulties. *Qualitative inquiry*, 15 (10), 1547–1551.

Castleden, H. and Garvin, T., 2008. Modifying photovoice for community-based participatory indigenous research. *Social science and medicine*, 66 (6), 1393–1405.

Coholic, D., 2010. *Arts activities for children and young people in need: helping children to develop mindfulness, spiritual awareness and self-esteem*. London: Jessica Kingsley.

Coholic, D., 2011. Exploring the feasibility and benefits of arts-based mindfulness-based practices with young people in need: aiming to improve aspects of self-awareness and resilience. *Child and youth care forum*, 40 (4), 303–317.

Coholic, D., Fraser, M., Robinson, B., and Lougheed, S., 2012. Promoting resilience within child protection: the suitability of arts-based and experiential group programs for children-in-care. *Social work with groups*, 35 (4), 345–361.

Coholic, D., Cote-Meek, S., and Recollet, D., in press. Exploring the acceptability and perceived benefits of arts-based group methods for aboriginal women: how arts-based methods can incorporate culture and contribute to healing. *Canadian social work review*.

Cole, A.L. and Knowles, J.G., 2008. Arts-informed research. *In*: J.G. Knowles and A.L. Cole, eds. *Handbook of the arts in qualitative research: perspectives, methodologies, examples, and issues*. Thousand Oaks, CA: Sage, 55–70.

Cox, C.T. and Cohen, B.M., 2000. Mandala artwork by clients with DID: clinical observations based on two theoretical models. *Art therapy: journal of the American art therapy association*, 17 (3), 195–201.

Cueva, M., 2011. 'Bringing what's on the inside out': arts-based cancer education with Alaska native peoples. *Pimatisiwin: a journal of aboriginal and indigenous community health*, 9 (1), 1–22.

Douglas, K. and Carless, D., 2009. Exploring taboo issues in professional sport through a fictional approach. *Reflective practice*, 10 (3), 311–323.

Douglas, K. and Carless, D., 2010. Restoring connections in physical activity and mental health research and practice: a confessional tale. *Qualitative research in sport and exercise*, 2 (3), 336–353.

Dufrene, P., 1990. Utilizing the arts for healing from a native American perspective: implications for creative arts therapies. *The Canadian journal of native studies*, 10 (1), 121–131.

Elkis-Abuhoff, D., Gaydos, M., Goldblatt, R., Chen, M., and Rose, S., 2009. Mandala drawings as an assessment tool for women with breast cancer. *The arts in psychotherapy*, 36 (4), 231–238.

Finley, S., 2008. Arts-based research. *In*: J.G. Knowles and A.L. Cole, eds. *Handbook of the arts in qualitative research: perspectives, methodologies, examples, and issues*. Thousand Oaks, CA: Sage, 71–81.

Gilbourne, D., 2010. 'Edge of Darkness' and 'Just in Time': two cautionary tales, two styles, one story. *Qualitative inquiry*, 16 (5), 325–331.

Gillies, V., Harden, A., Johnson, K., Reavey, P., Strange, V., and Willig, C., 2005. Painting pictures of embodied experience: the use of nonverbal data production for the study of embodiment. *Qualitative research in psychology*, 2 (3), 199–212.

Gravestock, H.M., 2010. Embodying understanding: drawing as research in sport and exercise. *Qualitative research in sport and exercise*, 2 (2), 196–208.

Guillemin, M., 2004. Undestanding illness: using drawings as a research method. *Qualitative health research*, 14 (2), 272–289.

Henderson, P., Rosen, D., and Mascaro, N., 2007. Empirical study on the healing nature of mandalas. *Psychology of aesthetics, creativity, and the arts*, 1 (3), 148–154.

Huss, E., 2009. A case study of bedouin women's art in social work: a model of social arts intervention with 'traditional' women negotiating western cultures. *Social work education*, 28 (6), 598–616.

Jung, C.G., 1973. *Mandala symbolism*. Princeton, NJ: Princeton University Press.

Kaomea, J., 2003. Reading erasures and making the familiar strange: defamiliarizing methods for research in formerly colonized and historically oppressed communities. *Educational researcher*, 32 (2), 14–25.

Kidd, S.A. and Kral, M.J., 2005. Practicing participatory action research. *Journal of counseling psychology*, 52 (2), 187–195.

Kovach, M., 2010. Conversational method in indigenous research. *First peoples child and family review*, 5 (1), 40–48.

Liebenberg, L., 2009. The visual image as discussion point: increasing validity in boundary crossing research. *Qualitative research*, 9 (4), 441–467.

Little Bear, L., 2000. Jagged worldviews colliding. *In*: M. Battiste, ed. *Reclaiming indigenous voice and vision*. Vancouver: UBC Press, 77–85.

Llewellyn, D.J. and Gilbourne, D., 2011. Representing applied research experiences through performance: extending beyond text. *In*: D. Gilbourne and M.B. Andersen, eds. *Critical essays in applied sport psychology*. Champagne, IL: Human Kinetics, 23–38.

Mason, J. and Davies, K., 2009. Coming to our senses? A critical approach to sensory methodology. *Qualitative research*, 9 (5), 587–603.

Packard, J., 2008. 'I'm Gonna show you what it's really like out here': the power and limitation of participatory visual methods. *Visual studies*, 23 (1), 63–77.

Patton, M.Q., 2002. *Qualitative research and evaluation methods*. 3rd ed. Thousand Oaks, CA: Sage.

Phoenix, C., 2010. Seeing the world of physical culture: the potential of visual methods for qualitative research in sport and exercise. *Qualitative research in sport and exercise*, 2 (2), 93–108.

Pink, S., 2003. Interdisciplinary agendas in visual research: re-situating visual anthropology. *Visual studies*, 18 (2), 179–192.

Ryba, T.V. and Schinke, R.J., 2009. Methodology as ritualized eurocentrism: introduction to the special issue. *International journal of sport and exercise psychology*, 7 (3), 263–274.

Schinke, R.J., Michel, G., Gauthier, A.P., Pickard, P., Danielson, R., Peltier, D., *et al.*, 2006. The adaptation to the mainstream in elite sport: a Canadian aboriginal perspective. *The sport psychologist*, 20 (4), 435–448.

Schinke, R.J., Peltier, D., Hanrahan, S.J., Eys, M.A., Recollet-Saikkonen, D., Yungblut, H., *et al.*, 2009. The progressive integration of Canadian indigenous culture within a sport psychology bicultural research team. *International journal of sport and exercise psychology*, 7 (3), 309–322.

Schinke, R., Yungblut, H., Blodgett, A., Eys, M., Peltier, D., Ritchie, S., *et al.*, 2010. The role of families in youth sport programming in a Canadian aboriginal reserve. *Journal of physical activity and health*, 7 (2), 156–166.

Slegelis, M.H., 1987. A study of Jung's mandala and its relationship to art psychotherapy. *The arts and psychotherapy*, 14 (4), 301–311.

Smith, L.T., 1999. *Decolonizing methodologies: research and indigenous peoples*. London: Zed.

Spaniol, S., 2005. 'Learned hopefulness': an arts-based approach to participatory action research. *Art therapy: journal of the American art therapy association*, 22 (2), 86–91.

Sparkes, A.C., 2002. *Telling tales in sport and physical activity: a qualitative journey*. Champaign, IL: Human Kinetics.

Sparkes, A.C. and Douglas, K., 2007. Making the case for poetic representations: an example in action. *The sport psychologist*, 21 (2), 170–189.

Swadener, B.B. and Mutua, K., 2008. Decolonizing performances: deconstructing the global postcolonial. *In*: N.K. Denzin, Y.S. Lincoln, and L.T. Smith, eds. *Handbook of critical and indigenous methodologies*. Thousand Oaks, CA: Sage, 31–43.

Van der Vennet, R. and Serice, S., 2012. Can colouring mandalas reduce anxiety? A replication study. *Art therapy: journal of the American art therapy association*, 29 (2), 87–92.

White, A., Bushin, N., Carpena-Mendez, F., and Ni Laoire, C., 2010. Using visual methodologies to explore contemporary Irish childhoods. *Qualitative research*, 10 (2), 143–158.

Wikwemikong Unceded Indian Reserve, 2012. *Wikwemikong unceded Indian reserve website* [online]. Available from: http://www.wikwemikong.ca/ [Accessed 10 December 2012].

Developing sport-based after-school programmes using a participatory action research approach

Nicholas L. Holt, Tara-Leigh F. McHugh, Lisa N. Tink, Bethan C. Kingsley, Angela M. Coppola, Kacey C. Neely and Ryan McDonald

Faculty of Physical Education and Recreation, University of Alberta, Edmonton, Alberta, Canada

This paper is based on a three-year research programme, the overall purpose of which was to develop, implement and evaluate sport-based after-school programmes for students in low-income areas of Edmonton, Alberta, Canada. In addition to presenting the results of this study, the other purpose of this paper was to provide an empirical example of participatory action research, depicting when and how community partners were engaged in the research process. Following several years of initial work in low-income communities, a need to create sport-based after-school programming was identified. The first action phase involved the creation and delivery of a multi-sport programme in two schools. Semi-structured interviews were conducted with 28 children and two teachers to evaluate programme content and benefits. Inductive analysis revealed that the programme provided children with new opportunities and helped them to learn social and personal life skills. In the second action phase, a revised programme was delivered to 35 children. Fourteen children and three teachers participated in interviews to share their views on programme content, benefits and challenges. There were difficulties relating to the children's skill level, behaviour and listening during the early stages of the programme. Nonetheless, by the end of the programme, children reported that they enjoyed activities based on creating optimal challenges and 'adventures' which engaged their imaginations. Children also learned fundamental movement, sport and life skills, some of which transferred to other areas of their lives.

Canadian guidelines call for children and adolescents to engage in 60 min or more of moderate-to-vigorous physical activity (MVPA) per day, but only 4% of Canadian girls and 9% of boys accumulate sufficient amounts of daily MVPA (Colley *et al.* 2011). Research conducted in other developed countries has also revealed that a large proportion of children and adolescents are inactive and lead sedentary lifestyles (Janssen *et al.* 2005). Researchers have suggested that the after-school period (from approximately 3 to 6 pm on weekdays) represents an important time for providing opportunities for physical activity (Pate and O'Neill 2009, Atkin *et al.* 2011). However, results from the 2007 to 2009 Canadian Health Measures Survey revealed that 6- to 19-year-olds accumulated an average of only 14 min of MVPA between 3 and 6 pm. The rest of the time (166 min) was spent in light physical activity or sedentary pursuits (Garriguet and Colley 2012). Thus, as the authors of the Active Healthy Kids Canada (2012) report card highlighted, 'Parents, caregivers, after-school program providers, and children and youth need to understand that the after-school period is an important window of opportunity for physical activity engagement' (p. 10).

Children from lower income families are more likely to be physically inactive and engage in sedentary pursuits than children from higher income families (Janssen et al. 2006). They often have insufficient financial resources to pay sport registration fees and other related costs that limit sustained participation (Holt et al. 2011) and restrict access to sport/leisure facilities (Gordon-Larsen et al. 2000). Additionally, for families living in low-income neighbourhoods, safety concerns may limit the amount of time children spend playing outdoors (Holt et al. 2009a). Researchers have identified a need for more planned and adult-supervised programmes in low-income areas (e.g. Humbert et al. 2006). After-school programmes may, therefore, provide affordable and safe places for children from low-income families to engage in physical activity (Active Healthy Kids Canada 2012).

Despite their promise, evidence for the effectiveness of after-school programmes is mixed. Pate and O'Neill (2009) reviewed studies examining after-school programmes designed to promote physical activity. Of the six randomised controlled trials reviewed, four produced significant increases in physical activity among children in the intervention group and two studies demonstrated trends toward increasing physical activity. Of the three quasi-experimental studies reviewed, two were effective in increasing children's physical activity. Atkin et al. (2011) recently conducted a more comprehensive review of 10 papers reporting nine studies (four of which had been included in the Pate and O'Neill review). Positive changes in physical activity were shown in three studies and no change was reported in six studies. Effective interventions were located in school settings whereas non-effective interventions were more likely to take place in combinations of school, home and community venues. There was also evidence that interventions targeting physical activity alone, rather than in combination with diet, were more effective. Nonetheless, Atkin et al. concluded that 'overall, findings indicate that interventions to promote physical activity delivered in the after-school setting have been ineffective to date' (p. 185). One reason for the limited effectiveness of after-school physical activity interventions may be the extent to which programmes are informed by, and relevant to, the needs of targeted communities (Witt 2004, Pate et al. 2007). As such, there is apparently a need for better understandings of how to create and deliver after-school programmes to promote physical activity among members of specific communities.

The current paper reports the results of a three-year research programme, the overall purpose of which was to develop, implement and evaluate sport-based after-school programmes for students in low-income areas of Edmonton, Alberta, Canada (a city which currently faces unprecedented levels of poverty and income inequality; Parkland Institute 2012). In addition to presenting the results of this research, the other purpose of this paper was to provide an empirical example of participatory action research (PAR), depicting when and how community partners were engaged in the research process.

Method

PAR is a way of approaching research as a collaborative enterprise founded on the assumption that academic researchers and community members can come together in some ways to create or change practices (Kemmis and McTaggart 2000, Brydon-Miller *et al.* 2011). Such participatory approaches are appropriate when researchers seek to understand the experiences of those involved, affected by or excluded from various forms of sport and physical activity (Frisby *et al.* 1997, 2005). Various researchers have demonstrated the merits of using PAR approaches when working with children and/or adolescents to address physical activity and sport opportunities within school settings (e.g. Bostock and Freeman 2003, Oliver *et al.* 2009, McHugh and Kowalski 2011, Enright and O'Sullivan 2012). Hence, PAR offered an appropriate methodological selection for this research project.

PAR does not refer to a singular methodological approach, but rather a collection of approaches that (usually) include a process of self-reflective cycles involving planning, acting and observing, and reflecting (Kemmis and McTaggart 2000, Stringer and Genat 2004). The current research was informed by an approach described by Frisby *et al.* (1997), who used PAR to examine access to physical activity services among low-income women. They based their approach on the original work of Green *et al.* (1995) and specifically described a five-phase research project. These phases were defining the problem (e.g. members of the community seek outside assistance from researchers to investigate a problem), building relationships (e.g. develop nonhierarchical partnerships with community members), community mobilisation (e.g. community members take on responsibility for portions of the project, which can include providing resources and expertise), data collection and analysis (e.g. participants may be involved to varying degrees in gathering, analysing and drawing conclusions from information), and action (e.g. changing existing services to accommodate newly revealed needs). In employing these broad steps, the current research was open, fluid and responsive to the needs of community partners and, therefore, the sequence of different phases of research was unique to this particular project. Hence, this research was an adapted version of the PAR approach reported by Frisby *et al.* (1997), which appeared to be appropriate given that Frisby and her colleagues have themselves presented papers depicting adaptations of the specific elements of their PAR approach (Frisby and Millar 2002, Frisby *et al.* 2005).

Research process

When using PAR, academic researchers enter into interactive relationships with community partners, who may be involved in some or all phases of the research project (Frisby *et al.* 2005). The current manuscript is intended to portray *when* and *how* various members of the research team (the academic researchers and the community partners)[1] were engaged in the research process in order to provide an empirical example of the execution of a PAR study. An overview of the process is depicted in Figure 1 and explained throughout the following sections. The principles underpinning the current research were consistent with the framework used by Frisby *et al.* (1997), but (as noted above) the sequence of events was unique to this particular study. Three main phases of the research are presented: the initial work (early community-based research with members of low-income communities in Edmonton), the first action phase (the After-School Sports Kids [ASSK] programme) and the second action phase (the TRY-Sport programme).

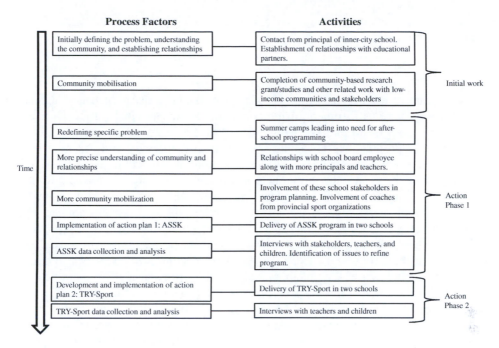

Figure 1.   Overview of research process.

Initial work

Initially defining the problem, understanding the community and establishing relationships

Frisby *et al.* (1997) explained that the first phase of PAR involves members of a community experiencing 'social problems' seeking assistance from other agencies and researchers to 'investigate the problem and identify alternatives for change' (p. 12). This perspective acknowledges the capacity of community members to identify issues relevant to their own lives. To establish context for the current research, it is necessary to briefly discuss some of NLH's (the lead academic researcher/author) initial community-based research in low-income areas of Edmonton, which can be traced back to the winter of 2005. NLH was teaching an undergraduate course on children's sport and physical activity. The course included fieldwork trips to inner-city and suburban neighbourhoods to compare and contrast opportunities for children to engage in sport and physical activity. Serendipitously, the principal of an inner-city elementary/middle school heard about the fieldwork trip through one of the undergraduate students and invited the class into the school to discuss the extracurricular sport and physical activity programmes it offered. The school was in an extremely 'disadvantaged' part of the city and had, according to the principal, adopted a policy that involved providing a range of extracurricular programming (e.g. sport, music and arts) to give students opportunities they may not have otherwise received. During this first meeting, in addition to discussing the programmes the school offered, the principal also expressed that she wanted some help in evaluating their value. Furthermore, she thought that establishing some connections with the university could add to the capacity of the school to provide sport and physical activity programming. Thus, the original definition of the 'problem' of providing and evaluating school-based extracurricular programming came from a member of the community.

Community mobilisation

The academic researchers became engaged in a gradual process of becoming more involved with various members of the community. The principal put NLH in contact with a school board employee responsible for the coordination and provision of extracurricular programmes to all the schools in the inner-city and a school board trustee (an elected official) who was deeply committed to children's health. With the support of these educational partners and accompanied by our increased understanding of some of the key issues, we (the academic researchers in collaboration with the school board trustee, employee and principal) successfully applied for a community-oriented research grant to explore sport and physical activity provision in the inner-city. One aspect of this research involved 'embedding' a research assistant in the school from September to May. The decision to embed a research assistant in the school was made collaboratively by the principal and NLH because her presence both facilitated the research process and provided additional 'staff' to add capacity to the school. That is, in addition to collecting data, the research assistant fulfilled the role of a general assistant, spending time with children from grades 5 to 9 in classroom and extracurricular settings. At the request of the school board trustee and employee, NLH also made presentations to the board of trustees, other school board employees and provincial government employees from the education ministry.

Two studies were published from this initial research with the school in question. These studies were based on interviews with 59 children and eight school staff, which were supplemented by interviews with 13 youth workers from several inner-city agencies involved in the provision of sport and physical activity opportunities. The first study (Holt *et al.* 2009a) examined opportunities and barriers to physical activity in the neighbourhood (as opposed to within the school per se). Although there were numerous physical activity opportunities in the neighbourhood (e.g. playgrounds, sport fields and evening programmes), children's access to these facilities was restricted because of concerns about 'stranger danger' (e.g. homeless people, drunks, drug users, prostitutes, gangs and bullies). There were also barriers to participation in evening programmes (i.e. programmes after 6 pm) because of problems with transportation, concerns about violence and staffing challenges.

The second study (Holt *et al.* 2011) examined school staff members' and children's perceptions of programmes offered within the school (i.e. physical education (PE) classes, intramural sports and sport teams) with a view to establishing factors that facilitated or impeded youth development. The findings highlighted the value of a specialist PE teacher who established clear boundaries during lessons while providing children with perceptions of choice. Children appeared to enjoy intramural sports (i.e. they were fun), but there were few attempts to create a developmentally appropriate atmosphere (that is, children were supervised during these sessions, with a supervisor-to-student ratio of 1–40 or 50, but there were few attempts to use particular pedagogical strategies such as those observed in the PE classes). In fact, there were numerous negative interactions between students during intramurals, which appeared to be at least partially related to the absence of structure. Coaches of the sport teams used a range of different techniques to promote social interactions and respect, and students reported learning about empathy and developing social skills. Holt *et al.* concluded that 'ways to incorporate the structure and developmental orientation of PE lessons, the "fun" of intramural sports, and the "life skills" focus of the sport teams should be explored' (p. 16). These studies, which were based on the views of various community stakeholders (including adults and children), informed the current research.

Action phase 1

Redefining specific problem

Soon after the completion of data collection for these two studies (i.e. Holt *et al.* 2009a, 2011), the original elementary/middle school was closed due to escalating costs and relatively low enrollment. Around this time, one of the co-authors of the current study (LNT) became involved with the research team as a Masters student and ultimately generated the initial idea for the research reported in the current paper. The impetus came when she was hired by a non-profit organisation to help create, deliver and evaluate summer sport camps for children in low-income areas of the city. The aim of this project was to develop a new strategy for the non-profit organisation to engage young people and their families. Partnering with the school board, four weeks of summer sports camps were delivered. Evaluations revealed that the children responded very positively to the camps, and the adult community members were pleased with the collaboration, which provided an indication that there was scope for creation of additional programming. But while summer camps were valuable, there remained a need to provide programming to children during the school year. Furthermore, in the face of a tight educational budget, schools faced even more difficulties in providing extracurricular programming than when the initial research (i.e. Holt *et al.* 2009a, 2011) took place. Through the summer camps and the partnerships with the non-profit organisation and school board employee, the need for after-school sport and physical activity programming during the school year was identified.

More precise understanding of community and relationships

The school board employee became an important partner because she placed a great deal of value on physical activity promotion and thought sport could play an important role in the lives of many children. For her, the summer camps seemed to represent an opportunity to 'rollout' physical activity/sport programming to schools. Around the same time, the after-school period was becoming a 'hot topic' in the province and several surveys/audits were being conducted (see City of Calgary 2008, Alberta Centre for Active Living 2012). This was set against a context of increasing concerns about children's engagement in physical activity – especially for young children in low-income areas (Humbert *et al.* 2006, Holt *et al.* 2009a, Pate and O'Neill 2009, Active Healthy Kids Canada 2012). The partnership with the school board employee was integral to moving from the summer camps project 'into' the after-school programming. She worked with principals in her school district to gauge their interest in after-school programming and ultimately facilitated the identification (and subsequent involvement) of two schools that were not only located in low-income neighbourhoods but would also benefit from after-school programme provision. These schools had few existing resources, a high proportion of new immigrant children, and the principals had favourable attitudes toward supporting the provision of sport-based programming. Through collaboration with the partner from the school board, the academic researchers developed a more precise understanding of the need to change existing service provision (which, in terms of sport and physical activity after-school programmes, was almost non-existent in some schools).

More community mobilisation

Having identified and established connections with two schools, members of these communities were mobilised in terms of providing resources and expertise. For example, the principals provided resources in terms of access to school gymnasia and teachers provided expertise in terms of logistical aspects of programme delivery. Together, the principals, teachers and academic researchers decided that the programme would run for three months in each school (in conjunction with specific phases of the school year) and on two afternoons per week (which was feasible for the schools and, from a research perspective, adequate engagement with the children to provide sufficient exposure to the activities). The programme was offered to children in grades 2 and 3 because the teachers thought these children would likely benefit the most from the programme if it provided them with skills and competence to play sport in the future (the academic researchers agreed with this recommendation because it was consistent with the literature and policy; Trost *et al.* 2008, Canadian Sport 4 Life [CS4L] 2012). Teachers also provided leadership in terms of specifically identifying and encouraging particular children to be involved in the programme. The programme was offered primarily to children who would not have other opportunities for extracurricular activities. Teachers identified these children and, after their registration, the programme was opened up to other children from grades 2 to 3 in the particular schools. Further, community mobilisation included the involvement of coaches from various provincial sport organisations (e.g. handball, wrestling, tennis and basketball) to help deliver the programme. The research team moved relatively quickly to the first action phase, but had yet to engage perhaps the most crucial group – the children themselves. This imbalance was addressed during the next phase of the research.

Implementation of action phase 1: ASSK

Frisby *et al.* (1997) suggested that prior to engaging in action, data should be gathered and analysed through methods such as surveys, interviews, focus groups or programme evaluations to engage participants and co-create knowledge that provides the basis for action plans. Although following the principle of engaging participants to co-create a basis for action, the formal data collection methods described by Frisby *et al.* were not used. Rather, as indicated in the previous sections, our team (which, at this point, included the academic researchers, a school board partner, principals and teachers) thought that we had sufficient understanding of the context, problem and community needs. Hence, the research team moved directly into the first stage of action and delivered the first iteration of the after-school programme, the ASSK programme (a name one of the children suggested), which was provided to 35 children from grades 2 to 3 at two schools. The programme operated out of the gymnasia and children were provided a healthy snack in addition to a range of games and sports. Two researchers/fieldworkers facilitated the programme activities. In addition to running sessions, they coordinated the involvement of the coaches from provincial sport organisations.

Although there was variation in the type of instruction provided by different coaches, in general, programme activities were based on fundamental movement and sport skills. These skills reflect the CS4L 'FUNdamentals' stage for children (targeted at girls aged approximately 6–8 years and boys aged 6–9 years). During this time, it is suggested that children should develop agility, balance, coordination and speed in a fun and challenging multi-sport environment with minimal focus on competition (CS4L 2012). These fundamental movement skills are intended to provide the foundation for teaching more sport-specific skills.

ASSK data collection and analysis

Formal data collection and analysis were completed after the delivery of the ASSK action phase to obtain participants' views of the programme – information subsequently used to help guide the next action phase. As part of the larger research study, semi-structured interviews were conducted with 19 adult stakeholders (e.g. coaches, members of non-profit organisations, school board members, etc.). Their data were not included in the current paper because these interviews focused on wider issues of sport and physical activity programming for children in low-income areas that are not directly relevant. However, data from two teachers interviewed were included because they provided examples of specific issues relating to what children may have learned through participating in ASSK. These teachers were also asked to comment on the strengths and weaknesses of the ASSK programme. Their data were used in conjunction with data generated during interviews with the children.

Twenty-eight of the 35 children who received the programme were interviewed to establish their views about the ASSK programme. Only those children who volunteered were interviewed. In total, 10 (of 14) students from one school and 18 (of 21) students from other school were interviewed. The children varied in age from 7 to 9 years old. In terms of ethnicity/countries of origin, 14 were White Canadians, 5 Aboriginal, 5 African, 1 South East Asian, 1 Chinese, 1 Hispanic, 1 East Indian and 6 children of Arabic descent. The ethnicity of one child was unknown. A total of 14 children spoke English as their second language.

Research Ethics Board and School Board approval was obtained to conduct all phases of the research. Teachers provided written informed consent. Parents provided written informed consent for their children, and the children provided verbal assent. Interviews were conducted at the school by a researcher/fieldworker and lasted approximately 30 min. The aim of the interviews was to establish children's views about the ASSK programme and how it might be improved in the future. Children were asked questions about the programme (e.g. What were the best/worst things about the programme?), instruction (e.g. What did the leaders teach during the programme?), programme delivery (e.g. If you could change the programme in any way, what would you change?) and a final summary question (If you could design a sports programme that you and all your friends could be in, what activities would you play?). Audio files from the interviews were transcribed verbatim and stripped of identifying information.

Data were subjected to an inductive content analysis procedure (Maykut and Morehouse 1994). Following transcription of the audio tapes, the transcripts were read several times by two researchers/fieldworkers to ensure their immersion in the data. The next step was to identify 'chunks' or 'units' of meaning in the data – a process called *unitising the data*. Units of data (i.e. quotes) were identified from the interview transcripts and similar quotes were grouped together as themes. This 'discovery' step is intended to identify a large array of potentially important issues (or themes). Next, similar themes were grouped together or abstracted into more general categories and (as recommended by Maykut and Morehouse) the constant comparative method (Glaser and Strauss 1967) was used to ensure that data coded in each theme/category were unique and distinct. Rules of inclusion were written to reflect the meaning captured by each category. The categories were reviewed by the academic researchers and later by the principals and some teachers. Finally, in writing this manuscript, the researchers selected the most pertinent findings that were relevant to the purpose of this research. These findings are reported below. Pseudonyms have been applied and, unless otherwise stated, the quotes were from interviews conducted with the children.

ASSK results

New opportunities

ASSK exposed children to new opportunities (i.e. activities many of the children had never played before). These opportunities were important because the children had few other opportunities to engage in sport programmes. Liz told us 'I've never been in a programme after-school … [And] my parents, they don't have enough money for a lot of sports things'. Similarly, Matt said, 'I learned some sports and some games … I play those games nowhere else'. A specific example outlining the lack of opportunities for one student was given by Anne (a teacher) who said, 'I was thinking about [name of student] because I think in that situation specifically if she can't do it [sport], not through home, like if it's not through school then she just doesn't get it'. The other teacher, Bev, reinforced these issues and said:

> I think just it was something that was really beneficial for the kids to have something to go to twice a week and to learn lots of new skills and to have an opportunity to be physically active for a good hour and a half at least twice a week when otherwise they probably would not have been doing that.

Social and personal life skills

Children described learning some social (e.g. making new friends) and personal (e.g. confidence) life skills through participating in ASSK. Meagan said she had learned 'How to cooperate with others' and 'to meet new people and to learn new things'. Anna said, 'I feel like I'm learning that, that to play as a team. If there's a person left out who has no partner you let them join [in] …' The teachers also noted these opportunities to learn social skills. In fact, Bev (teacher) thought the social skills could be particularly important because:

> I think that some of our kids don't really get a lot of that support at home in terms of good social skills and things and so helping them to learn those skills, which will be helpful in any setting, is good.

Additionally, the programme was viewed as a context where students could try new things and improve their confidence. A specific example was given by Anne (teacher) who described the improvement she had seen in one of her student's confidence. She said:

> I think someone like [name of student], I think just because he's kind of an all over [the place] kind of kid, being successful there I think just helped him, you know, whether we saw it transfer into the classroom I don't know but I think for him it was good. Just a little confidence, yeah, built some confidence for him.

This example also reflected another important issue; namely that the teacher was unsure as to whether or not the skills the child learned transferred into the class-room.

Action phase 2

Development and implementation of action phase 2: TRY-Sport

Given that PAR is a collaborative and reflective process that seeks to transform practice through action (Kemmis and McTaggart 2000), the next phase of this research involved further refining and redeveloping the programme based on the data obtained and analysed during the previous phase. Even though the analysis was reviewed by principals and teachers, the process was driven by the academic researchers, which differed from the Frisby *et al*'s. (1997) approach (they had more involvement from community members at a comparable stage of their research). That said, there were numerous examples from the children and teachers through which they voiced a need for the continued delivery of the programme as it pro-vided opportunities the children would not otherwise receive. Social and personal life skills were reported even though ASSK did not include an intentional approach to developing such skills. Therefore, in refining the programme, the academic researchers decided to capitalise on these apparent strengths of the programme context and more intentionally target life skills. Furthermore, because a teacher expressed doubts about whether the life skills helped the children in the classroom, life skills were taught in a manner that may allow 'transfer' to other areas of their lives (cf. Papacharisis *et al*. 2005). Teamwork and confidence were selected because these life skills were identified through the previous phase of the research. The academic researchers added a third life skill (leadership) because research suggests this can be learned within sport settings (e.g. Hellison *et al*. 2008, Holt *et al*. 2008, 2009b).

A notable recommendation that the academic researchers made, which was supported by principals and teachers, was to *not* involve coaches from provincial sport organisations in the delivery of the revised programme. Their previous involvement was valuable and facilitated the inclusion of a range of sports. How-ever, the academic researchers thought, and the principals and teachers agreed, that it was possible to create a programme using a fewer number of sports and still address a range of movement and life skills. Also, facilitating the attendance of coaches was a demanding and time-intensive task that would lend itself to challenges in the long term because these organisations have limited resources and often a high turnover in staff (cf. Holt *et al*. 2009a). Another issue was that different coaches used varying teaching techniques and styles, so it was difficult to ensure the developmental appropriateness of the pedagogy, which may be an important aspect of programme delivery in low-income school settings (Holt *et al.* 2011).

The academic researchers also made a recommendation to focus on three sports. Again, this recommendation was supported by the school partners. The academic researchers wanted to focus on three sports (soccer, basketball and volleyball) because they would cover a broad range of fundamental movement skills (running, jumping, kicking, throwing, striking, etc.). Also, these three sports required minimal equipment which was important because (a) schools did not have financial resources to buy equipment and (b) we would not be able to rely on the coaches, as we did in Phase 2, to bring sport-specific equipment. The name of the programme was changed to TRY-Sport, and goals of the programme were to teach fundamental movement and sport skills (using soccer, volleyball and basketball) and life skills (teamwork, leadership and confidence). Unlike during the first action phase, when one of the children 'named' the ASSK programme, we (the academic researchers) named TRY-Sport because of the focus on three sports/life skills and to emphasise that the programme was an opportunity for children to 'try' sports.

TRY-Sport was delivered by three researchers/fieldworkers to children at two schools in low-income areas. The team (academic researchers, principals and teachers in this case) supported some parents' requests to attend the programme, which, as it turned out, was useful for translating instructions to the younger children who did not have a strong command of English. The programme was opened to younger children (i.e. grades K-3). This recommendation came from the principals and teachers – again because of the view that younger children would benefit from being exposed to the programme.

From a pedagogical perspective, some activities involved asking children to provide incidences of how the teamwork needed to execute a particular game might help them in the classroom or at home. The children were then expected to try to apply some of these skills in their daily lives. Then, in a subsequent session, the researchers/fieldworkers used reflective techniques (Holt *et al.* 2007, Jones *et al.* 2011) and asked children to provide specific examples of how they had used these skills in their lives. Sessions also included activities designed to teach children fundamental movement skills in ways that engaged their imagination (Anderson 2001). Children were provided opportunities for input and choices over certain activities and the researchers/fieldworkers sought to create optimal challenges – pedagogical strategies intended to promote intrinsic motivation in physical activity and sport settings (Mandigo and Holt 2000, 2006, Mandigo *et al.* 2008). An example of a session plan has been included in the appendix.

TRY-Sport data collection and analysis

TRY-Sport was delivered to 35 children (from grades K-3) attending two schools in low-income areas. During the programme, the researchers/fieldworkers maintained logs that included observations and critical reflections on their involvement and issues related to programme content and delivery, detailed examples of which have been reported elsewhere (Holt *et al.* in press). Following the programme, the researchers/fieldworkers interviewed 14 children (7 boys and 7 girls) from grades 2 and 3 from a range of different ethnic backgrounds (we did not obtain specific demographic information). The youngest children (i.e. K – grade 1) were not interviewed due to their limited language skills. Three teachers (one full-time teacher and two teaching aides) were also interviewed.

Children were asked about their perceptions of the activities in which they were engaged, the skills they may have learned and the extent to which these skills may have helped them in other areas of their lives. Questions included: If you were describing the programme to a kid who was thinking of joining us, what would you say? Tell me about your favorite parts of the programme. What did you learn about from being in the programme? What were the parts of the programme you liked the least? Tell me what leadership (teamwork/confidence) means. What did you learn about leadership (teamwork/confidence) during the programme? If you could change the programme in any way what would you do? Interviews with the children which lasted for approximately 20–25 min were transcribed verbatim, stripped of identifying information and assigned pseudonyms. The teachers were also asked to provide their views of the programme and, although interviews with the teachers were free-flowing and conversational, they covered most of the same issues the children had been asked to discuss. The same analysis principles described previously were applied to the data and the key findings are reported below.

TRY-Sport results

Difficulties encountered

Before discussing some of the benefits of the programme, it is important to make it clear that the researchers/fieldworkers faced several difficulties. For example, at the beginning of TRY-Sport, the researchers/fieldworkers had concerns about the children's skill level, behaviour and listening. In terms of skill level, the researchers/fieldworkers had apparently over-estimated the fundamental movement skills that the children would possess to such an extent that they could not run some of the games and activities initially planned. Indeed, as one of the fieldworkers noted in her journal:

> Just from observing this week, their actual physical skills aren't as strong as I would have thought. I'm probably just assuming kids can run, jump, and throw. But I guess if you are never taught properly, you don't really learn – so I guess that's where we come in.

As the reflection implies, the researchers/fieldworkers soon realised the need to focus more on teaching fundamental movement skills and continued to adapt the programme activities to cater for a range of skill levels.

The researchers/fieldworkers also had trouble, during the early stages of the programme, simply getting the children to listen. One of the teachers remarked on this and said 'I think it was just difficult for the reason that they went to school all day in a structured environment. Then they came to after-school programme [and didn't want to listen]'. Furthermore, a teacher suggested a reason for some of the behavioural issues we initially faced was:

> All these kids are like, um they're new, newer kids [i.e. newcomers to Canada] and so they, they've been living like in refugee camps or whatever. Basically their life is like you fight first for whatever … There's like 10 kids in a household that's how they solve their problems right. Mom is not gonna be focused on each kid and so, problem solving, they'll just solve their own problems.

The researchers/fieldworkers and teachers discussed the behavioural issues and devised a system in which teachers would attend the programme and help ensure the children were listening. As one teacher said 'I just figured my role as trying to like keep them engaged and keep them paying attention because I wanted them to learn'.

Finally, it took time for some of the children to trust the researchers/fieldworkers. An important suggestion made by one of the teachers was that, in the future, it would be useful for the instructors to come into the school before the start of a programme to get to know the children. She said:

> … Like before the program even starts … Just coming in and being like 'hey I'm [name of instructors], we're, we're gonna be here, we're gonna be hanging out with you guys … We're gonna teach you some cool stuff in gym.' … It just takes time and like their trust, which sometimes isn't always easy to gain from these kids. Yeah, not always simple.

Benefits of programme

Optimal challenges and adventures. As the programme progressed, the children had positive views of the ways in which the researchers/fieldworkers attempted to engage their imaginations. For example, one activity was called the 'Amazon Adventure' that placed some fundamental movement skills (i.e. jumping and kicking) within the playful context of an imaginary jungle setting. Dana liked this activity and particularly enjoyed 'catching the coconuts, catching the balls, and pretending them as coconuts [*sic*] when he [instructor] threw them up'. Discussing another activity set in an imaginary beach environment, Samuel's comment highlighted both the value of the imaginative approach and the provision of choice. He said:

> … Right before the beach family dance ... We were in the gym and I asked if we could do a beach adventure. And [that is] what we did ... We set out hula hoops and tried to bounce the ball into the sand. The hula hoop was the sand. And then when the tide came in we would all run into the hula hoop.

Referring to another activity that was based on the notion of optimal challenges, John said he liked:

> Us tryin' to clap our hands and throwin' the ball in the air, seeing how much times we can clap our hands … I loved them … That it was a bit of a challenge to do it ... It has to be a little of a challenge or else people won't be interested in it … [And] I can shoot in the big hoop now pretty well. It's kinda like a cannon, you have to aim then fire.

These examples, and many others, suggested that the programme was delivered in a manner that positively engaged the children's imagination.

Fundamental movement and sport skills. One feature of data reported in the previous theme was that each child also referred to specific fundamental movement skills targeted (i.e. catching for Dana, bouncing a ball for Samuel and throwing and shooting a ball for John). As the programme progressed, the children were able to move from mastering fundamental movement skills to skills associated with the three different sports we taught. For example, talking about soccer, Julie told us,

> I learned that we don't use our tip of the foot [to kick] but we use it in the middle part and side. And I learned that 'cause I used to kick it with my toe before. Well I didn't know [that] 'cause I never doing soccer before [sic].

Alan said,

> I learned how to play basketball proper and I learned how to spike the ball [in volleyball] and how to hit the ball with my head [in soccer] and how to try to trick people by putting the ball between your legs and stuff.

Ian mentioned that he got better at some volleyball skills and said 'all of the teachers said, "oh you're getting good at volleyball," I said "[it's] all because of the thing [i.e. TRY-Sport]"'. Similarly, Jordan said:

> Well like I play basketball [but] I kinda didn't know a bunch of moves, so they [instructors] were teaching me. 'Cause you could go bounce, pass and then pass it back 'cause if you jump up then they can pass it to you and you can get a goal [basket] … I would say that it's fun. So that's really good and I love it and I hope they come to this school again.

Teachers also recognised some of the improvements made by the children. One teacher remarked 'they [the children] liked being good at stuff too, so a lot of them did get a lot better at things … [One of the girls], she just loved it, and she was so cute'. And another teacher said:

> You guys actually taught how to play sports. Instead of saying 'OK, go play soccer' you guys taught how you dribble a ball or the correct form of how to throw a volleyball. Like it's teaching them the right way instead of just being like 'OK do this, these are the rules, do whatever you want with it' sort of thing. So I thought that was good.

Indeed, the strategy of teaching fundamental movement and sport skills seemed to have some positive consequences *after* the programme ended. A teacher said:

> When you guys left and we started playing soccer with them they really enjoyed it. Before they were just like 'we don't wanna play soccer.' Then when you guys left and [then] they loved soccer … Every time, like now we go outside, the Grade 2s and 3s, they'll just take a soccer ball. Before they hated soccer. But I guess now that they know the rules and they know how to play properly they enjoy it more.

Life skills

There was variation in the children's responses when it came to discussing life skills they may have learned by participating in TRY-Sport. Some examples in relation to the three main life skills targeted (teamwork, leadership and confidence) are provided below.

Teamwork. Most children were able to provide specific examples of teamwork they had learned in TRY-Sport. Julie said she had learned that

> working together is better and then you can like win a game maybe, or sometimes if the other team wins, it doesn't matter if you win or lose, and you just did a good job still, and you did teamwork still.

Alan gave another example of teamwork when he said:

> It means that you have to tell your team the plan that you want to work ... You have to pass the ball to your team and then you're doing teamwork. And if he [teammate] says [he is] open and then nobody else is paying attention then you pass it to that teammate and then you let people have the ball instead of you always having it.

Similarly, Sarah talked about how teamwork helped her team play better. She said:

> Like if you were working together playing soccer and you were kicking the ball and you just kept it during the game and you wouldn't pass it to someone on your team that is not teamwork. Teamwork is like passing it to the other ball like in soccer, passing it to the other person and passing it and then the other person shoots a goal.

These examples show that teamwork was a concept the children were able to understand and learn. Teachers also noted improvements in teamwork. One told us:

> Like before, it's like one kid will have the ball and then just like, everyone is against each other ... But now they're getting [it]. They're like realising 'oh it's two teams' and they're passing ... And when they score they sort of like celebrate with each other instead, instead of just like one person.

Confidence. The words of the children suggested that many of them had trouble expressing the concept of confidence. For example, when asked about confidence Julie said, 'We did talk about it and when we were over there [pointing to school gymnasium] we talked a little bit of confidence. I'm not sure as I remember.' When Sean was asked what confidence means he said, 'Like I can't explain it'. When Claire was asked the same question, she actually gave a description of concentration and behaviour. She said, 'OK. It means you're focusing on what you're doing and you're not fooling around'. One of the children who appeared to have a stronger grasp of the idea of confidence was Beth. When asked how she felt about learning basketball, she said, 'I felt proud of myself when I figured it out and I felt proud of the other people figuring it out and I was feeling that I could learn how to play basketball and stuff'. In this sense, her feeling of pride may reflect a growing sense of confidence.

There were, however, examples from teachers that suggested there was some success in terms of the children learning about confidence. One said that she had seen a change in one of the students and said '[name of student] is a little bit louder and he seems more confident [now], you know he's a bright kid ... [but] his participation and his confidence level seems higher'. Referring to another student, a teacher told us he was 'coming out of his shell' a little more and 'he was excited to go [to TRY-Sport] ... I think he needs it definitely, he's coming along, he's wanting to be part of the activities like more and more like that'. Overall, confidence was a life skill the children had difficultly expressing, but the teachers provided some insights that they witnessed children growing in confidence.

Leadership. Leadership was particularly difficult for the children to understand and/ or express. It appeared to be the most poorly articulated component of the TRY-Sport programme. For example, when we asked children about leadership, quite often they would refer to good behaviour rather than leadership behaviours per se. Sarah said:

> Leadership means to be good and not be bad and not follow the rules... Like if you said for all of us to sit down and be quiet and we didn't sit down and be quiet that wouldn't be so much leadership I think.

Other children provided different perspectives. For Alan, leadership meant:

> How you treat people and how you do things. 'Cause you have to think what you're gonna say before you actually say it 'cause it might hurt somebody's feelings or it might just be rude or something. And it means that if you wanna be a leader then you have to do what you're told ... Yeah, I learned that you're not the only one who's important, everybody's important.

One reason children described leadership in these ways may have been because, due to the initial concerns about behaviour and listening, the researchers/fieldworkers often explained leadership in terms of being a good role-model for other students (i.e. good behaviour demonstrates being a good leader in the class). Additionally, a teacher explained why she thought some of the children may have struggled to express learning about leadership. She said 'I'm sure it did resonate with them but maybe not in the way that they realised it would'. Hence, children had some difficulties understanding the concept of leadership, suggesting that it had not been taught in an effective manner.

Transferability of life skills. Despite some children having difficulty expressing concepts of confidence and leadership, there were examples that the skills learned in TRY-Sport helped them in other areas of their lives. For example, a teacher said 'In the classroom, those skills do transcend into the classroom ... It should become part of you ... part of your everyday life'. Some children talked about how they had used the concept of teamwork in their school activities. This tended to be expressed through helping other children. Alan said that he learned 'to help people when they need it'. When asked to give an example, he went on to tell us of a time he demonstrated leadership skills 'when [name of student] needed help I helped her with the [schoolwork activity] cause she couldn't figure out what, where a story would go in, so I helped her'. And Jordan told us the following story:

> In the classroom I would say like if somebody has a problem. Like we got somebody from Lebanon he doesn't know how to speak English and so we get somebody to help him.
>
> *Interviewer*: OK. And do you think some of the team work skills that you learned in TRY-Sport help you in the classroom?
>
> *Jordan*: Yeah.
>
> *Interviewer*: How do you think that helps you?
>
> *Jordan*: I think it helps me 'cause [name of student], that's in there and he gets upset 'cause he can't do it. And so I help him and you know what he always does? He always says thank you and he tries to repay me by helping me.

Claire provided examples of transfer of skills to her home rather than school life. She said:

I didn't learn so much for school but I did learn that being fair is very important … When I was being fair and being a good leader when I was playing with my little brother. Like if we were playing a game and I would always win then sometimes I would let him win 'cause sometimes he would get a little sad so I would let him win the next game.

Interviewer: OK. How else might you have been a good leader at home?

Claire: By helping my little brother, like if he wants to learn a new sport sometimes then I would help him.

In some other cases when children were asked about what skills they learned in TRY-Sport that may have helped them in other areas, they provided examples that did not appear to directly relate to skills targeted. For example, Beth said, 'I used to not think that I could do math and then I got better, and then I got more trust in myself to do it'. Ian said that he learned 'Don't be shy with girls … and sit beside girls if you like to and listen' and similarly, Moe said that he learned about 'Sitting beside girls, be nice to other people and always listen to the one that's talking … Listening, sitting beside girls'. Hence, there was some evidence for the transfer of life skills, but not necessarily in the ways that had been targeted.

Discussion

The overall purpose of this research was to develop, implement and evaluate sport-based after-school programmes for students in low-income areas of Edmonton, Alberta, Canada. In addition, the other purpose of this paper was to provide an empirical example of PAR, depicting when and how community partners were engaged in the research process. This research was responsive to calls to promote physical activity and include community partners in the creation and delivery of after-school programming, especially for children from low-income neighbourhoods (Holt *et al.* 2009a, Pate and O'Neill 2009). In particular, the involvement of community partners may be an important element in creating effective programming and overcoming some of the limitations of existing after-school physical activity programmes (Pate and O'Neill 2009, Atkin *et al.* 2011).

Findings revealed that the programmes provided new opportunities for many of the children. The successes reported in terms of fundamental movement and sport skills are particularly noteworthy because the children's skill level was so low at the start of TRY-Sport and the researchers/fieldworkers had trouble running planned activities. The fact that children reported learning such skills (which was corroborated by teachers) may be important in preparing them for a lifetime of sport and physical activity participation (Trost *et al.* 2008). In fact, after the researchers/fieldworkers left one of the schools, the children were requesting to play sports they did not play before, which the teacher attributed to the skills they learned through TRY-Sport. Although these findings are promising indications of success, in the future it will be vital that research include more formalised assessment of fundamental movement and sport skills and long-term follow-up. To this end, new initiatives to measure fundamental movement and sport skills using the concept of physical literacy may offer an important contribution to the literature that will advance research in this area (Tremblay and Lloyd 2010).

Adolescents and young adults can learn a range of life skills through their participation in sport, including teamwork, leadership, respect and initiative (e.g. Holt *et al*. 2008, Holt *et al*. 2009b). It is generally accepted that the extent to which youth sport participants learn life skills is contingent upon intentional instruction and positive interactions with coaches, parents and peers (Holt and Neely 2012). Some instructional life skills programmes are available (see Hellison *et al*. 2008, Petitpas *et al*. 2008), and there is promising evidence that children who received such programmes reported learning about goal setting, problem-solving and positive thinking (Papacharisis *et al*. 2005). The current findings add to the life skills literature by revealing some successes *and* challenges associated with a reflective and integrated approach to teaching transferable life skills. Specifically, the children could grasp and report examples of teamwork but they appeared to have less well-developed understandings of leadership and confidence. In part, this could be related to the children's developmental stage and their cognitive ability to understand complex abstract constructs like leadership and confidence, whereas teamwork is more concrete and tangible. Another reason may be that TRY-Sport was based on three team sports, which may have been best-suited to promoting teamwork due to the need for individuals to work together to achieve personal and group goals (Holt *et al*. 2009b).

Reflections on the research process

In this section, we, the academic researchers, consider some of the relational elements of this research process. A strength was the long-standing involvement of the academic researchers within the community along with the specific relationships that were cultivated for this after-school research programme. Such relationships are key factors in the success of PAR projects (Boog 2003, Stringer and Genat 2004, McHugh and Kowalski 2009), and particularly important during the early stages of research (Fletcher 2003). Indeed, in the early stages of the current research, the high level of engagement/involvement from members of the educational community helped shape and define the research. This level of engagement/involvement translated into a great deal of 'momentum' and the research moved quite quickly into the first action phase.

Within PAR, there is a balance between 'participatory' and 'action' phases. Although there was clearly a strong participatory aspect of the current research, it was very action oriented (indeed, there were two action phases). As noted above, the initial work and relationships with various educational partners helped establish a problem that was clearly defined and quite localised, which facilitated the move to the first action phase. However, with the early adoption of action, there is a risk that it may neither be fully informed by nor relevant to community members' needs. One implication researchers may wish to consider from the empirical example of PAR provided in this paper is the timing of moving toward action phases. There may be a 'perceived need' to move into action quickly to create change, but such action may not always be desirable if the research team does not represent relevant partners or if members of the team are not fully engaged in the process of change.

In the case of the current research, children's views may not have been fully represented. Before discussing this further, it is important to note that children *were* involved in some ways. For example, they had choices and input into particular activities. This pedagogical approach was founded on some tenets of self-determination theory (SDT; Ryan and Deci 2000), where it is proposed that individuals strive to fulfil three basic psychological needs; competence, relatedness and autonomy. SDT is comprised of five 'mini-theories', one of which is cognitive evaluation theory (CET). CET specifically addresses the effects of social contexts on intrinsic motivation, such as how factors such as rewards and control influence intrinsic motivation for activities. Providing perceptions of choice and opportunities to engage in optimally challenging activities are pedagogical strategies consistent with CET (Mandigo and Holt 2000, 2006, Mandigo *et al.* 2008). That is, they are attempts to increase children's sense of autonomy within a structure with clear boundaries – strategies that may be particularly important in inner-city school settings (Holt *et al.* 2011). This theoretical orientation provided a way of including children's perspectives in keeping with the participatory elements of the research.

However, perhaps the children were not adequately engaged throughout all stages of this research. There was not, for example, a 'leadership group' of children involved in some of the planning decisions. Such leadership groups have been created as a feature of other PAR studies, but they tend to include adults (Frisby *et al.* 1997) or adolescents (McHugh and Kowalski 2011) rather than children. From a PAR perspective, if community members are considered experts in their daily lives and activities, then it would be appropriate to have engaged the children more, particularly in terms of 'bigger picture' issues about how such after-school programming could play a positive role in their lives. After all, this was ultimately the underlying intention of the entire research project. Perhaps, there was a tacit assumption of children as 'passive' recipients of the programme. But, if the children were too young to be engaged in these bigger picture issues or as a 'leadership group', then why were they old enough to participate in research interviews? These decisions – from our perspective as academic researchers – may have been partially self-serving. We interviewed the children and they became participants who provided data to publish in a study; but upon reflection, we question whether they were truly engaged in the process as 'co-researchers'.

Macauley *et al.* (1999) argued that PAR can include various degrees of participation, and that the specific roles and contributions of team members may change throughout the duration of a project. There were instances in which some adult community partners were less involved. The most obvious example was our (the academic researchers') recommendation to exclude the provincial sport organisations and their coaches. The principals and teachers supported this recommendation, but the coaches/organisations were not adequately consulted. Gosin *et al.* (2003) questioned whether participants need to be involved in all stages of a project and the most important factor is the extent to which the target communities benefit from the decisions made. In the current research, the target communities were located in the schools, so the decision was made for the benefit of the schools and the students, not for the benefit of the coaches/provincial sport organisations. By excluding the coaches, we (the academic researchers) thought we could devote our resources to creating pedagogically consistent sessions, and assumed that by using the PE literature, we could engage the children in developmentally appropriate ways. But, the views of coaches and members of provincial sport organisations (or children for that matter) about this decision were not obtained. Other researchers may wish to consider how to make decisions to change the direction of programmes that are more inclusive and consistent with the tenets of PAR.

Conclusion

The grant that funded this research has ended and, as a consequence, the programmes are not being delivered at this time. In an attempt to maintain contact and visibility with the schools, the academic researchers are currently working to deliver 'sports days' during which children from various schools will be brought together to receive TRY-Sport programming free-of-charge. However, it is challenging for academic researchers working at research-intensive universities to provide social programming in the absence of a clear research agenda (and funding). As Walsh (2006) suggested, university faculty may have expertise in their academic discipline but they rarely have knowledge of inter-organisational collaboration needed to run community programmes. And yet, academics may hope to support the creation of programmes that eventually become self-governed. To this end, some members of the research team are expanding upon the after-school project and working with school communities to identify locally relevant physical activity/sport practices, with a particular focus on working with Aboriginal youth.

In summary, after-school programmes offer an attractive approach for promoting physical activity but evidence of their effectiveness is mixed (Atkin *et al.* 2011). Findings contributed to the fundamental movement, sport and life skills literature and informed the after-school programming literature by demonstrating ways in which programmes that are relevant to participants' needs can be created and delivered. This study may also contribute to the research methods literature by providing an empirical example of how and when participants were engaged in the research process, hopefully revealing some of the intricacies of conducting PAR. Given the low levels of physical activity participation among children in Canada (Colley *et al.* 2011) and other developed countries (Janssen *et al.* 2005), our research may offer a valuable platform that informs future after-school programming and provides viable strategies to enhance the effectiveness of future research.

Acknowledgements

We would like to thank all the people who contributed to this research. Some of the research presented in this article was completed as partial fulfillment of LNT's Master's degree. This research was supported by grants from the Social Sciences and Humanities Research Council of Canada and KidSport Canada.

Note

1. The term 'research team' refers to all the people involved in this research project. The research team was comprised of several 'sub-groups' – children, teachers and principals from several schools; school board employees and trustees; coaches from provincial sport organisations; and the academic researchers. We have tried, wherever possible, to stipulate the particular sub-group involved at various phases of the research.

Notes on contributors

Nicholas L. Holt is a professor in the Faculty of Physical Education and Recreation at the University of Alberta. He conducts research examining psychosocial aspects of youth sport and physical activity.

Tara-Leigh F. McHugh is an assistant professor in the Faculty of Physical Education and Recreation at the University of Alberta. Her work primarily focuses on physical activity among Aboriginal youth.

Lisa N. Tink was a MA student in the Faculty of Physical Education and Recreation at the University of Alberta.

Bethan C. Kingsley is a PhD student in the Faculty of Physical Education and Recreation at the University of Alberta.

Angela M. Coppola is a PhD student in the Faculty of Physical Education and Recreation at the University of Alberta.

Kacey C. Neely is a PhD student in the Faculty of Physical Education and Recreation at the University of Alberta.

Ryan McDonald was an undergraduate student in the Faculty of Physical Education and Recreation at the University of Alberta.

References

Active Healthy Kids Canada, 2012. *Active Healthy Kids Canada report card on physical activity for children and youth*. Available from: http://www.activehealthykids.ca/Report-Card/PhysicalActivity.aspx.

Alberta Centre for Active Living, 2012. *What's happening in after-school programs? Findings from an environmental scan of after-school programs in Alberta*. Available from: http://www.centre4activeliving.ca/publications/research-reports/2012-after-school/report.pdf.

Anderson, A., 2001. *Learning strategies: the missing 'think' in physical education and coaching*. Toronto: Sports Books.

Atkin, A.J., Goreley, T., Biddle, S.J.H., Cavill, N., and Foster, C., 2011. Interventions to promote physical activity in young people conducted in the hours immediately after-school: a systematic review. *International journal of behavioral medicine*, 18 (3), 176–187.

Boog, B.W.M., 2003. The emancipatory character of action research, its history and the present state of the art. *Journal of community and applied social psychology*, 13 (3), 426–438.

Bostock, J. and Freeman, J., 2003. 'No limits': doing participatory action research with young people in Northumberland. *Journal of community and applied social psychology*, 13 (6), 464–474.

Brydon-Miller, M., *et al.*, 2011. Jazz and the banyan tree: participatory action research. *In*: N.K. Denzin and Y.S. Lincoln, eds. *Handbook of qualitative research*. 4th ed. Newbury Park, CA: Sage, 387–400.

Canadian Sport 4 Life, 2012. *Learn about Canadian 4 Life*. Available from: http://www.canadiansportforlife.ca/.

City of Calgary, 2008. *Critical hours: a plan to invest in Calgary's children*. Calgary: Community and Neighbourhood Services.

Colley, R.C., Garriguet, D., Janssen, I., Craig, C.L., Clarke, J., and Tremblay, M.S., 2011. Physical activity of Canadian children and youth: accelerometer results from the 2007 to 2009 Canadian health measures survey. *Health reports*, 22 (1), 15–21.

Enright, E. and O'Sullivan, M., 2012. Listening to young people's voices in physical education and youth sport research. *In*: K. Armour and D. Macdonald, eds. *Research methods in physical education and youths sport*. London: Routledge, 120–132.

Fletcher, C., 2003. Community-based participatory research relationships with Aboriginal communities in Canada: an overview of context and process. *Pimatiswim: a journal of aboriginal and indigenous, community health*, 1 (1), 27–62.

Frisby, W., Crawford, S., and Dorer, T., 1997. Reflections on participatory action research: the case of low-income women accessing local physical activity services. *Journal of sport management*, 11 (11), 8–28.

Frisby, W. and Millar, S., 2002. The actualities of doing community development to promote the inclusion of low income populations in local sport and recreation. *European sport management quarterly*, 2 (3), 209–233.

Frisby, W., *et al.*, 2005. Putting 'participatory' into participatory forms of action research. *Journal of sport management*, 19 (4), 367–386.

Garriguet, D. and Colley, R.C., 2012. Daily patterns of physical activity participation in Canadians. *Health reports*, 23 (2), 1–6.

Glaser, B. and Strauss, A., 1967. *The discovery of grounded theory*. Chicago, IL: Aldine.

Gordon-Larsen, P., McMurray, R.G., and Popkin, B.M., 2000. Determinants of adolescent physical activity and inactivity patterns. *Pediatrics*, 105 (6), E83.

Gosin, M.N., Dustman, P.A., Drapeau, A.E., and Harthun, M.L., 2003. Participatory action research: creating an effective prevention curriculum for adolescents in the Southwestern US. *Health education research*, 18 (3), 363–379.

Green, L.W., George, A., Daniel, M., Frankish, C.J., Herbert, C.P., Bowie, W.R., *et al.*, 1995. *Study of participatory research in health promotion: review and recommendations for the development of participatory research in health promotion in Canada*. Ottawa: Royal Society of Canada, Institute of Health Promotion Research.

Hellison, D., Martinek, T., and Walsh, D., 2008. Sport and responsible leadership among youth. *In*: N.L. Holt, ed. *Positive youth development through sport*. London: Routledge, 49–60.

Holt, N.L. and Neely, K.C., 2012. Positive youth development through sport: a review. *Revista Iberoamericana de Psicologia de Ejercicio y el Deporte (IberoAmerican journal of sport psychology)*, 6 (2), 299–316.

Holt, N.L., Tamminen, K.A., and Jones, M.I., 2007. Promoting positive youth development through teaching games in physical education. *Health and physical* education, 3 (Autumn), 8–13.

Holt, N.L., Tink, L.N., Mandigo, J.L., and Fox, K.R., 2008. Do youth learn life skills through their involvement in high school sport? *Canadian journal of education*, 31 (2), 281–304.

Holt, N.L., Cunningham, C-T., Sehn, Z.L., Spence, J.C., Newton, A.S., Gall, G.D.C., *et al.*, 2009a. Neighborhood physical activity opportunities for inner city children and youth. *Health and place*, 15 (4), 1022–1028.

Holt, N.L., Tink, L.N., Black, D.E., *et al.*, 2009b. An interpretive analysis of life skills associated with sport participation. *Qualitative research in sport and exercise*, 1 (2), 160–175.

Holt, N.L., Kingsley, B.C., Tink, L.N., and Scherer, J., 2011. Benefits and challenges associated with sport participation by children and parents from low-income families. *Psychology of sport and exercise*, 12 (5), 490–499.

Holt, N.L. et al., in press. Using critical incident reflection in qualitative research: transferable skills for sport psychologists? *In*: Z. Knowles, D. Gilbourne, D. Cropley, and L. Dugdill, eds. *Reflective practice in the sport and exercise sciences: contemporary issues*. London: Routledge.

Humbert, M.L., Chad, K.E., Spink, K.S., Muhajarine, N., Anderson, K.D., Bruner, M., *et al.*, 2006. Factors that influence physical activity participation among high- and low-SES youth. *Qualitative health research*, 16 (4), 476–483.

Janssen, I., Katzmarzyk, P., Boyce, W.F., Vereecken, C., Mulvihill, C., Roberts, C., *et al.*, 2005. Comparison of overweight and obesity prevalence in school-aged youth from 34 countries and their relationships with physical activity and dietary patterns. *Obesity reviews*, 6 (2), 123–132.

Janssen, I., Boyce, W.F., Simpson, K., and Pickett, W., 2006. Influence of individual- and area-level measures of socioeconomic status on obesity, unhealthy eating, and physical inactivity in Canadian adolescents. *American journal of clinical nutrition*, 83 (1), 139–145.

Jones, M.I., Lavallee, D., and Tod, D., 2011. Developing communication and organization skills: the ELITE life skills reflective practice program. *The sport psychologist*, 25 (2), 159–176.

Kemmis, S. and McTaggart, R., 2000. Participatory action research. *In*: N.K. Denzin and Y. S. Lincoln, eds. *Handbook of qualitative research*. Thousand Oaks, CA: Sage, 567–605.

Macauley, A.C., Commanda, L.E., Freeman, W.L., Gibson, N., McCabe, M.L., Robbins, C., *et al.*, 1999. Participatory research maximizes community and lay involvement. *British medical journal*, 319 (7212), 774–778.

Mandigo, J.L. and Holt, N.L., 2000. Putting theory into practice: how cognitive evaluation theory helps us motivate children in physical activity. *Journal of physical education, recreation and dance*, 71 (1), 44–49.

Mandigo, J.L. and Holt, N.L., 2006. Elementary students' accounts of optimal challenge in physical education. *The physical educator*, 63 (4), 170–184.

Mandigo, J.L., Holt, N.L., Anderson, A., and Sheppard, J., 2008. Children's motivational experiences following autonomy-supportive games lessons. *European physical education review*, 14 (3), 407–415.

Maykut, R. and Morehouse, P., 1994. *Beginning qualitative inquiry: a practical and philosophic guide*. London: Falmer.

McHugh, T.-L.F. and Kowalski, K., 2009. Lessons learned: participatory action research with young aboriginal women. *Pimatisiwin*, 7 (1), 117–131.

McHugh, T.-L.F. and Kowalski, K., 2011. "A new view of body image": a school-based participatory action research project with young aboriginal women. *Action research*, 9 (3), 220–241.

Oliver, K.L., Hamzeh, M., and McCaughtry, N., 2009. Girly girls can play games: 5th grade girls negotiate self-identified barriers to physical activity. *Journal of teaching in physical education*, 28 (1), 90–110.

Papacharisis, V., Goudas, M., Danish, S., and Teodorakis, T., 2005. The effectiveness of teaching a life skills program in a sport context. *Journal of applied sport psychology*, 17 (3), 247–254.

Parkland Institute, 2012. *A social policy framework for Alberta: fairness and justice for all.* Available from: http://parklandinstitute.ca/downloads/reports/ABPolicyFramework_2012_ web.pdf [Accessed 21 November 2012].

Pate, R.R. and O'Neill, J.R., 2009. After-school interventions to increase physical activity among youth. *British journal of sports medicine*, 43 (1), 14–18.

Pate, R.R., Saunders, R., Dishman, R.K., Addy, C., Dowda, M., and Ward, D.S., 2007. Long-term effects of a physical activity intervention in high school girls. *American journal of preventive medicine*, 33 (4), 276–280.

Petitpas, A.J., Cornelius, A., and Van Raalte, J., 2008. Youth development through sport: it's all about relationships. *In*: N.L. Holt, ed. *Positive youth development through sport*. London: Routledge, 61–70.

Ryan, R.M. and Deci, E.L., 2000. Self-determination theory and the facilitation of intrinsic motivation, social development, and well-being. *American psychologist*, 55 (1), 68–78.

Stringer, E.T. and Genat, W.J., 2004. *Action research in health*. Upper Saddle River, NJ: Pearson Education.

Tremblay, M.S. and Lloyd, M., 2010. Physical literacy measurement: the missing piece. *Physical and health education journal*, 76 (1), 26–30.

Trost, S.G., Rosenkranz, R.R., and Dzewaltowski, D., 2008. Physical activity levels among children attending after-school programs. *Medicine and science in sports and exercise*, 40 (4), 622–629.

Walsh, D., 2006. Best practices in university-community partnerships: lessons learned from a physical-activity-based program. *Journal of physical education, recreation, and dance*, 77 (4), 45–49.

Witt, P.A., 2004. Programs that work: developing quality after-school programs. *Journal of park and recreation administration*, 22 (4), 103–126.

Appendix. Example of lesson plan

Date: Tuesday 24 January 2012

Sport: Basketball

Warm-Up: Fundamental movements	Animal moves; Giant steps (lunges), bounding leaps (from one foot to other), hops (same foot), jumps (two feet), skipping, galloping, side shuffles, crab walk, frog jumps. 'Ryan Says': Lunges, jumping jacks, balancing, etc.

(Continued)

Appendix (*Continued*)

Skill: Ball handling	Every kid with a ball, in circle, over-under, through the legs, around the world, big dribble, little dribble, etc. Optimal challenge: Throw and clap game
Practice	Explain dribble. Do on the spot dribble, running dribbles, zig-zag dribbling, red-light, green-light with dribble.
Game	Dribble relays
Life skill: Confidence	Talk about getting better with the optimal challenge. Ask how did you feel after each try? Focus on concept of building confidence through practice.

Challenging and transforming power relations within community-based participatory research: the promise of a Foucauldian analysis

Matias I. Golob and Audrey R. Giles

School of Human Kinetics, University of Ottawa, Ottawa, Canada

Community-based participatory research (CBPR) advocates claim that by engaging community members to participate as equal partners in research that addresses issues relevant to the community, participatory methodologies can contribute to decreasing local health inequities and help build capacity for social change. There are, however, considerable concerns about the under-theorisation of power within CBPR approaches and the possibility of the marginalisation of research participants occurring in the very research processes that are meant to overcome such problems. Such critiques often engage with post-structuralist theories, notably the work of French philosopher Michel Foucault, and point towards the possible dominating effects of CBPR for marginalised communities. While these critiques offer valuable insights, they have not critically engage with Foucault's understanding of power as productive; that is, while power acts as a constraint on action, its effects are never only repressive – the exercise of power always simultaneously both inhibits and enables action. Through examples of CBPR projects that have addressed new Canadians' diverse health promotion needs, in this paper we argue that by attending to the ways in which power both inhibits and enables community members' actions, we will be better positioned as researchers to recognise and minimise the potential dominating effects of CBPR.

Introduction

Community-based participatory research (CBPR) is as an overarching term used to characterise research that strives for maximum community engagement on issues relevant to the community engaged in the research. While there are some nuances that differentiate the many terms that have been used to describe CBPR approaches – e.g. participatory action research, action research, feminist participatory action research (FPAR) and community-based research – all of them express a deep commitment to enhance the relevance of research by ensuring that community members are equitably involved in co-determining all aspects of the research process (Kemmis and McTaggart 2000). CBPR advocates claim that by engaging community members from groups of individuals understood to be marginalised (e.g. ethno-cultural minority immigrants, economically disadvantaged, indigenous people) in research, these individuals actively form and communicate their own meanings and understandings of a particular issue. As a result, participatory methodologies can contribute to building capacity for social change (Reason and Bradbury 2008, Minkler and Vallerstein 2011). Indeed, one of the main advantages of CBPR for community health issues is the reciprocal capacity building of community members, academics and service providers through partnerships (Israel *et al.* 1998). Academics and service providers gain an understanding of community members' epistemology of health and wellness – e.g. how they understand physical activity fitting within their social and cultural understandings of health and wellness – and in so doing, learn how to use their skills and knowledge to best serve the community's particular needs and interests. Members of marginalised communities develop a more sophisticated understanding of the health issue in question – e.g. how physical activity can promote health and wellness – and use their expertise of the cultural and social contexts of the health issue to produce solutions and build momentum for social change. CBPR approaches thus represent a pragmatic response by academics and social activists who believe that research focused on strategies, policies and programmes aimed at tacking social problems should be developed with the consultation and participation of the people affected by the research findings (Kindon *et al.* 2007).

There are, however, considerable concerns about the under-theorisation of power within CBPR approaches and the possibility of the marginalisation of research participants occurring in the very research processes that are meant to overcome such problems (Chambers 1997, Kemmis and McTaggart 2000, Kesby *et al.* 2007). A substantial literature suggests that by 'empowering' marginalised individuals to analyse and transform their lives through equitable involvement in the research process, CBPR approaches can challenge deep-rooted power inequities in the knowledge production process (see Gaventa and Cornwall 2006). Drawing from a structuralist account of power, where power is taken to be a commodity that can be possessed and redistributed, an understanding of CBPR as empowering otherwise marginalised individuals implies that some people and groups of people are positioned outside of power relations (Kemmis and MgTaggart 2000).

More recently, scholars have extended a post-structuralist critique to the theorisation of power within CBPR approaches (see e.g. Chambers 1997, Cooke and Kothari 2001, Hickey and Mohan 2005, Kesby *et al.* 2007). Drawing on the writings of Foucault and Gordon (1980) and Foucault (1983, 1990), post-structuralists do not see power as a commodity some individuals and groups possess, but as an *effect*: an action or strategy exercised by some in an attempt to influence or act upon the possibilities of action of other people. Yet, to date, much of the focus of a Foucauldian analysis has centred on the dominating effects of power relations within CBPR. For example, some authors (e.g. Henkel and Stirrat 2001, Kothari 2001) have argued that CBPR approaches should be conceived as instruments of regulation or even domination mobilised to control the actions of community members who participate/ collaborate in the research. By virtue of their position of 'authority' as experts, university-based academics and staff at community organisations can govern how a particular topic can be meaningfully talked about and reasoned about, and thus how knowledge about it is produced and disseminated (Henkel and Stirrat 2001). Indeed, some authors have suggested that CBPR processes merely reproduce existing power relations. As a result, a failure to critically examine relations of power within CBPR undermines its foundational goal of creating equity between researchers and community members (Israel *et al*. 2006).

It is our contention that while such critiques offer valuable insights for CBPR researchers, a focus on CBPR as a technology of domination does not fully engage with Foucault and Gordon (1980) and Foucault's (1983, 1990) understanding of power as *productive*; that is, while power acts as a constraint on action, its effects are never only repressive – the exercise of power always simultaneously inhibits and enables action (Fraser 1989, Shogan 1999). In other words, what such critiques by and large do not do is consider the exercise of power as the condition of possibility for an individuals' self-(trans)formation. Hence, instead of seeing CBPR merely as a technology of domination, in this paper we draw more broadly on Foucault's unique conceptualisation of power and, in so doing, facilitate a discussion of CBPR as not only repressive, but also enabling and productive.

A Foucauldian approach to understanding how power relations produce action within CBPR allows us to recognise how discourses – understood here as written, spoken, non-verbal and visual communication strategies that, in expressing a knowledge claim about a specific subject, mediate or organise an individual's inter-actions with the social world (Foucault and Gordon 1980) – act as constraints that simultaneously inhibit and enable community members' self-formation as subjects of power relations. Such an application of Foucault's work, we argue, not only offers a more optimistic account of CBPR outcomes, but also presents researchers with important insights that can help minimise the potential of CBPR approaches as a form of power that has dominating effects.

New Canadians' health promotion needs

In order to make our argument accessible to those who are not familiar with Foucauldian theory, we draw on findings from CBPR research that has already been conducted to address health disparities among new Canadians, a group defined as having resided in Canada for five years or fewer (Statistics Canada 2008). Research has indicated that, upon arrival to Canada, immigrants consistently report very good to excellent health and display health characteristics that equal or exceed those of Canadian-born residents (Perez 2002, Newbold 2005, 2009, Ng *et al*. 2005). Generally referred to as the 'healthy immigrant effect,' several reason for this observation have been suggested, including differences in the sociocultural aspects of diet and physical activity that exist between the immigrants' place of origin and Canada (Seefeldt *et al*. 2002). Additionally, Canadian immigration policies have been developed to select prospective permanent residents on the basis of education, language ability and job skills – all of which have been correlated with healthy life-styles (Hyman 2004). Nevertheless, over time, this healthy immigrant effect is lost; epidemiological evidence has indicated that, with increasing length of residence in Canada, immigrants have an increased risk of transitioning to poorer health (Perez 2002, Seefeldt *et al*. 2002, Newbold 2009). For example, Perez (2002) reported that recent immigrants to Canada have superior health when compared with the Canadian-born population in terms of chronic conditions (e.g. cardiovascular disease, diabetes mellitus and cancer), even after controlling for observables, and that the odds of reporting chronic conditions rises with time in Canada.

While more studies are required to better understand the pathways that lead to a decline in health status among new Canadians, research has suggested recent immigrants who originate from non-Western cultures and societies[1] (who are considered minorities and have less established population cohorts) are often uninformed about or unfamiliar with the health and social services available to them in Canada, and in some instances are underserved or excluded by local health and social services (Magalhaes *et al*. 2010). For example, qualitative researchers have attributed new Canadians' under participation in leisure-based physical activity to problems associated with sociocultural and economic adaptation, noting that immigrants who originate from non-Western cultures and societies often have different beliefs, attitudes and behaviours related to leisure activity in comparison to the general population (see e.g. Tirone and Shaw 1997, Tirone 2000, Stack and Iwasaki 2009, Golob 2010). Such findings have produced a discourse that suggests that new Canadians who originate from non-Western cultures and societies have a low level of understanding that leisure-based physical activity can promote and preserve health, and an associated discourse that points to the marginalisation of new Canadians' unique cultural contexts in which leisure-based activities may take place.

In the past two decades, CBPR approaches have received increasing attention from university-based academics and community members interested in building capacity for positive health outcomes with new Canadians, particularly those who originate from non-Western cultures and societies. Researchers have employed CBPR approaches to understand and address issues associated with low rates of breast cancer screening (Ahmad *et al*. 2011), mental well-being (Simich *et al*. 2009), and sport and recreation access (Frisby *et al*. 2005, Frisby 2011), among others. How the health disparity under investigation is understood and the power relations at work in addressing it are at the very heart of the CBPR process, which is meant to facilitate the equal sharing of power between academic experts and community members who are experts on their own lives. By applying Foucault's unique conceptualisation of power, CBPR researchers interested in building capacity for positive health outcomes may be better prepared to work with community members from groups of individuals understood to be marginalised in a way that attends to ways in which power relations simultaneously inhibit and enable action in the research process.

Foucault, power and CBPR

Foucault's writings on power and power relations have challenged assumptions of how individuals can transgress relations of dominance. In contrast to the juridical account of power, which rests on the assumption that some individuals and groups of individuals are positioned outside of power relations (Kemmis and McTaggart 2000), Foucault and Gordon (1980) did not view power as a commodity that can be accumulated, possessed and therefore redistributed. Power, according to Foucault (1990), is not inherent within 'powerful' individuals and groups; rather, 'power is everywhere; not because it embraces everything, but because it comes from everywhere' (p. 93). In other words, power does not emanate from a central source but circulates throughout the entire social body. In this view, power circulates through the various and shifting positions that individuals occupy within a complex network of discourse, practices and relationships that position some as powerful, and that justify and facilitate their authority in relations to others (Clegg 1989). Therefore, individuals are never in a position that is exterior to relations of power.

Foucault (1990) thus implied that power is something that is relational, something that is embodied and enacted rather than possessed, and therefore better understood as an effect: an action or strategy exercised by some to guide and shape others' conduct. As subjects and objects of power relations, individuals have the ever-present capacity to exercise power in ways that not only affirm but also resist dominant relations of power. Correspondingly, for Foucauldian scholars questions such as 'who has power?' or 'where, or in what, does power reside?' are changed to what Foucault termed the 'how' of power: 'How do institutions, dominant groups, and individuals exercise power through the use of strategies, techniques, and procedures?' and 'how do these strategies, techniques, and procedures give power its effect?'

Foucault's unique conceptualisation of power as productive, relational and only existing through action has three important implications for thinking about CBPR: (1) participation in CBPR can enable marginalised individuals to access the power/knowledge nexus; (2) the exercise of power acts as a constraint that simultaneously inhibits and enables actions; and (3) the exercise of power is a necessary condition of possibility for change.

CBPR can enable otherwise marginalised individuals to access the power/knowledge nexus

According to Foucault and Gordon (1980), power and knowledge are inextricably enmeshed in a circular loop: power produces and sustains knowledge, while knowledge induces and extends the effects of power. In other words, power and knowledge are reliant on each other for their existence. In this view, power/knowledge produces the conditions and effects of knowledge production: power/knowledge positions some individuals as authorised to offer authoritative knowledge claims (e.g. academics) and concomitantly exclude the knowledge claims of others (e.g. members of marginalised groups, such as new Canadians who originate from non-Western cultures and societies), which thus acts to valorise some statements as 'truth' and render others as irrelevant or illegitimate.

Appropriately, some authors (e.g. Chambers 1997, Kemmis and McTaggart 2000) have argued that CBPR approaches enable marginalised peoples' access to Foucault's power/knowledge nexus. For instance, Kemmis and McTaggart (2000) suggested that as participants in all aspects of the research process, from formulating the research question through to the final interpretation and dissemination of results, community members gain the capacity to actively form and communicate their own meanings and understandings of the issue under investigation. As a result, they argue, CBPR challenges the ways in which power is embedded and reinforced in conventional research methodologies. Similarly, Chambers (1997) reasoned that through a dynamic and collaborative process of planning, acting and reflecting, marginalised individuals are able to lay claim to their own distinctive versions and visions of reality, and thus acquire the 'power to' and 'power within' that restores their agency as active subjects of power relations. Accordingly, from a Foucauldian perspective, CBPR approaches represent a setting for community members to exercise power. To illustrate, researchers have reported language to be an important barrier to health research with recent immigrants to Canada who originate from non-Western cultures and societies (Isaacs *et al.* 2013). Through the use of participatory methodologies, linguistically diverse new Canadians can gain the capacity to share their insights in and through the participation of staff from immigrant serving agencies that are fluent in the languages of choice (Ahmad *et al.* 2011).

Power as constraints on action

For Foucault, the exercise of power produces constraints on people's actions; as a result, researchers can explore both the inhibiting and enabling dimensions of power relations (Fraser 1989, Shogan 1999, Weedon 1999). Foucault (1990) argued that power is not simply a coercive force that limits, prohibits and obstructs action; rather, power makes us what we are. According to Foucault and Gordon (1980, p. 119), what makes the exercise of power accepted 'is simply the fact that it doesn't only weigh on us as a force that says no, but that it traverses and produces things, it induces pleasure, forms knowledge, produces discourse.' For this reason, the exercise of power ought to be seen as a key element in the very formation of individuals and the practices they attempt to perform. Indeed, from a Foucauldian perspective, prevailing discourses act as constraints that simultaneously inhibit and enable how an individual, as a subject and object of power relations, understands and constructs her/himself and the social actions that she/he attempts to perform (Fraser 1989).

Correspondingly, we can infer that the discursive constructions of a particular issue act as constraints to the processes of investigation within CBPR, but in a way that always both inhibits and enables the actions of CBPR participants. Indeed, from a Foucauldian perspective, CBPR approaches create the conditions for community members to identify and become critically aware of the limits and creative possibilities of the multiple and perhaps contradictory discourses that inform their actions. From this vantage point, CBPR researchers would be encouraged to question how the discursive constructions of the issue under investigation act as constraints that effect the actions of all individuals who participate/collaborate in the research process. For example, Frisby (2011) conducted FPAR with recent immigrant Chinese women, an immigrant service agency and recreation staff in Vancouver, British Columbia to identify and discuss promising physical activity inclusion practices. In their research, a considerable amount of time was spend identifying and problematising discourses surrounding Chinese immigrants leisure interests and needs, including a prevailing discourse that suggests Chinese immigrants are interested in badminton, table tennis and Tai Chi. Such a discourse serves to homogenise Chinese immigrant women, which leads to the assumption that if these activities are offered by recreation providers, then the physical activity levels of Chinese immigrants will be addressed. Nevertheless, Frisby (2011) reported the discourse was helpful for recreation staff to learn about more about Chinese immigrant women's leisure interests and needs and to think beyond simplistic physical activity inclusion strategies (e.g. subsidised costs result in increased participation).

The exercise of power is a necessary condition of possibility for change

Third, and building on the last point, through a Foucauldian lens, the exercise of power enables the possibility for critical reflection and deliberate self-transformation. The main reason for this is that in his later works, Foucault (1983, 2000) conceived of the exercise of power as a necessary precondition for the possibility of self-formation. According to Foucault (2000, p. 286), 'a person understands and constructs him/herself as a particular subject through 'models that he [*sic*] finds in his culture and are proposed, suggested, imposed upon him by his culture, his society, and his social group'. In other words, because a subject cannot be positioned outside of power relations, the self is understood as constituted by power relations, yet as capable of constituting oneself in and through her/his affirmation of and or resistance to a set of historically situated discourses. Indeed, Foucault (1990) rejected the assumption that exercises of power and practices of resistance are mutually exclusive: 'Where there is power, there is resistance, and yet, or rather consequently, this resistance is never in a position of exteriority in relation to power' (p. 95). Moreover, Foucault (1983) maintained that the exercise of power is 'always a way of acting upon an acting subject or acting subjects by virtue of their acting or being capable of action' (p. 220). Hence, a 'minimal freedom' is possible – and only possible in a field defined precisely by the structuring work of power relations (Thompson 2003). Correspondingly, the discursive constructions of an issue under investigation in a CBPR project not only transmits and reproduces power, but following Foucault (1990, p. 101), also 'undermines it and exposes it, renders it fragile and makes it possible to thwart it' (p. 101), which thus implies that an individual's transgression from relations of dominance is inherently always a possibility. To exemplify, in a participatory action research project that explored perceptions of mental health and adaptation strategies among immigrants to Canada from non-Western countries, Simich *et al.* (2009) reported that the approach enabled a dialectical cultural negotiation process. Through participation in the research process, culturally diverse immigrants to Canada gained the ability identify, problematise and negotiate a perceived feeling of social exclusion and powerlessness associated with the mental health system in Canada.

To summarise, Foucault's understanding of power and power relations has far reaching implications for thinking about CBPR outcomes. Contrary to the juridical conception of power, where power is viewed as an essentially negative, repressive and prohibitive force, Foucauldian theory suggests that because power is the product of force relations between free subjects, the exercise of power does not only inhibit, but in fact can enable individuals to engage in practices that have the potential to transgress relations of domination. As we will argue in the final section of this paper, this point is particularly important for theorising how, from a Foucauldian perspective, researchers can minimise relations of domination within CBPR, since it suggests that the exercise of power is a necessary condition for the possibility of critical reflection and deliberate self-transformation. In order to exemplify the importance of attending to issues of power and power relations within CBPR, in the next section we engage with Foucault's work on two technologies of power – the technologies of domination and the technologies of the self, to show how the discursive constructions of new Canadians' health promotion needs may be conceptualised to simultaneously inhibit and enable participants' self-formation as subjects of power relations.

CBPR as a form of governance

In his later works, Foucault (1994, 2008) offered a general theory of how power is exercised in the *biopolitical* management of individuals, which he termed *governmentality*. Effective governance in modern democratic societies, Foucault (1994) argued, is not about coercion or the suppression of a subject's agency, but rather the cultivation of a subject's agency in particular ways. In other words, for Foucault the 'rational' ordering of modern individuals is accomplished through the installation of capacities for self-management (Miller and Rose 2008). Through the development of knowledge practices (e.g. statistics) and the installation of institutions and practices of policing (e.g. health clubs and weight scales) individuals gain the capacity to pursue, through their own means, practices of self-(trans)formation. Governmentality can therefore be conceived of as the 'link' Foucault developed to analyse the connections between macro-level techniques employed to control or regulate whole societies or groups (what he called 'technologies of domination') and self-techniques used by individuals to (trans)form oneself as a subject of power relations (what he called 'technologies of the self'). A closer examination of these two technologies of power, and of their points of interconnection, is useful to reveal the various ways in which power effects the actions of CBPR participants.

CBPR as a technology of domination

From a Foucauldian perspective, power relations construct individual subjectivities. In his early works, Foucault and Gordon (1980) and Foucault (1995) focused on how being 'known' or categorised can act to constrain people to certain ends. That is, how modes of knowledge production and organisation 'discipline' and 'normalise' people's behaviours and social practices such that they 'determine the conduct of individuals and submits them to certain ends or domination, an objectivising of the subject' (Foucault 1994, p. 146). Some authors (e.g. Henkel and Stirrat 2001, Kothari 2001) have engaged with Foucault's early work to argue that CBPR processes govern participants' actions because they propose or impose boundaries and rules of inquiry that exclude other procedures and mechanisms of knowledge production. Specifically, these authors have contended that CBPR approaches are mechanisms of domination and manipulation as participants' actions are dictated and determined by dominant discourses. For instance, Henkel and Stirrat (2001) suggested that the participatory approach is tantamount to what Foucault and Gordon (1980) called 'subjection' – that individuals are empowered not to construct their own knowledge, but to serve the interests of a dominant group: 'as citizens of the modern state; as consumers in the increasingly global market; as responsible patients in the health system; as rational farmers; as participants in the labour market, and so on' (Henkel and Stirrat 2001, p. 182). In other words, these authors argued that CBPR constitutes an exercise of power that has dominating effects.

Following this line of thought, CBPR approaches in health research could be seen as attempts to govern marginalised individuals in particular ways that serve and maintain the interests of a dominant group. In other words, CBPR approaches in this view can be perceived as reinforcing, rather than challenging, existing power relations. For example, Kresby *et al.* (2007) suggested domination might be evident when individuals in positions of authority (e.g. academic experts) provide community members with specific discourses to propose or impose a particular form of conduct on participants – e.g. equality discourses act as 'resources' that specify how community members can talk and what they can talk about in the research process. To illustrate, a CBPR project developed to explore how leisure-based physical activity programmes could be made more accessible for marginalised new Canadians implies particular discourses about the relationship between health inequalities and leisure pursuits that produce the parameters within which some leisure pursuits become more acceptable than others (Golob and Giles 2011). For instance, prevailing discourses surrounding the health benefits derived from certain leisure-based physical activity activities (e.g. swimming reduces the risk of osteoarthritis among adults) (Bryan and Katzmarzyk 2009) act to prescribe, define and frame what counts as appropriate health-promoting leisure pursuits and simultaneously 'problematises' other leisure pursuits (e.g. activities that sustain cultural distinctiveness such as volunteering for a local ethnic community) (Golob and Giles 2011). Thus, the discursive construction of health-promoting leisure pursuits acts to privilege and enable new Canadians' participation in certain leisure pursuits while simultaneously rendering other leisure pursuits irrelevant or illegitimate.

CBPR projects aimed primarily at improving recent immigrants' access to mainstream health-promoting leisure activities, while laudable, can be therefore conceived as a disciplinary technology exercised to regulate immigrant participants' conduct by constituting 'regimens of truth' by which they may understand and live their lives in a new host country. Because health care in Canada is publicly funded, university-based researchers and staff at community organisations are inclined to legitimise their work on the basis of dominant health promotion discourses that suggest engagement in leisure-based physical activity can address health inequalities among new Canadians (Golob 2010). However, such work could be seen as problematic in Canada because it normalises mainstream leisure pursuits and thus contradicts a public policy discourse that constructs leisure as a practice of choice, freedom, and self-determination (Interprovincial Sport and Recreation Council 1987). That is to say, CBPR initiatives for health promotion that are framed in light of dominant discourses that suggest appropriate leisure pursuits for sustaining health and wellness can be seen to impose the leisure meanings and practices of dominant groups on newcomers, and thus be seen as exploitative and manipulative. Consequently, although CBPR approaches may appear to seek just or benevolent processes for knowledge production that can transform relations of power, they nevertheless can constitute an exercise of power that cultivates community members' agency in particular ways and thus can reproduce the very inequalities in power relations that researchers seek to challenge (Kothari 2001).

Dominant discourses surrounding a health issue do not, however, inherently repress community members who participate/collaborate in the research process. That is, dominant discourses do not solely restrict or limit participants' actions; rather, they have a 'discursive effect' (Markula and Pringle 2006, p. 29), as they can enable CBPR participants' capacities for critical reflection and deliberate self-transformation (for more on CBPR and participants' critical self-reflection within an Aboriginal context, see Blodgett *et al.* 2010a, 2010b). Indeed, CBPR approaches should also be seen as helping recent immigrants to understand and take action to sustain health and well-being in a new sociocultural and economic environment. For example, Frisby (2011) reported that identifying and discussing inclusion mechanisms for recent Chinese immigrant women to participate in community sport and recreation enabled the emergence of new skills and capacities among study participants. According to Frisby, through the research process, the Chinese immigrant women participants developed a sense of 'trust' with recreation staff, and recognised themselves as 'links' and 'contacts' between community recreation centres and the Chinese community who could communicate the city's leisure access policy to other co-ethnics who had recently arrived. Hence, while dominant discourses surrounding the health promotion needs of recent Chinese immigrant women (e.g. subsidising sport and recreation costs will increase leisure-based physical activity participation) (Frisby *et al.* 2005) inhibited other ways to understand and approach the issue under investigation (e.g. recent immigrants to Canada want to sustain cultural difference in the realm of leisure) (Golob and Giles 2011), they concurrently enabled action geared towards increasing leisure-based physical activity participation among new Canadians. This reiterates the point that exercises of power always simultaneously inhibit and enable action. Thus, to understand the effect of dominant discourses in CBPR, it is essential for researchers to consider how power relations influence the self-formation of community members. To continue this line of argumentation, we now turn to Foucault's writing on the technologies of the self.

CBPR and technologies of the self

In addition to acting as a technique of domination, through a Foucauldian lens, CBPR processes can also be seen to simultaneously enable an individual to understand and (trans)form her/himself as a particular subject within power relations. In his later work, beginning with the second volume of *The History of Sexuality*, Foucault (1994) was interested in the process by which individuals 'think about themselves, act for themselves, and transform themselves within power relations' (Rail and Harvey 1995, p. 167) – how individuals respond to and make sense of the regimes of truth by which they understand and form a relationship to oneself. According to Foucault (1994, p. 146), in all societies we find techniques that

> permit individuals to effect by their own means, or with the help of others, a certain number of operations on their own bodies and souls, thoughts, conduct, and way of being, so as to transform themselves in order to attain a certain state of happiness, purity, wisdom, perfection, immorality.

Through self-techniques, an individual thus constitutes 'himself [*sic*] as a moral subject of his own actions' (Foucault 2000, p. 263). While a discussion of the ethical relationship to oneself is beyond the scope of this paper, the point we seek to draw out is that power relations do not eliminate or undermine any meaningful conceptualisation of the self; instead, the complex, multiple and shifting relations of power in an individual's social field should be seen to enable new conceptions of the self and new forms of subjectivity (Foucault 1983). By taking up the position of a subject in and through those relations – that is, in becoming self-reflexive of the multiple and perhaps even contradictory discourses that inform their conceptions of the self, individuals are capable of engaging in deliberate practices of self-(trans)formation.

Thus, in addition to having a dominating effect, CBPR approaches can be seen to create a space in which marginalised individuals can invent new subjectivities by critically reworking present ones. That is, through the process of critical reflection, participants gain a 'minimal freedom' to deliberatively self-(trans)form in relation to and as dictated and determined by dominant discourses. To illustrate, Frisby *et al.* (2005, p. 371) conducted FPAR in partnership with Women Organizing Activities for Women (WOAW) to tackle 'restrictive policies and practices hindering access to community-based recreation programmes for women [including women immigrants] on low income.' In this example, women participants came together with community partners and university researchers in an attempt to tackle social exclusion in community recreation facilities. Their findings suggested that participation in the research process enabled women with low incomes to problematise how exclusion is discursively (re)produced and to take action that facilitated their participation in community recreation programmes (e.g. advocate for affordable child care). Thus, while the discursive production of leisure-based physical activity as a health promoting activity can be understood to inhibit diverse leisure meanings and forms, it must simultaneously be seen to enable the development of strategies for CBPR participants' participation in health-promoting physical activity – in effect, as supporting CBPR participants' capacity for the possibility of work on the self to be achieved.

It is this limited type of agency that has been the focus of post-structuralist critiques of CBPR, which contend that individuals in positions of authority (e.g. academic experts) impact the conduct of community members through the installation of capacities for self-techniques. In the prevailing critique, community members' engagement in the technologies of the self are governed all along by discourses provided by individuals in positions of authority (e.g. Canadian physical activity guidelines that recommend adults accumulate at least 150 min a moderate-to-vigorous intensity physical activity per week to sustain health and well-being) (Canadian Society for Exercise Physiology 2013), 'to induce participants to reconstitute themselves as reflective agents engaged in a programme of critical self-regulation and analysis' (Kesby *et al.* 2007, p. 20). Yet, Foucault's (1983, p. 220) understanding that power is always 'a way of acting upon an acting subject' allows for a more dynamic approach to understanding the various ways in which discourse effects community members self-(trans)formation. According to Thompson (2003, p. 122), from a Foucauldian perspective

> power relations necessarily presuppose that all parties involved in such relations have the ability, even in the most extreme cases, to choose amongst a range of structural options. This sort of freedom is, in turn, only possible in a field defined precisely by the structuring work of governance.

Agency is therefore at stake in and through the actions of community members – not in the sense an 'essential freedom,' but rather in the form of a 'minimal freedom.' Because community members are always in a position of power, the freedom to self-(trans)form as a subject of power relations is offered through the discourses that provide the resources and techniques to do so. Hence, domination and freedom are two sides of the same coin.

As has been exemplified through an examination of CBPR projects that have addressed new Canadians' diverse health promotion needs, Foucault's work on the technologies of domination and the technologies of the self can be used to demonstrate the various ways in which how power effects the actions of CBPR participants. Accordingly, rather than conceptualising CBPR approaches as dominating instruments that function to suppress particular actions or as a strategy that fosters an individual's agency, it is more useful to think of these two outcomes as occurring simultaneously.

Implications for CBPR researchers

Now that we have provide an overview of Foucault's work on power and power relations and how they relate to CBPR, we turn our attention to a discussion of

how health researchers can minimise the potential of CBPR as an exercise of domination. We argue that CBPR initiatives should not be seen as operating independent
of power relations; that CBPR researchers should instead attend to the ways in
which power relations act as constraints that simultaneously inhibit and enable the
actions of community members who participate/collaborate in the research process;
that we should consider CBPR approaches as affording marginalised individuals the
opportunity to problematise and potentially dismantle essentialist notions of the self;
and, that CBPR's outcomes are unpredictable.

CBPR does not operate independent of power relations

Following Foucault, CBPR initiatives should not be seen as operating independent
of power relations. As a result, CBPR researchers should not attempt to eliminate
power relations in the research process, but instead attend to the ways in which
power relations effect the actions of participants who collaborate/participate in the
research process. Indeed, the exercise of power is a condition of possibility for individual subjectivity (Foucault 1983). As such, power should be seen to create the
conditions for CBPR participants to critically reflect on the limits and creative possibilities of the multiple, and perhaps contradictory discourses that inform the issue
under investigation. Returning to the discursive construction of new Canadians'
health promotion needs, university-based academics and staff at community organisations would be urged to interrogate how dominant discourses surrounding the
research problem (e.g. engagement in leisure-based physical activity promotes
health and wellbeing) are taken up and acted upon by recent immigrants to Canada
from non-Western cultures and societies who participate/collaborate in the research
process: 'Are new Canadians cognisant of the health gains derived from leisure-
based physical activity?' 'How do new Canadians recognise and problematise such
discourses?' and 'How do new Canadians affirm or resist such discourses through
their actions?' Indeed, Foucault (1995) did not deny that forms of domination might
exist; nevertheless, to understand how power relations are produced and sustained,
or challenged and transgressed, Foucault and Gordon (1980) and Foucault (1990)
suggested we interrogate *how* power is exercised through the practices, techniques
and procedures that give it effect.

CBPR as enabling community members' critical awareness

Accordingly, we further argue that researchers ought to think of CBPR initiatives as
settings for community members to interrogate the limits and creative possibilities
of social constraints; that is, we should consider CBPR approaches as affording
otherwise marginalised individuals the opportunity to take up the position of a subject who is able to problematise and potentially dismantle essentialist notions of the
self produced and sustained through relations of power/knowledge. To illustrate, we
return to our example of a project developed to address new Canadians' health promotion needs through leisure-based physical activity. Instead of seeing prevailing
discourses as factors that act to only inhibit new Canadians' leisure pursuits, we
should see them as also enabling individual participants to become critically aware
of the multiple and perhaps contradictory discourses that inform their leisure actions
(e.g. ethnicity, religion, family roles). In other words, the discursive production of
new Canadians' health promotion needs should be seen and understood as a

necessary precondition for the possibility of action; a 'resource' that new Canadians who participate/collaborate in the research process can use to identify, problematise and make sense of their leisure behaviours in a new sociocultural environment. The exercise of power within CBPR should therefore be considered as a precondition for community members' actions, as it is in the taking up of the regimes of truth that an individual can interrogate the limits of one's subjectivity and with it the potential for creating new types of subjectivities.

Mere critique is not enough, however, to transform relations of power or discourse (Markula and Pringle 2006). Critical awareness is practical in the sense that it is oriented towards possible action. Indeed, Foucault (1983) suggested questioning that which is presented to us as natural and as normal opens up the space for a possible reworking and transformation of the self. For this reason, the key for the transformation power relations or discourse lies in the actions of CBPR participants, as individual actions upon acting subjects inform the form of change. Put somewhat differently, it is through the interrogation of the limits and creative possibilities of constraints exercised in and through discourse that community members evoke the possibility for transgression. Returning once more to new Canadians' health promotion needs, CBPR processes can yield new insights about the problem at hand that can transform discourse. As was illustrated through Frisby *et al.*'s (2005) example, low-income women's (including immigrants') under participation in leisure-based physical activity may be attributed to perceptions that public sport and recreation facilities are hostile environments designed to serve the needs and interest of dominant groups. Yet, through CBPR processes, the participants were able to identify and problematise the delivery of public recreation services, and take action that facilitated their participation in leisure-based physical activity (Frisby *et al.* 2005). Thus, CBPR approaches ought to be grounded in the understanding that power relations are dynamic and that all participants, as subjects within power relations, have the ever-present capacity to modify power relations through action upon action.

CBPR's outcomes are unpredictable

Lastly, a Foucauldian approach recognises that the type of change, if any, in power relations or discourses is highly dependent on individual actions. Community members who participate/ collaborate in the research process are not a homogeneous group of individuals who are united in their interpretation of the issue under investigation. Indeed, the transgression of power relations is about an individual's deliberate work on the limits of one's subjectivity, inventing new subjectivities by critically reworking the present ones (Foucault 1983). As such, CBPR initiatives are unpredictable in outcome; it is not possible to anticipate how participants' actions can transgress power relations or discourses. However, as we have argued in this paper, it is important to note that an individual's deliberate self-transformation is always constrained (i.e. inhibited and enabled) by the discursive construction of the issue under investigation, as it conditions the field of possibility for individual subjectivity. In other words, the exercise of power is a necessary condition for the possibility of critical reflection and deliberate self-transformation. Thus, researchers should consider CBPR as a tool used in the service of marginalised individuals' own self-formation and as enabling new skills and capacities for marginalised individuals' transgression of relations of dominance. For example, in terms of addressing health disparities among recent immigrants to Canada, we ought to see CBPR approaches as an important step in building reciprocal capacity for positive health outcomes: understanding how to sustain health and wellbeing in a new sociocultural environment is part of the personal adaptation process for immigrants, just as understanding immigrants' diverse perceptions and health promotion needs is part of the social adaptation process for health care providers and institutions.

Conclusion

In this paper, we engaged with Foucault's work to argue that by attending to the ways in which power always both inhibits and enables action, we will be better positioned as researchers to recognise CBPR's strengths and limitations, and thus better prepared for its potential outcomes. Because an individual is inherently always capable of recreating him/herself as a subject of power relations, we stress the need for researchers to facilitate participants' ability to critically analyse the limits and creative possibilities of the multiple and perhaps even contradictory discourses that inform the research process. Critical reflection establishes the opportunity for deliberate self-transformation (Foucault 1983). However, critical self-transformation does not necessarily lead to a transgression of power relations or discourse (Markula and Pringle 2006). As such, CBPR researchers ought to also critically reflect on how they and others exercise power in the research process. By uncovering how all participants exercise power – and especially how such exercises always serve to both enable and inhibit subjects' actions, we can formulate approaches to research that are better able to meet participants' needs. For example, dominant discourses surrounding the health gains derived from leisure-based physical activity offer new Canadians resources and techniques they can use to sustain health and wellbeing in a new socio-cultural environment. Thus, from a Foucauldian perspective, CBPR approaches can set in motion processes by which marginalised people can, in concert with researchers and staff at community organisations, critically analyse the nature, meanings and understandings of their health promotion needs in order to develop strategies that meet their needs.

Note

1. In Canada, and in many other high-immigrant receiving countries such as the USA, the UK and Australia, the largest proportions of new permanent residents originate from non-Western countries. This contrasts Canadian immigration patterns before the 1970's, when nearly all newcomers arrived from Western and Central Europe and the USA (Statistics Canada 2007).

Notes on contributors

Matias I. Golob is a PhD candidate in the School of Human Kinetics at the University of Ottawa.

Audrey R. Giles is an associate professor in the School of Human Kinetics at the University of Ottawa.

References

Ahmad, F., Mahmood, S., Pietkiewicz, I., McDonald, L., and Ginsburg, O., 2011. Concept mapping with South Asian immigrant women: barriers to mammography and solutions. *Journal of immigrant minority health*, 14, 242–250.

Blodgett, A.T., Schinke, R.J., Peltier, D., Wabano, M.J., Fisher, A., Eys, M.A., *et al.*, 2010a. 'Naadmaadmi': reflections of Aboriginal community members engaged in sport psychology co-researching activities with mainstream academics. *Qualitative research in sport and exercise*, 2 (1), 56–76.

Blodgett, A.T., Schinke, R.J., Fisher, L.A., Yungblut, H.E., Recollet-Saikkonen, D., Peltier, D., *et al.*, 2010b. Praxis and community-level sport programming strategies in a Canadian aboriginal reserve. *International journal of sport and exercise psychology*, 8 (3), 262–283.

Bryan, S.N. and Katzmarzyk, P.T., 2009. Are Canadians meeting the guidelines for moderate and vigorous leisure-time physical activity? *Applied physiology nutrition and metabolism*, 34 (4), 707–715.

Canadian Society for Exercise Physiology, 2013. *Canadian physical activity guidelines for adults: 18–64 years*. Available from: http://www.csep.ca/CMFiles/Guidelines/CSEP-Info-Sheets-adults-ENG.pdf [Accessed June 2013].

Chambers, R., 1997. *Whose reality counts? Putting the first last*. London: Intermediate Technology.

Clegg, S.R., 1989. *Frameworks of power*. London: Sage.

Cooke, B. and Kothari, U., 2001. *Participation: the new tyranny?* London: Zed Books.

Foucault, M., 1983. Afterword: the subject and power. *In*: H. Dreyfus and P. Rabinow, eds. *Michel Foucault: beyond structuralism and hermeneutics*. Chicago, IL: University of Chicago Press, 208–226.

Foucault, M., 1990. *The history of sexuality: the will to knowledge*. Vol. 1. London: Penguin books, Vol. 1.

Foucault, M., 1994. *The use of pleasure: the history of sexuality*. Vol. 2. London: Penguin books.

Foucault, M., 1995. *Discipline and punish: the birth of the prison*. New York: Vintage Books.

Foucault, M., 2000. On the genealogy of ethics: an overview of work in progress. *In*: P. Rabinow, ed. *Essential works of Foucault 1954–1984: ethics, subjectivity and truth* (Trans. Robert Hurley and others). London: Penguin.

Foucault, M. and Gordon, C., 1980. *Power/knowledge: selected interviews and other writings, 1972–1977*. New York: Pantheon Books.

Fraser, N., 1989. Foucault on modern power: empirical insights and normative confusions. *In*: N. Fraser, ed. *Unruly practices: power, discourse, and gender in contemporary social theory*. Minneapolis, MN: University of Minnesota Press, 17–34.

Frisby, W., 2011. Promising physical activity inclusion practices for Chinese immigrant women in Vancouver, Canada. *Quest*, 63 (1), 135–147.

Frisby, W., Reid, C., Millar, S., and Hoeber, L., 2005. Putting participatory into participatory forms of action research. *Journal of sport management*, 19, 267–386.

Gaventa, J. and Cornwall, A., 2006. Challenging the boundaries of the possible: participation, knowledge and power. *International development studies*, 37 (6), 122–128.

Golob, M., 2010. Correlations between policy discourse and leisure constraints among ethnic minorities: a case study of recent arrivals to Canada. *Annals of leisure research*, 13 (1), 27–46.

Golob, M. and Giles, A.R., 2011. Canadian multicultural citizenship: constraints on immigrants' leisure pursuits. *World leisure journal*, 53 (4), 312–321.

Henkel, H. and Stirrat, R., 2001. Participation as spiritual duty: empowerment as secular subjection. *In*: B. Cooke and U. Kothari, eds. *Participation: the new tyranny?* New York: Zed Books, 168–184.

Hickey, S. and Mohan, G., 2005. *Participation: from tyranny to transformation? Exploring new approaches to participation in development*. London: Zed Books.

Hyman, I., 2004. Setting the stage: reviewing current knowledge on the health of Canadian immigrants: what is the evidence and where are the gaps? *Canadian journal of public health*, 95 (3), 14–18.

Interprovincial Sport and Recreation Council, 1987. *National recreation statement*. Available from: http://lin.ca/resources/html/statement.htm [Accessed April 2010].

Isaacs, S., Valaitis, R., Newbold, K.B., Black, M., and Sargeant, J., 2013. Brokering for the primary healthcare needs of recent immigrant families in Atlantic, Canada. *Primary health care research and development*, 14, 63–79.

Israel, B.A., Schulz, A.J., Parker, E.A., and Becker, A.B., 1998. Review of community-based research: assessing partnership approaches to improve public health. *Annual review of public health*, 19, 173–202.

Israel, B.A., Krieger, J., Vladhov, D., Ciske, S., Foley, M., Fortin, P., *et al.*, 2006. Challenges and facilitating factors in sustaining community-based participatory research partnerships: lessons learned from the Detroit, New York City, and Seattle Urban Research Centers. *Journal of urban health*, 83 (6), 1022–1040.

Kemmis, S. and McTaggart, R., 2000. Participatory action research. *In*: N.K. Denzin and Y. S. Lincoln, eds. *Handbook of qualitative research*. 2nd ed. Thousand Oaks, CA: Sage, 567–603.

Kesby, M., Kindon, S., and Pain, R., 2007. Participation as a form of power: retheorising empowerment and spatialising participatory action research. *In*: S. Kindon, R. Pain, and M. Kesby, eds. *Participatory action research approaches and methods: connecting people, participation and place*. New York: Routledge, 19–25.

Kindon, S., Pain, R., and Kesby, M., 2007. Participatory action research: origins, approaches and methods. *In*: S. Kindon, R. Pain, and M. Kesby, eds. *Participatory action research approaches and methods: connecting people, participation and place*. New York: Routledge, 8–18.

Kothari, U., 2001. Power, knowledge, and social control in participatory development. *In*: B. Cooke and U. Kothari, eds. *Participation: the new tyranny?* New York: Zed Books, 139–152.

Magalhaes, L., Carrasco, C., and Gastaldo, D., 2010. Undocumented migrants in Canada: a scope literature review on health, access to services, and working conditions. *Journal of immigrant minority health*, 12, 132–151.

Markula, P. and Pringle, R., 2006. *Foucault, sport and exercise: power, knowledge and transforming the self*. London: Routledge.

Minkler, M. and Vallerstein, N., 2011. *Community-based participatory research for health: from process to outcomes*. 2nd ed. San Francisco, CA: Joseey-Bass.

Miller, P. and Rose, N., 2008. *Governing the present: administering economic, social, and personal life*. Cambridge: Polity Press.

Newbold, K.B., 2005. Health status and health care of immigrants in Canada: a longitudinal analysis. *Journal of health services and responsible policy*, 10 (2), 77–83.

Newbold, K.B., 2009. Health care use and the Canadian immigrant population. *International journal of health services*, 39 (3), 545–565.

Ng, E., *et al.*, 2005. Dynamics of immigrants' health in Canada: evidence from the National Population Health Survey. *Statistics Canada*. Available from: www.statcan.gc.ca/pub/82-618-m /2005002/pdf/4193621-eng.pdf [Accessed September 2010].

Perez, C.E., 2002. Health status and health behaviour among immigrants. *Health reports-statistics Canada*, 13 (Supplement), 1–13.

Rail, G. and Harvey, J., 1995. Body at work: Michel Foucault and the sociology of sport. *Sociology of sport journal*, 12, 164–179.

Reason, P. and Bradbury, H., 2008. Introduction. *In*: H. Bradbury and P. Reason, eds. *Handbook of action research: participative inquiry and practice*. 2nd ed. Thousands Oaks, CA: Sage, 1–10.

Seefeldt, V., Malina, R.M., and Clark, M.A., 2002. Factors affecting levels of physical activity in adults. *Sports medicine*, 32 (3), 143–168.

Shogan, D., 1999. *The making of high performance athletes*. Toronto: University of Toronto Press.

Simich, L., Maiter, S., and Ochocka, J., 2009. From social liminality to cultural negotiation: transformative processes in immigrant mental wellbeing. *Anthropology and medicine*, 16 (3), 253–366.

Stack, J. and Iwasaki, Y., 2009. The role of leisure pursuits in adaptation processes among Afghan refugees who have immigrated to Winnipeg, Canada. *Leisure studies*, 28 (3), 239–259.

Statistics Canada, 2007. *Portrait of the Canadian population in 2006, 2006 census.* Ottawa, ON: Ministry of Industry, Report No. 97-550-XIE.

Statistics Canada, 2008. *2006 census: immigrants in Canada: a portrait of the foreign-born population.* Available from: http://www.statcan.gc.ca/pub/85f0033m/2008018/findings-resultats-eng.htm [Accessed September 2010].

Thompson, K., 2003. Forms of resistance: Foucault on tactical reversal and self-formation. *Continental philosophy review*, 36 (2), 113–138.

Tirone, S.C., 2000. Racism, indifference and the leisure experiences of South Asian Canadianteens. *Leisure/Loisir*, 24 (1), 89–114.

Tirone, S.C. and Shaw, S.M., 1997. At the center of their lives: Indo Canadian women, their families and leisure. *Journal of leisure research*, 29 (3), 225–244.

Weedon, C., 1999. *Feminism, theory and the politics of difference.* Oxford: Blackwell.

Growing up in the Kayamandi Township: I. The role of sport in helping young people overcome challenges within their community

Meredith A. Whitley[a], Laura A. Hayden[b] and Daniel Gould[c]

[a]Department of Exercise Science, Health Studies, Physical Education, & Sport Management, Adelphi University, Garden City, NY, USA; [b]Department of Counselling and School Psychology, University of Massachusetts, Boston, MA, USA; [c]Institute for the Study of Youth Sports, Michigan State University, East Lansing, MI, USA

While the growth of the sport-for-development movement has coincided with the establishment of a number of sport-for-development organisations, many of these organisations have been top-down development projects or outside-in globalisation projects, which are not as effective as they could be. In an effort to address the gap in the literature on inside-up sport-for-development programmes, this study focused on one specific community in South Africa that is being served by various sport programmes. Interviews were conducted with 40 participants, divided into three sub-groups: community members, coaches and athletes. The methodological framework of the study, a description of the community and the role of sport in the community are described in detail. Additionally, the barriers that prevent young people from participating in sport are addressed, along with a look at how sport can help young people overcome the challenges of growing up in this community. The practical implications of these findings are also addressed, with a focus on how to support existing sport programmes in these communities, develop coaching education programmes to better serve young athletes and design and implement new sport programmes within similar communities.

While sport has long been recognised as a means of improving the physical and mental health of those involved, the term 'sport-for-development' is a more recent social construct in which sport is positioned as a tool for social development to allow both individuals and communities to pursue and realise their potential (Okada and Young 2011). During the late 1990s, the sport-for-development construct transitioned from fragmented, ad hoc interventions to a well-defined movement with the establishment of a number of sport-for-development organisations, including the Edusport Foundation in Zambia in 1999, Magic Bus in Mumbai in 1999 and EMIMA (a Swahili acronym for sport, physical activity and education) in Tanzania in 2001 (Kidd 2008, Coalter 2010). This rapid growth within the sport-for-development movement has since continued, with increasing numbers of organisations (e.g. Right To Play and Mathare Youth Sport Association [MYSA]) involved in a variety of sport-for-development projects, along with the formation of the International Platform on Sport and Development (Spaaij 2009a).

Positioning sport as a tool for development is now supported by key policy-makers throughout the world, with the United Nations labelling 2005 as the Year of Development and Peace through Sport (United Nations 2005) and the World Economic Forum committing to sport for development and peace in 2006 (United Nations 2006). There has even been a push for sport to be linked to the Millennium Development Goals, which include the eradication or reduction of poverty, hunger and child mortality and the promotion of education and gender equality (Van Eekeren 2006). The United Nations (2003) supports the use of sport as a viable and practical tool in helping to achieve these goals, which has led even more donors and development agencies to incorporate sport into their universal development strategies (Levine *et al.* 2008).

This fascination with the sport-for-development movement has also occurred in South Africa, where a series of public–private partnerships have used sport in hopes of achieving a range of developmental goals. This began with the formation of the Australia-South Africa Development Programme in 1993, in which the Australian Agency for International Development and the South African Government have partnered to provide funding and support for a series of sport-for-development initiatives over the past two decades (Burnett 2001, 2010). These initiatives have been value-based programmes focusing on sport participation and the development of sport skills for all young South Africans, regardless of their race, ethnicity or financial status (Burnett *et al.* 1999, Burnett 2006). Additionally, Sport and Recreation South Africa has created the School Sport Mass Participation Programme, designed to help build communities through the provision of structured opportunities for young people to participate in sport and recreation programmes (2008). The overarching goals of this programme are to increase the level of participation in sport and recreation, raise sport's profile in South African communities, increase South Africa's sporting success at international events and educate the public about HIV/AIDS while also reducing the crime rate. Both of these national programmes have been evaluated by Burnett (2001, 2006, 2010, 2011), with findings indicating that these programmes have led to increased opportunities in new sports, sustained participation in sports and limited social change in terms of empowerment, equity and access to participation and decision-making opportunities for community members.

Although Burnett's research has indicated that these programmes are having a positive impact, many scholars and practitioners within the sport-for-development movement would argue that these programmes are not as effective as they could be, given that these are all top-down development projects (Allender *et al.* 2006, Mintzberg 2006). This is one of three distinct development approaches that Mintzberg has defined within the sport-for-development movement, with the others being the outside-in globalisation approach and the inside-up indigenous development approach. The top-down development approach refers to programmes that have been pre-designed and are carried out in a number of different contexts. It assumes that the recipients in each community will benefit in prescribed ways, and that, over time, the community will begin to take ownership of the programme. Although there are certainly benefits to this approach, there are many concerns related to these top-down development projects, such as: (a) the power and politics in the sport and development relationship, including the potential for top-down programmes to align with capitalism (Darnell 2007, Black 2010); (b) concerns about whether these programmes are even addressing the needs of the community (Allender *et al.* 2006); (c) the potential for these programmes to be used for gaining social control and regulation (Spaaij 2009b, Darnell and Hayhurst 2011, Hartmann and Kwauk 2011) and (d) concerns over whether these programmes will be fully embraced by the communities in which they are located (Mintzberg 2006). Both the Australia-South Africa Development Programme and the School Sport Mass Partici-pation Programme are top-down development projects, with the South African Government overseeing the design, implementation and evaluation of both of these programming efforts. The external researcher has acknowledged the lack of buy-in from the communities in which the School Sport Mass Participation Programme was implemented (Burnett 2010).

Another development approach within the sport-for-development movement is the outside-in globalisation approach, which often involves the formation of strate-gic partnerships between external non-governmental organisations and the recipients of these programmes (Mintzberg 2006). There has been a proliferation of these types of sport-for-development programmes (Armstrong and Giulianotti 2004, Pisani 2008), with Right To Play being one of the most well-known and well-funded organisations. These programmes are often based on pre-conceived global agendas stipulated by international agencies, such as the Millennium Development Goals by the United Nations, leading critics to claim that these predefined parame-ters and objectives may lead to sport-for-development programmes that do not address local issues or needs (Kidd 2008, Coalter 2010).

Given concerns about dependency and global agendas with outside-in develop-ment approaches and the concerns regarding power, politics and community owner-ship with top-down development projects, it is no surprise that there has been a call for more inside-up development programmes. This development approach refers to widespread community involvement in the design, implementation and evaluation of sport-for-development programmes, with the main focus on addressing the local needs of the community. The MYSA is one example of an inside-up sport-for-development programme that is located in Kenya, as this association established locally-based aims, objectives and principles (Willis 2000, Hognestad and Tollisen 2004). While some of the outside-in and top-down development projects are com-munity based, the MYSA and other inside-up development projects are community-driven, leading to local ownership and greater buy-in from community members. This matches the findings of the Sport for Development and Peace International Working Group (2008), which reported that the most effective programmes empower their participants and foster local ownership.

Unfortunately, there is a critical gap in the literature on inside-up sport-for-development programmes, even though there are a number of these programmes in communities throughout South Africa. In order to understand the impact of these programmes on the individuals and communities being served and, ultimately, to demonstrate best practices across communities, it is necessary for these sport-for-development programmes to be studied in the context of their respective communi-ties. Along with this call for community-driven research, there has also been a call for research methods that address alternative knowledges or voices, as the current body of literature is largely focused on programmers from top-down and outside-in development approaches (Parameswaran 2008, McEwan 2009, Hayhurst and Frisby 2010, Darnell and Hayhurst 2011). There is also the concern that researchers have primarily relied on quantitative evaluation methods instead of also using qualitative methods that are more likely to lead to a more nuanced and in-depth understanding of these programmes and the individuals' experiences at the ground level (Levermore 2011). Therefore, a need exists to supplement existing research by conducting qualitative research that will give voice to individuals at the ground level, leading to a better understanding of their experiences and realities (Bartlett *et al.* 2007, Genat 2009) and allowing people from different social and cultural backgrounds to describe their sport experiences in their own words, which is often overlooked by Western researchers (Coakley 2003).

To fill this void in the literature and give voice to those individuals who are involved in inside-up programming efforts, this study focused on one specific community in South Africa that is being served by a number of sport programmes: the Kayamandi Township. In order to develop a comprehensive understanding of the Kayamandi Township, the sport programmes and the coaches and athletes involved, this study was designed as a qualitative investigation in which interviews were conducted with community members, coaches and athletes from the Kayamandi Township. Speaking with three different subsets of the population within the community enhanced the findings through the process of data triangulation, adding rigour, breadth and depth to this investigation (Patton 2001, Denzin and Lincoln 2005). Another strength of this research was that coaches and athletes interviewed were from a variety of sport programmes within the community. This addressed another limitation of past research studies (Lindsey and Banda 2011), which have focused solely on individual sport-for-development programmes (e.g. Gasser and Levinsen 2004, Sugden 2006) or on singular sport-for-development organisations (e.g. Armstrong 2004, Coalter 2007), instead of examining a broad selection of programmes within one community. By focusing on one South African community, the aim of the current investigation was to develop a comprehensive understanding of the Kayamandi Township and the role of sport within this community.

Given the size of this study, all the data cannot be presented in a comprehensive manner in one manuscript. Therefore, this first manuscript will provide an underlying coherency to a series of articles that will explore this data. This manuscript will present information common to all future articles: (a) the methodological framework of the study; (b) a detailed description of the Kayamandi Township, including the challenges that young people face growing up in this community; (c) the role of sport in the Kayamandi Township; (d) the barriers that often prevent young people from becoming involved or continuing involvement in sport and the strategies that coaches use to help athletes overcome these barriers and (e) how sport can help young people overcome the challenges they face growing up in the Kayamandi Township and the strategies that coaches use to help their athletes. For the purposes of the current manuscript, the focus will be on: (a) the challenges for young people growing up in this community; (b) the barriers to sport participation for these individuals and (c) the strategies that coaches in the Kayamandi Township have developed to overcome these barriers and increase the number of young people involved in sport.

Method

Participants

Since this was an exploratory study of a community and population who have not previously shared their lived experiences and everyday realities, we wanted to obtain rich data from a variety of perspectives (Kvale 1996, Tashakkori and Teddlie 2010). Therefore, interviews were conducted with three groups of individuals from the Kayamandi Township: coaches, community members and athletes. Following ethical clearance from an American university and a South African university, qualitative interviews were conducted with a total of 40 participants. Selected participants were required to be past or current residents of the Kayamandi Township and able to speak and understand conversational English. The community members and coaches were required to be at least 18 years old, while the athletes were between the ages of 9 and 20. Using these criteria for inclusion, the final sample consisted of 10 coaches, 11 community members and 19 athletes.

For the sub-group comprised of coaches from the Kayamandi Township, these 10 participants (9 males and 1 female) were between the ages of 22 and 37 ($M = 28.4$, SD $= 7.0$), with one coach choosing not to divulge his age. All of these coaches had experience coaching in the Kayamandi Township, with an average of 4.42 years of coaching experience (SD $= 3.57$). Participants had coached a variety of sports, including soccer, mountain biking, running, bicycle motocross (BMX), netball, futsal and indigenous games, with the settings ranging from school sport teams to local club teams to unstructured sport experiences for the young people of the Kayamandi Township. Two of the coaches had reached Grade 10 within their high school, while four had graduated from high school and the others had a mixture of degrees from technical colleges and universities. Three coaches reported no experience in any type of coaching education programme, while the rest of the coaches discussed experiences ranging from just one training course to a more comprehensive coaching education programme.

As for the sub-group of community members from the Kayamandi Township, these 11 participants (5 males and 6 females) were between the ages of 20 and 69 ($M = 42.0$, SD $= 15.8$). There was a wide range in educational experiences, with two community members without a high school degree, five who had completed high school and four with post-secondary educational experience. Two individuals were unemployed at the time of their interviews and one of the older community members was retired. Those who were currently employed included a police officer, a pastor, someone who produced crafts at a local shop and two community members who worked in the sporting environment in the Kayamandi Township, although neither of these individuals was a coach at the time of the interviews. Participants' experiences in sport ranged from no sport experience to childhood sport experience to young adult sport experience.

For the sub-group comprised of athletes from the Kayamandi Township, these 19 participants (11 males and 8 females) were between the ages of 9 and 20 ($M = 16.2$, SD $= 3.0$). All of the participants were students at the time of their interviews, with the majority of participants attending one of the schools within the Kayamandi Township ($n = 15$). The sports represented included soccer, mountain biking, stick fighting, netball, athletics (i.e. track and field) and BMX. Sport experiences ranged from playing in organised clubs to playing for school teams or simply participating in unorganised games and/or practices in the community. Only two participants were living with both of their parents at the time of their interviews, with the other participants living with their mothers, close family members, siblings and/or adoptive parents.

Procedures

Following the recommendation of Krueger and Casey (2000), all of the interviews were conducted by the same individual, who was trained extensively in qualitative research methodology, extremely knowledgeable of the research topic and heavily involved in the development of the interview guides. The interviewer was a white female doctoral student in her mid-twenties from the USA who had conducted research and outreach efforts with a variety of marginalised populations prior to this experience, including with recent immigrants and young refugees from a wide range of countries now living in the USA. In order to minimise the potential for cultural misunderstanding, mistrust and resistance toward the research study (Blodgett *et al.* 2010), the interviewer intensively studied the community and spent a considerable amount of time in the Kayamandi Township. This began 10 months prior to the data collection period, at which time she visited the Kayamandi Township and began her intensive study of the community through direct and indirect observation and developing personal and professional relationships with a variety of coaches, community members and athletes.

Following her introduction to the Kayamandi Township, from her home university in the USA, she maintained an ongoing dialogue with members of the community while continuing to develop her education about the community through reading additional materials pertaining to the Kayamandi Township, other townships in South Africa and the political, cultural and social history of South Africa. Upon her return to the Kayamandi Township for data collection over a span of three months, she reconnected with the individuals she met 10 months earlier while also engaging in numerous conversations and building relationships based on respect and trust with coaches, community members and athletes in the community, as recommended by Goodkind and Decon (2004). The focus of these relationships was on the interviewer's interest in learning about the Kayamandi Township and the coaches, community members and athletes' experiences in this community, evidenced by the interviewer continually asking questions and asking permission to attend and/or observe different community events and sporting practices and games.

Since the interviewer was not connected with any governmental or organisational mission that could be related to a top-down development project or an outside-in globalisation approach (Mintzberg 2006), she stressed her interest in giving a voice to the individuals at the ground level, leading to a better understanding of their experiences and realities. There were many indications of the respect and trust that developed between the interviewer and the coaches, community members and athletes, such as a youth sport coach inviting her to participate in team practices, a community member inviting her into his home and an athlete asking her to attend her netball practices and games. At the conclusion of her 3-month stay, the interviewer spent an estimated 200 h in the Kayamandi Township developing and nurturing these relationships while observing the daily life and sporting environment in the community, with data collection not beginning until the second month of her stay. This time spent in the township afforded the interviewer the opportunity to develop a strong understanding of the community, culture and customs, which, in turn, allowed her to ask culturally sensitive and pertinent follow-up interview questions. She also worked with several community members to design and deliver two sport-based development programmes for the children and youth of the Kayamandi Township, which enabled the interviewer to develop stronger relationships with many of the community members, as it was clear that she was not in the community simply to conduct a research study, but was interested in collaborating with community members to design and implement programmes that would contribute to the development of their young people. This experience also allowed the interviewer to develop a better understanding of the realities of conducting a sport-based programme in the Kayamandi Township, leading to stronger practical implications from the research findings. It is important to note that there was no crossover with the individuals who participated in these sport-based programmes and those who served as participants in the present study.

Focusing on the interviewer's ontological and epistemological assumptions that framed this study, she embraced a constructivist ontology, with the belief that there are multiple versions of reality constructed by individuals, along with an interpretivist epistemology, with the assumption that direct knowledge of the phenomena under study is not possible, resulting in indirect indications of phenomena (Strauss and Corbin 1994, Weed 2009). The underlying aim of this research study was to explore the multiple versions of reality perceived by the 40 participants of the study; however, in line with the objectivist, scientific paradigm identified by Sparkes (2002), it was impossible to remove the interviewer's and second and third investigators' roles in the study design, data collection, data analysis and writing phases of the study, making it difficult to directly capture the experience of the participants (King 2009). Therefore, the study design, data collection, data analysis and writing phases were conducted with a focus on constructing the participants' understanding of their experiences and everyday realities while also including the investigators' interpretations of the participants' rich descriptions in the interview transcripts. This approach is similar to the use of interpretative phenomenological analysis (Smith and Osborn 2003) to guide the study, although this approach was not directly employed.

As for the study participants, snowball sampling techniques were used, with the interviewer relying on her contacts within the community as well as each participant to recommend other individuals to contact. Given the strong relationships that the interviewer developed with a variety of coaches, community members and athletes, a number of individuals were used to begin snowball sampling. Additionally, the selection of participants was also purposive in nature, with the interviewer deliberately working toward a sample that would include coaches, community members and athletes, along with a range of ages and both male and female participants with a range of educational and professional experiences. This ensured a representative sample and increased the range of data exposed (Lincoln and Guba 1985), resulting in a more rigorous and comprehensive study. Given the fact that there were very few female coaches in the Kayamandi Township, there was a disproportional number of males to females for the sub-group of coaches; however, the percentage of female coaches interviewed was proportionate to the percentage of female coaches within the Kayamandi Township. For the coaches and athletes, there was also a focus on ensuring that a variety of sports and sport settings (e.g. school, community and club) would be represented in the final sample.

All of the interviews were conducted within the Kayamandi Township. In order to foster an atmosphere conducive to sharing personal information and experiences, each participant was asked to choose his or her preferred interview location within the community, as this decision increased the likelihood that participants would feel comfortable and empowered by the interviewer (Elwood and Martin 2000, Goodkind and Decon 2004). Some participants chose to be interviewed in their homes or businesses, while other participants asked to be interviewed in a private room at a local non-profit organisation. Prior to the start of each interview, the participants were informed of the following: (a) the purposes of the study, with a particular focus on how the findings from this study could be used to benefit the community, which has often been overlooked in studies of marginalised populations (Smith 1999, Kral *et al.* 2002); (b) their confidentiality rights; (c) their right to refuse to answer specific questions and (d) the option of ending the interview at any time. The participants then read and signed an informed consent form. For the athletes who were under 18 years of age, informed consent forms were signed by their parents prior to the interview, with the participants signing informed assent forms at the beginning of the interview, thus signifying their voluntary participation in the study. Incentives were not offered as a means to recruit participants, with the participants taking part in the study under their own volition. The length of interviews varied between the three sub-groups within the sample, with coaches' interviews lasting an average of 52 min, community members speaking for an average of 42 min and athletes speaking for an average of 33 min.

Interview guides

Following the guidelines set by Kvale (1996), a semi-structured format was used for the interviews, with three separate interview guides constructed for the three sub-groups interviewed:[1] coaches, community members and athletes from the Kayamandi Township. These interview guides allowed a specific set of questions to be posed to all participants within each sub-group, although the interviewer was free to ask additional probes and follow-up questions to explore any unexpected issues and topics that arose in each interview. The interview guides were developed from a combination of factors, including the previous literature on positive youth development (Larson 2000, Lerner *et al.* 2005), community youth development (Garbarino 1995, Benson *et al.* 1998), coaching (Smith *et al.* 1979, Jones *et al.* 2004, Jones 2009) and life skills development (Hellison and Walsh 2002, Hellison 2003, Petitpas *et al.* 2005). Additionally, a review of qualitative research methods was used in the development of the interview guides (Lincoln and Guba 1985, Kvale 1996, Tashakkori and Teddlie 2010). Following the construction of each interview guide, an expert knowledgeable in these fields and in qualitative research critiqued the guides to ensure the questions were clear and applicable. To minimise the potential for cross-cultural misunderstanding during the interviews, the interview guides were also reviewed by a South African university professor and an individual who worked in a non-profit organisation in the Kayamandi Township.

While there were similar questions posed in all of the interviews, the interview guides were designed specifically for each sub-group. The major components of the interview guide for the coaches included their own experiences coaching in the Kayamandi Township, basic information on their athletes and teams, their knowledge of sports within the Kayamandi Township, their personal goals for their athletes and a discussion regarding life skills development and success as a coach. The interview guides for community members focused on the participants' knowledge of sports within the community and discussions regarding whether sport could be helpful to the athletes as well as the Kayamandi Township at large. The interview guides for athletes focused on their experiences as athletes, including barriers and issues related to sport participation and continuation, their views of their coaches and their teams, their perceptions of the support for sports within the community and their view on the role of sport as it affects them as athletes, community members and future professionals.

Data analysis

Given that the purpose of the study was exploratory in nature, the analysis procedures centred on finding patterns rather than generating and/or testing theories (Tashakkori and Teddlie 2010). The audio recordings of the interviews were transcribed verbatim and then checked for accuracy by the interviewer. The interviewer and a second member of the research team (with extensive training and experience with cultural sensitivity and transnational research) then independently performed a comprehensive inductive content analysis that was guided by constant comparison and critical reflection. This analysis procedure began with reading each transcript several times for familiarity, leading to the open coding of raw meaning units, followed by the creation and organisation of lower and higher order themes (Côté et al. 1993). At the conclusion of each level of analysis, an iterative consensus validation process was followed by the two researchers, with the transcripts being reviewed and discussed to reach consensus when differences arose (Greenleaf et al. 2001). Additionally, at the conclusion of the analysis procedures, the two researchers reviewed the higher order themes, lower order themes and raw meaning units to ensure that the way they were categorised and ordered was both the most logical and meaningful way to organise the participants' remarks. A third investigator was also used as a peer debrief throughout the analysis procedures as well as the final stage of analysis, with this individual bringing his vast knowledge and experience in sport-based youth development and global sport and development into the analysis procedures. Additionally, this third investigator had previously visited the Kayamandi Township and was familiar with the community and South Africa at large, leading to a more nuanced understanding of the history, culture and society.

To evaluate the methodological rigour of this study, the criteria of fairness, ontological authenticity, educative authenticity, catalytic authenticity and tactical authenticity prescribed by Guba and Lincoln (2005) were utilised (Sparkes and Smith 2009), which will now be explored. With three different groups of individuals from the Kayamandi Township (coaches, community members and athletes), multiple points of view were shared by the participants, with the interviewer developing strong relationships that were based on respect and trust with the participants throughout the duration of the data collection period. This allowed the interviewer to conduct each interview in a comfortable, supportive environment in which participants shared their thoughts, feelings and experiences without fear of judgement and with the interviewer continually highlighting the importance of their lived experiences and everyday realities. Additionally, the interviews were constructed in a way that fostered a sense of discovery and learning, with the participants encouraged to deeply reflect on their own experiences and realities and consider what actions could be taken in the future, whether by the individual participants or by the community at large. As for increasing the likelihood that the data analysis revealed the multiple realities experienced by the participants and was not diluted or distorted by the interviewer, the data analysis procedures also included multiple coders, the process of iterative consensus validation and the use of a peer review (Lincoln and Guba 1985, Tashakkori and Teddlie 2010).

Limitations

Several limitations of the study design must be acknowledged, beginning with the participant pool. One sub-group of participants was comprised of current or former athletes, thereby overlooking the rest of the young people in the community; however, this limitation was determined to be acceptable as the focus of the study was on this subset of the population. Another limitation was the requirement for each participant to be able to speak and understand conversational English, which could have limited the sample. There was also the possibility that the interviewees may have reacted negatively to the interviewer's skin colour, gender and/or nationality, as the interviewer was not part of the community, resulting in the interviewer not receiving the most accurate information from participants. There was also the possibility that the interviewer and her fellow researchers misinterpreted the data due to their Western lens. While methods were employed to minimise the possibility of these limitations from occurring, such as time spent in the community, relationship building and intensive study of the history, culture and society, these limitations still must be acknowledged.

Results and specific discussion

The inductive content analysis of the 40 interviews yielded 2446 raw meaning units, which coalesced under 411 lower order themes and, ultimately, 176 higher order themes. These data were organised under 30 general dimensions. These general dimensions are explored in the following section, along with an in-depth review of select higher order and lower order themes.[2] The final general dimension is addressed in the discussion section, as the focus is on the practical implications and recommendations for parents, coaches and programme providers to help young people overcome the barriers to sport participation and reap the benefits of sport within the Kayamandi Township.

The Kayamandi Township

Underserved community

The setting of this study was the Kayamandi Township, which was originally built to house black migrant labourers employed on the Stellenbosch farms, and is now largely comprised of black residents from the ethnic clans of the Xhosa. When asked to describe the Kayamandi Township, the study participants ($n=22$) discussed the 'undesirability' of the community, with a high rate of crime, poor living conditions and a dangerous environment, while highlighting positive aspects of the community, such as the friendly people and fun activities. While there are a number of issues within the Kayamandi Township, the majority of coaches ($n=8$), community members ($n=8$) and athletes ($n=15$) still saw it as a welcoming place with kind people who are determined to create a better future for the next generation. In fact, one community member described this area as a 'vibrant community where all sorts of activities take place', while another community member explained how the 'people of Kayamandi are very friendly'. This was an unexpected finding, which may not have emerged if the investigators had not taken an inside-up development approach, listening to the voices of the individuals at the ground level.

Despite this shared pride in their community, the Kayamandi Township is still a low-income, underserved community with a range of challenges and issues. As one community member accurately stated, this is a 'relatively poor community' with the unemployment rate estimated at 34% (University of Stellenbosch 2001). This poverty has led to a variety of issues, beginning with the high number of informal dwellings and shacks made of wood, aluminium, plastic and other low-cost building materials, with the size of these dwellings averaging 5 m^2 of floor space (Barnes 2002, Lindner 2006). These poor living conditions were actually one of the most cited lower order themes in this study, with one athlete discussing how 'there are too many shacks … people need houses'. Due to substantial issues with the sewage system and water and refuse removal in this overcrowded community, there is a high prevalence of disease, including tuberculosis and diarrhoea (Barnes 2002). The study participants were aware of the health-related issues present in the community, with a particular focus on the prevalence and transmission of HIV/AIDS. This turned into a discussion surrounding the unhealthy sexual behaviour that often occurs within the Kayamandi Township, such as 'people getting HIV and AIDS disease while they know that you can prevent HIV by carrying a condom'.

Other study participants ($n = 10$) discussed the high rate of pregnancy at a young age, with one athlete acknowledging that 'there are too many girls who are pregnant in Kayamandi'. This matches previous findings within the community that only 5% of the women who had children were older than 30 years when they first gave birth, with around 42% of women bearing their first child while they were still in school (University of Stellenbosch 2001). Along with these high rates of disease and unhealthy sexual behaviour, the Kayamandi Township also sees high rates of malnutrition (Turcotte 2003). One athlete in the present study discussed how some girls procured food through prostitution, explaining how 'others being prostitute, because they don't have money for food'.

Substance use

The second most frequently cited higher order theme throughout the study was that of substance use within the Kayamandi Township. This theme included concerns over alcohol, with one community member sharing how 'our young people are so involved in young ages in alcohol' and an athlete explaining how youth 'like drinking'. Drug use is another reality in the Kayamandi Township, including both marijuana and tic (methamphetamine), with a boxing coach describing how 'the problem, the challenges that we face outside of boxing … is the drugs'. Along with alcohol and drug use, there was also a focus on smoking, as the young people 'smoke all the time'. This focus included cigarette smoking and 'smoking glue', which was cited by a few of the participants as being a trend in the township at that time.

Crime

The poverty combined with the substance use and severe overcrowding have a large impact on the crime rate, with the study participants ($n = 31$) acknowledging that there are a series of behavioural issues (e.g. robbery, murder, etc.) that have created a very dangerous environment in the community. One community member stated, 'you must always be on alert that you can be robbed', and an athlete described how 'when you walk at night, you get robbed. People take your stuff or sometimes they come into your house and then they steal things there'. This was confirmed by a female community member, who explained how 'you must go [walk] with some-one, like a guy or someone you can trust … because you can't walk alone at night, 'cause it's dangerous'. In fact, as the interviewer became embedded in the community, her hosts always insisted she be escorted between locations.

Educational issues

There are also issues with the public school system, with overcrowded educational institutions (Lindner 2006), as confirmed by one community member in the study, who explained that

> here in Kayamandi … this class is about 50, plus 40 … in the classroom. Then, there's only one teacher. I don't think one teacher can go to each student and know [teach] how to read.

The study participants openly discussed these issues, with one athlete describing how the 'teachers of Kayamandi, they are also irresponsible because some of them are not professional trained and some of them are not even past Standard 10'. There were also concerns regarding the post-secondary education options for young people from the Kayamandi Township, as 'there's no money for them [the high school graduates] to go to the tertiary level'.

Lack of support

The final set of themes that arose from the data centred on the support that the young people receive as they grow up in the Kayamandi Township. Beginning with the community, the participants ($n = 19$) discussed how they perceived a largely unsupportive and negative community environment in which young people were surrounded by negative peer pressure and, at times, mean people who were not helping them think about and actively work toward their futures. As one community member described, peer pressure is a serious issue for young people, 'because if I see my friend doing something bad, I don't have the guts to tell him or her that, "this is not good." I just want to do, "cause I want to be cool"'.

Additionally, an overall lack of parental guidance and support emerged as challenges for young people growing up in the Kayamandi Township. As one community member explained, 'you'll find kids doing bad things because the parents didn't teach … they are not open enough to talk about other stuff'. An athlete echoed this sentiment with these words: 'to the parents, I could say some of them are not encouragers … some are tearing their children down. And they do not want to give their children money to pay for essential things'. The participants discussed a variety of reasons for this lack of support, including the fact that there were many single parents and children without their biological parents in the community. As one community member explained, 'in our community, we do have some kids that don't have parents, some of their parents have died because of AIDS'. Another issue is the distant parent–child relationships that are often caused by parents working long hours, which may create the following scenario: 'in the morning, when I [the child] wake up, my mother is not there. She's gone already to work. She comes back and sleeping … no one cares about what's happening in anyone's life'.

Sport in the Kayamandi Township

The study participants cited 21 different sports in existence within the Kayamandi Township, with soccer being the most frequently cited sport, followed by netball, rugby, basketball and mountain biking. These sports ranged from club sports to school sports to unstructured community practices and games, with young people participating in a variety of these sport opportunities. The coaches and community members discussed how sport was an integral part of the community, with one of the community members sharing how 'you can't have a community without sport' and another community member explaining how 'generation to generation, sport has played a very significant part of the community'. Additionally, it was believed that sport helped contribute to the development of the Kayamandi Township, with one participant explaining that sport 'is indeed a way forward that we can be able to build our communities'. The reasons that young people participate in sport within this community range from achieving sport success, developing their personal identity and feeling competent to developing close relationships, having fun and staying busy.

Lack of sport resources

Despite the shared belief in the power of sport for the young people of the Kayamandi Township, a number of barriers were identified that often prevented young people from getting involved in sport or even caused athletes to discontinue their sport participation (see Figure 1). The most significant barrier is the lack of sport resources, which emerged as the most frequently cited higher order theme in the

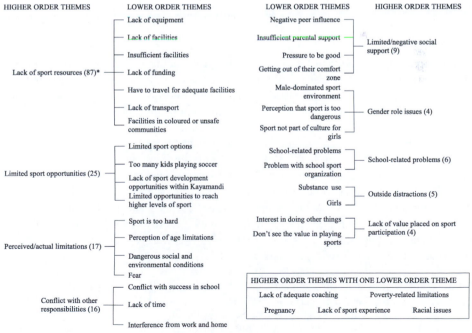

* The number stands for the number of raw meaning units in the higher order theme.

Figure 1.   Perceived barriers to sport participation.

study. While funding was the underlying issue for this lack of sport resources, the implications of this lack of funding included the lack of sport-specific equipment, as the athletes 'don't have the basics, like some cones to jump, jump, jump and do some specific exercises'. Other athletes are unable to 'play soccer because they don't have money to the buy boots [soccer cleats]'. There was also a concern about the lack of facilities in the community, since there are 'no sports facilities here in Kayamandi. There's no fields'. According to one athlete,

> here in Kayamandi, got two fields, but those two fields are not good enough for play, because … there is no time to take care of that field, to just give the field water so it can grow grass. There's no time, so the field becomes so messy.

This has a direct impact on the experiences of young athletes, with one athlete discussing how 'we don't really practice, because we don't have a field to practice'. As one coach explained, 'if we could get some funds, it would be much better because we can have our own fields'. This lack of facilities has led some young people to play in the streets, which can be a significant health issue, given the poor water and waste removal within the streets of the Kayamandi Township (Barnes 2002). For other teams, it is often necessary for them to travel outside the community for practices and games, although the teams generally do not have the funding to provide or pay for any type of transportation to the practice and/or game locations. This results in athletes having to 'pay for ourselves', which is a significant issue for many athletes, given the poverty within the Kayamandi Township. An athlete explained how 'it's a lot of money. Because sometimes we can't go to the games, because we don't have money and we have to pay the transport, so we don't go to the games'.

Responsibilities

An additional barrier preventing young people from being involved in sport was the various responsibilities young people held, beginning with their educational responsibilities. As one athlete described, 'you need to choose between soccer and school'. A number of young female participants cited household responsibilities as a significant limitation, as 'boys and girls are treated different. Girls like at the age of 8 years, they know they've got house responsibilities, so they act like moms'. These household responsibilities generally include cooking for the family, cleaning the household, picking up water from public taps and providing childcare for younger siblings and relatives. Since they can take up time, these responsibilities prevent some young people from playing 'soccer, because there is too much work at home'. Also, children are often expected to help at their parents' work places or to gain employment on their own, thus contributing to the family's income. One soccer player described the following scenario:

> My friend used to play soccer, but his mother decided to open a shebeen [bar] at his home, so he must sell the beers for customers … So he must serve the beers to the people, so he can't get enough practice. So he's not fit. So when he does go to the soccer field, even though we can give him a chance, he doesn't do enough … he doesn't get enough soccer. He loves soccer, but … work is a very, very, very crucial part.

Lack of coaches and social support

An additional barrier cited by the participants was the lack of coaches in general as well as a lack of coaches who were highly trained and competent in the sport they were coaching. One athlete acknowledged how 'we don't have a coach', while a community member described how difficult it was for those without training to coach: 'It's like us teaching them [the athletes] how to play, but we are not that professional enough to teach them'. Another frequently cited theme was the amount of social support that the athletes received, with some participants discussing the lack of parental support ($n = 4$).

> It's their background, maybe at home she or he is not being supported by the parents. Sometimes when your parents are not supporting you, you start saying, 'what's the point of doing it if my family is not supporting me?'

Another athlete explained how her family problems caused her to step away from her sport: 'I stop playing netball, because I have a lot of problem for my family. So I have to stop doing sports to focus on those problem'. This negative environment extended outside the family unit, with participants identifying the negative influence of peer pressure. In the words of an athlete, 'I think that if you are influenced enough by friends, they are going to stop you. You are not going to play'.

Coaching strategies for overcoming barriers

When the coaches were asked to reflect on the strategies used to help their athletes (or potential athletes) overcome these barriers to sport participation, only five coaches offered strategies. The most frequently cited theme was managing the resources that were available to the coaches by facilitating practices at multiple locations and bringing equipment for the athletes to use. One coach talked about asking the parents for donations, although this was not a huge success, given the financial realities within the Kayamandi Township. The final theme focused on training the current athletes, with the hope that this would generate outside interest and help current athletes stay committed to their sport.

Role of sport in overcoming challenges

Prevents bad situations and decisions

When participants were asked to reflect on how sport participation could help young people in the Kayamandi Township face the challenges and issues present in this community, the majority of the participants discussed how sport removes athletes from bad situations and prevents athletes from making bad decisions because it keeps them busy, makes them too tired to get into trouble and gets them out of the community during 'dangerous times'. According to one athlete, 'sport gives me a reason not to go to drink', while another athlete acknowledged that 'if I was staying at home doing nothing, maybe I would be the one who's monkeying around. So it helped me a lot. Sport helped me a lot to stay out of bad things'. These quotations demonstrate how sport is helping athletes 'stay busy', because sport 'distracts the children from doing all the wrong things'. The athletes discussed the importance of being 'busy' as to not get involved in bad situations or make bad choices. One of the coaches explained how some athletes 'are scared of the effect of drug using. So they think, 'if I go and play sport, from there I'll be tired. I will have to go to sleep'. Another athlete explained that

> if we're participating in sport, most of the time you spend there. You do not have time to go and smoke or do some sort of stuff. Especially most children are using alcohol on Fridays and Saturdays.

The participants agreed that sport 'gives you something to do, to focus on', which is critical for young people in the Kayamandi Township who are often bored and surrounded by negative peer pressure.

Team membership

Another central theme that was cited by a number of participants was the positive impact that team membership had on athletes, helping them overlook the negative peer pressure from influences outside of their teams and providing them with a sense of belonging that was often missing from their home lives. In the words of one athlete, 'you fit in with your teammates. If you fit with your teammates ... then at home, everything's fine'. Another athlete described the positive influence of teammates on their lives outside of sport:

> We keep visiting one another to talk about things and what's bad, what's good, and so forth. And that helps us a lot, because we're asking each other, on the field, off the field, at home, out of home. So while helping each other in school, out of school. So I think it's been helpful for us.

Coaching strategies for overcoming challenges

Although the previous section indicated the ways in which mere participation in sport helped young people face some of the challenges in the Kayamandi Township, the coaches in this study also discussed the strategies that they use to help their athletes face these challenges (see Figure 2). The most cited strategy was to provide individual support to the athletes, ranging from building close relationships with

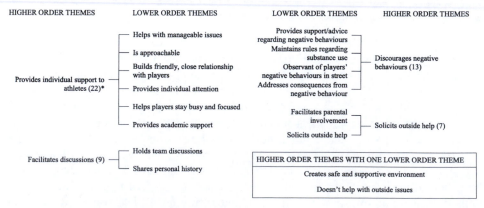

* The number stands for the number of raw meaning units in the higher order theme.

Figure 2.   Strategies for coaches dealing with players' challenges.

athletes to providing individual attention to each athlete on their teams. According to one coach, you need to 'become like a friend ... because if you are like a coach, then you're already creating a distance' between you and the athletes. Another coach described how important it was to truly care for and support his athletes:

> In sports, in order for the kids to achieve something, you have ... [to] love them first. If they see that there is love for them, they will love what they will be doing, and whatever you teach, they will listen attentively. They will listen. They will listen to you with curiosity, because they are listening from a person whom they love.

Along with simply caring for their athletes, the coaches ($n = 4$) discussed the importance of creating an environment in which athletes felt safe and supported by the coaches and their teammates. This environment often allowed the coaches to facilitate discussions amongst the athletes, during which the athletes shared experiences and issues with one another while supporting each other. In the eyes of one participant, team discussions can be incredibly helpful, as the coaches 'find kids which have different problems. But in there, if one of them speak about his or her problem, everyone will talk, will speak'. These team discussions also provided opportunities for the coaches to share their own life experiences, which helped the athletes realise that others have had similar experiences and overcome these challenges and have productive and happy lives. Therefore, the coaches would 'share anything with them [the athletes] and maybe show them the right path'.

Although there was a large focus on facilitating discussions, some coaches also identified needing to discourage any negative behaviours, such as alcohol use, drug use and stealing. As one coach described, 'I'm telling them that, "this is not the way to go. You can't drink and at the same time do sports. They don't mix. You should do one at a time. So, you choose which one you want best". Another coach discussed his team rule on substance use: 'one thing with our club, we don't drink, we don't smoke. That is a policy'. While this strategy is not always effective, it is more likely to have a larger impact on athletes if they first have strong relationships with their coaches that are built on trust and respect, which was a priority of many of the coaches.

Practical implications

There are a number of practical implications for the future based on the lived experiences and everyday realities shared in this qualitative study. While the investigators acknowledge that implementing all the presented implications may not be feasible due to the high levels of absolute poverty within the Kayamandi Township and similar communities, the investigators did not want to limit the implications that were shared and, rather, wanted to enable community members to choose which implications were the best fit for their community. Additionally, it is possible that some communities may choose to begin with one or two practical implications, with the intention of addressing additional implications in the future when funding is secured and/or certain milestones are reached. For example, the MYSA is a great example of a sport-for-development programme with an inside-up indigenous development approach that began with basic programming efforts that have since been refined and expanded with outside funding from partnerships and donors within Kenya and abroad (Hognestad and Tollisen 2004).

Moving onto the first practical implication, if there is an interest in supporting the sport programmes already in existence in communities similar to the Kayamandi Township, it is important that these programmes are provided with basic resources, such as equipment, facilities and travel accommodations. One athlete from the study agreed with this assessment, calling for the community to 'improve our facilities', while another athlete explained how 'if we've got some facilities, then … they [the young people] are going to participate, most of them, in all junior levels'. These recommendations match the findings of Dennerlein and Adami (2004), who highlighted the need for at least three recreational areas, two sport fields and five playgrounds to be built within the Kayamandi Township in order to meet the current needs of the community. By increasing these basic sport resources, current sport programmes are more likely to be sustainable in the foreseeable future; however, the findings also revealed that any attempt to upgrade facilities and equipment must be well designed and protected, as vandalism and theft are more likely because of the extreme poverty (e.g. stealing a basketball backboard for a house roof). Another opportunity to improve the current sport experiences within the Kayamandi Township centres on the provision of developmental opportunities within and outside of the Kayamandi Township, such as sport training opportunities for young athletes, coupled with a greater selection of sport options. The overwhelming focus on soccer and, for females, netball was identified as a barrier for many young athletes in the Kayamandi Township, since athletes uninterested in playing these sports did not have many other sport options. In order to increase the number of young people who are involved in sport, there must be a range of sport options easily available.

In South African communities such as the Kayamandi Township, there is a need for the development of coaching education programmes that will help current and future coaches become more knowledgeable about their role as a coach. This recommendation is a direct response to the finding that many coaches had extremely limited training, which led to suboptimal experiences for the athletes. These coaching education programmes should not only focus on basic coaching mechanics, motivational techniques and life skills education, they should also include a realistic explanation of how coaches can increase athletes' involvement in sport. For example, if coaches want to increase female athletic involvement, they may need to spend time convincing mothers of the importance of involvement while demonstrating how involvement would not interfere with household duties. One of the most surprising results of this study was that the coaches did not have many strategies to overcome the barriers to sport participation that exist in the Kayamandi Township.

The study findings have suggested that one of the most significant barriers and frustrations with sport participation is the lack of parental support with their children's sport participation; therefore, there is also a need to develop parent education programmes in order to create a more supportive and positive familial climate for the young people in the Kayamandi Township. According to one community member, it is 'a matter of educating parents as well about the importance of sport for their children'. Another community member explained:

> If you want to motivate a child to play a sport, their father must have the motivation himself to do something around him. That will make the child to say, 'I want to be like my dad.' The mother must do something, the child will say, 'I want to be like my mom.'

Some study participants also acknowledged that it was not just the parents who needed to be more involved in and supportive of sports in the Kayamandi Township, but that there is a need to 'involve the community, the parents, and the schools'.

As for designing and implementing new sport programmes within communities such as the Kayamandi Township, it is critical to first focus on the basic human needs, such as feeding the athletes and ensuring they are healthy, as it may be challenging for athletes to participate in sport if they are hungry, thirsty, sick and/or abused. Once these basic needs have been reached, coaches can focus on athletes' sport needs, such as ensuring that there are safe places to play, good fields and the necessary equipment. This also includes training coaches on sport-specific techniques, such as how to help young players improve their shot in netball. The final step in the implementation of a well-designed sport programme would be the integration of life skills education into the sport environment, with coaches being trained through the aforementioned coaching education programmes to intentionally use strategies and techniques specifically designed to foster and teach these skills (Gould and Carson 2008). This type of life skills training has been achieved with the MYSA in Kenya (Hognestad and Tollisen 2004), although the AIDS educational components and other life skills education are not integrated into the sport environment, which has been recommended by researchers and practitioners as the best way to foster skill acquisition (Hellison and Walsh 2002, Petitpas *et al.* 2005). It is also imperative that each sport programme be adapted to fit the culture and context of each specific community. In order to adapt, coaches and community members from that community must be involved in design and implementation, as these individuals have the institutional knowledge of the community. This idea matches Giulianotti's (2011) call for greater community involvement in the design and implementation of sport-for-development programmes. In fact, Hognestad and Tollisen (2004) suggest that the main reason for the success of the MYSA compared with more traditional aid programmes is the fact that community members are heavily involved in the design and implementation of the MYSA, despite its dependency on outside funding. This highlights the need for a shared sense of ownership of sport programmes (as achieved with MYSA), leading to a greater chance of sustainability and the potential for more impact within the community.

General discussion

As indicated by the findings of this study, there are many challenges that young people face when growing up in the Kayamandi Township, ranging from hunger and unemployment to health challenges, such as HIV/AIDS, to dealing with substance use and a myriad of family problems. However, in interviewing coaches, community members and athletes, sport emerged as a tool that has helped young people in the Kayamandi Township face these challenges. The study participants identified many benefits from mere participation in sport. For example, they stated that sport practices take the young athletes off the streets and keep them busy, thus preventing them from getting into trouble during after-school hours. Additionally, playing sports is tiring, decreasing the likelihood of young people getting into trouble after practice. Although these benefits are not necessarily linked to specific programming within the sport setting, they are still critical to the safety of the young people and may be seen as the building blocks to an effective programme.

As for the role of the coaches in facing these challenges, the coaches discussed the strategies they have found to be effective in helping their athletes face these challenges. Since the coaches were aware of the cultural practices and the unfortunate realities of living in the Kayamandi Township, many chose to incorporate certain strategies that would counteract these factors. For example, many of the athletes do not have a strong and supportive family structure and often feel a sense of loneliness and a need for belonging, so the coaches worked hard to create a safe and supportive environment in which the athletes would feel welcomed and loved. These strategies were tailored for the sport environment within the Kayamandi Township, once again highlighting the need for community involvement in the design, implementation and evaluation of sport-for-development programmes (Mintzberg 2006, Giulianotti 2011). Additionally, since it is uncommon for parents to have personal, in-depth discussions with their children about the challenges of growing up in the Kayamandi Township, such as practising safe sex and the perils of alcohol and drug use, the coaches structured their practices to ensure that these discussions could occur among teammates. In this way, the coaches were using their deep understanding of the community to address many of the gaps in support, guidance and education for their athletes. Therefore, although most of these coaches did not report any type of coaching education or training, their knowledge and understanding of cultural practices within the community proved to be immensely helpful to their athletes.

The lack of training for many of the coaches was highlighted by some participants ($n=6$), with the athletes and coaches discussing how this limited their experiences in sports. Coach training is not only important for teaching sport skills but in achieving social-emotional development and life skill sport objectives, as recent evidence studying underserved youth in the USA has shown that the use of specific coaching strategies was significantly related to greater youth developmental gains (Gould *et al.* 2011). If coaching education programmes could be tailored to this specific community, there is the possibility that these coaches could have an even greater impact on their athletes. It is possible that a well-designed, culturally relevant coaching education programme could provide coaches with the expertise to help athletes realise their full potential; however, following the recommendations of Giulianotti (2011) and Mintzberg (2006), it is critical for coaches to be involved in the design, implementation and evaluation of this type of coaching education programme.

Future research directions

While the current study addressed the phenomena of interest through qualitative means, it would be prudent to address the role of sport participation on youth development through quantitative means in hopes of capturing additional material not identified through interviews with community members, coaches and athletes. Adopting a qualitative approach afforded the investigators an opportunity to explore participants' perceptions, which is limiting in that the accuracy of the interviews relied on the honesty and self-awareness of participants and provided non-generalisable data; however, the goal of the current study was to explore participants' perspectives, suggesting that a qualitative approach was appropriate. Employing a quantitative or mixed method approach would yield more outcome-based data and allow future researchers to address the relationship between sport participation and particular markers and measures of success, such as academic achievement, self-efficacy and subjective well-being, which all contribute to optimal youth development.

Additionally, the process of conducting this study yielded implications for future researchers in relation to gathering accurate and meaningful data by highlighting the importance of developing long-term relationships based on mutual trust and respect with community stakeholders. More specifically, future researchers can benefit from soliciting community stakeholders' input in designing culturally sensitive and relevant areas of exploration in the hopes of producing high quality transnational research that captures the voice and experiences of the community under investigation. Future researchers can connect their research with service agendas by providing constructive and tangible feedback to community stakeholders based on the findings of their research studies. For example, providing a summative report that outlines the results of a study and, most importantly, the practical implications of that study, may provide the community the guidance it needs to modify existing or implement new programmes to contribute to youth development in particular areas.

Future researchers might also consider collaborating with coaches on ways to expand their arsenal of coaching strategies to meet athlete needs and, subsequently, assess if they are more effective than coaches who are untrained. Additionally, in order to increase female involvement in sport, future researchers can design and implement an intervention to increase maternal support for their daughters' sport participation in order to assess the relationship, if any, between maternal support and girls' sport participation. Finally, researchers are in a position to assist community members in learning how to use evaluation data to approach the government and other funders to provide some of the physical assets needed to improve the community.

Acknowledgement

Funding for this study was provided by the Institute for the Study of Youth Sports at Michigan State University.

Notes

1. The three separate interview guides are available upon request from the first author.
2. Complete tables of the results of all analyses are available upon request from the first author.

Notes on contributors

Meredith A. Whitley is an Assistant Professor in the Department of Exercise Science, Health Studies, Physical Education, & Sport Management at Adelphi University. Her research interests centre on sport as a powerful tool for positive change in the lives of underserved children and youth throughout the world.

Laura A. Hayden is the Graduate Programme Director and Online Programme Coordinator of the School Counselling programme at the University of Massachusetts Boston. Her research focuses on the psychosocial development of urban youth through physical activity, the role of the school counsellor in facilitating school-based social support programs and the relationship between social justice and effective student support in urban schools.

Daniel Gould is the Director of the Institute for the Study of Youth Sports and Professor in the Department of Kinesiology at Michigan State University. Specialising in sport psychology, his current research focuses on how coaches teach life skills to young athletes, youth leadership development through sport and the role parents play in youth sports experience.

References

Allender, S., Cowburn, G., and Foster, C., 2006. Understanding participation in sport and physical activity among children and adults: a review of qualitative studies. *Health education research*, 21 (6), 826–835.

Armstrong, G., 2004. The lords of misrule: football and the rights of the child in Liberia, West Africa. *Sport in society*, 7 (3), 473–502.

Armstrong, G. and Giulianotti, R., 2004. *Football in Africa: conflict conciliation and community*. Basingstoke: Palgrave Macmillan.

Barnes, J.M., 2002. *Report on water quality analysis of the Plankenburg River*. Tygerberg: University of Stellenbosch.

Bartlett, J., Iwasaki, Y., Gottlieb, B., Hall, D., and Mannell, R., 2007. Framework for aboriginal-guided decolonizing research involving Me'tis and First Nations persons with diabetes. *Social science & medicine*, 65 (11), 2371–2382.

Benson, P.L., Leffert, N., Scales, P.C., and Blyth, D.A., 1998. Beyond the 'village' rhetoric: creating healthy communities for children and adolescents. *Applied developmental science*, 2 (3), 138–159.

Black, D., 2010. The ambiguities of development: implications for development through sport. *Sport in society*, 13 (1), 121–129.

Blodgett, A.T., Schinke, R.J., Peltier, D., Wabano, M.J., Fisher, L.A., Eys, M.A., *et al.*, 2010. 'Naadmaadmi': reflections of aboriginal community members engaged in sport psychology co-researching activities with mainstream academics. *Qualitative research in sport and exercise*, 2 (1), 56–76.

Burnett, C., 2001. Social impact assessment and sport development: social spin-offs of the Australia-South Africa Junior Sport Programme. *International review for the sociology of sport*, 36 (1), 41–56.

Burnett, C., 2006. Building social capital through an 'active community club'. *International review for the sociology of sport*, 41 (3), 283–294.

Burnett, C., 2010. Sport-for-development approaches in the South African context: a case study analysis. *South African journal for research in sport, physical education and recreation*, 32 (1), 29–42.

Burnett, C., 2011. Engaging sport-for-development for social impact in the South African context. *The social impact of sport: cross-cultural perspectives*, 12 (9), 84–97.

Burnett, C., Hollander, W.J., Uys, J.M., De Bruin, G.P., and Lombard, A.J.J., 1999. *The Australia-South Africa Sport Development Programme: an impact study of the junior sport component*. Johannesburg: Department of Sport and Movement Studies, Rand Afrikaans University.

Coakley, J., 2003. *Sports in society: issues and controversies*. 8th ed. New York: McGraw-Hill.

Coalter, F., 2007. *A wider social role for sport: who's keeping the score?* London: Routledge.

Coalter, F., 2010. The politics of sport-for-development: limited focus programmes and broad gauge problems? *International review for the sociology of sport*, 45 (3), 295–314.

Côté, J., Salmela, J.H., Baria, A., and Russell, S.J., 1993. Organizing and interpreting unstructured qualitative data. *The sport psychologist*, 7 (2), 127–137.

Darnell, S.C., 2007. Playing with race: right to play and the production of whiteness in 'development through sport'. *Sport in society*, 10 (4), 560–579.

Darnell, S.C. and Hayhurst, L.M.C., 2011. Sport for decolonization: exploring a new praxis of sport for development. *Progress in development studies*, 11 (3), 183–196.

Dennerlein, J. and Adami, K., 2004. *Sustainable district development in Kayamandi*. Frankfurt: University of Applied Sciences Frankfurt Main.

Denzin, N. and Lincoln, Y., eds., 2005. *Handbook of qualitative research*. 3rd ed. Beverly Hills, CA: Sage.

Elwood, S.A. and Martin, D.G., 2000. 'Placing' interviews: location and scales of power in qualitative research. *Professional geographer*, 52 (4), 649–657.

Garbarino, J., 1995. *Affirmation and acceptance: creating identity for children*. San Francisco, CA: Jossey-Bass.

Gasser, P.K. and Levinsen, A., 2004. Breaking post-war ice: open fun football schools in Bosnia and Herzegovina. *Sport in society*, 7 (3), 457–472.

Genat, B., 2009. Building emergent situated knowledges in participatory action research. *Action research*, 7 (1), 101–115.

Giulianotti, R., 2011. Sport, peacemaking and conflict resolution: a contextual analysis and modelling of the sport, development and peace sector. *Ethnic and racial studies*, 34 (2), 207–228.

Goodkind, J.R. and Decon, Z., 2004. Methodological issues in conducting research with refugee women: principles for recognizing and re-centering the multiply marginalized. *Journal of community psychology*, 32 (6), 721–739.

Gould, D. and Carson, S., 2008. Life skills development through sport: current status and future directions. *Sport & exercise psychology reviews*, 1 (1), 58–78.

Gould, D., Flett, M.R., and Lauer, L., 2011. The relationship between psychosocial development and the sports climate experienced by underserved youth. *Psychology of sport & exercise*, 13 (1), 80–87.

Greenleaf, C., Gould, D., and Dieffenbach, K., 2001. Factors influencing Olympic performance: interviews with Atlanta and Nagano US Olympians. *Journal of applied sport psychology*, 13 (2), 154–184.

Guba, E. and Lincoln, Y., 2005. Paradigmatic controversies, contradictions and emerging confluences. *In*: N. Denzin and Y. Lincoln, eds. *Handbook of qualitative research*. 3rd ed. London: Sage, 191–216.

Hartmann, D. and Kwauk, C., 2011. Sport and development: an overview, critique, and reconstruction. *Journal of sport & social issues*, 35 (3), 284–305.

Hayhurst, L.M.C. and Frisby, W., 2010. Inevitable tensions: Swiss and Canadian sport for development NGO perspectives on partnerships with high performance sport. *European sport management quarterly*, 10 (1), 75–96.

Hellison, D., 2003. Teaching personal and social responsibility in physical education. *In*: S.J. Silverman and C.D. Ennis, eds. *Students learning in physical education: applying research to enhance instruction*. Champaign, IL: Human Kinetics, 241–254.

Hellison, D. and Walsh, D., 2002. Responsibility-based youth programs evaluation: investigating the investigators. *Quest*, 54 (4), 292–307.

Hognestad, H. and Tollisen, A., 2004. Playing against deprivation: football and development in Nairobi, Kenya. *In*: G. Armstrong and R. Giulianotti, eds. *Football in Africa*. Basingstoke: Palgrave Macmillan, 210–226.

Jones, R.L., 2009. Coaching as caring (The smiling gallery): accessing hidden knowledge. *Physical education and sport pedagogy*, 14 (4), 377–390.

Jones, R.L., Armour, K.M., and Potrac, P., 2004. *Sports coaching cultures: from practice to theory*. London: Routledge.

Kidd, B., 2008. A new social movement: sport for development and peace. *Sport in society*, 11 (4), 370–380.

King, S., 2009. Sociocultural sport studies and the scientific paradigm: a response to John Smith. *Qualitative research in sport and exercise*, 1 (2), 101–106.

Kral, M.J., Burkhardt, K.J., and Kidd, S., 2002. The new research agenda for a cultural psychology. *Canadian psychology*, 43 (3), 154–162.

Krueger, R.A. and Casey, M.A., 2000. *Focus groups: a practical guide for applied research*. 4th ed. Thousand Oaks, CA: Sage.

Kvale, S., 1996. *Interviews: an introduction to qualitative research interviewing*. Thousand Oaks, CA: Sage.

Larson, R.W., 2000. Toward a psychology of positive youth development. *American psychologist*, 55 (1), 170–183.

Lerner, R.M., Almerigi, J.B., Theokas, C., and Lerner, J., 2005. Positive youth development: a view of the issues. *The journal of early adolescence*, 25 (1), 10–16.

Levermore, R., 2011. Evaluating sport-for-development: approaches and critical issues. *Progress in development studies*, 11 (4), 339–353.

Levine, R., Lloyd, C., Greene, M., and Grown, C., 2008. *Girls count: a global investment & action agenda*. Washington, DC: Center for Global Development.

Lincoln, Y.S. and Guba, E., 1985. *Naturalistic inquiry*. Beverly Hills, CA: Sage.

Lindner, M., 2006. *Evaluation study on the effects of the child mind project: a school-based life skills programme on HIV/AIDS and sex education at a primary school in a South African semi-urban environment (Kayamandi, Stellenbosch)*. Thesis (PhD). Freien Universität.

Lindsey, I. and Banda, D., 2011. Sport and the fight against HIV/AIDS in Zambia: a 'partnership approach'? *International review for the sociology of sport*, 46 (1), 90–107.

McEwan, C., 2009. *Postcolonialism and development*. London: Routledge.

Mintzberg, H., 2006. Developing leaders? Developing countries? *Development in practice*, 16 (1), 4–14.

Okada, C. and Young, K., 2011. Sport and social development: promise and caution from an incipient Cambodian football league. *International review for the sociology of sport*, 47 (1), 5–26.

Parameswaran, R., 2008. Reading the visual, tracking the global: postcolonial feminist methodology and the chameleon codes of resistance. *In*: N. Denzin, Y. Lincoln, and L.T. Smith, eds. *Handbook of critical and indigenous methodologies*. Thousand Oaks, CA: Sage, 407–428.

Patton, M.Q., 2001. *Qualitative research and evaluation methods*. 2nd ed. Thousand Oaks, CA: Sage.

Petitpas, A.J., Cornelius, A.E., Van Raalte, J.L., and Jones, T., 2005. A framework for planning youth sport programs that foster psychosocial development. *The sport psychologist*, 19 (1), 63–80.

Pisani, E., 2008. *The wisdom of whores: bureaucrats, brothels and the business of AIDS*. London: Granta Books.

Smith, L.T., 1999. *Decolonizing methodologies: research and indigenous peoples*. London: Zed Books.

Smith, J.K. and Osborn, M., 2003. Interpretative phenomenological analysis. *In*: J.A. Smith, ed. *Qualitative psychology: a practical guide to research methods*. London: Sage, 51–80.

Smith, R.E., Smoll, F.L., and Curtis, B., 1979. Coach effectiveness training: a cognitive-behavioral approach to enhancing relationship skills in youth sport coaches. *Journal of sport psychology*, 1 (1), 59–75.

Spaaij, R., 2009a. The social impact of sport: diversities, complexities and contexts. *Sport in society*, 12 (9), 1109–1117.

Spaaij, R., 2009b. Sport as a vehicle for social mobility and regulation of disadvantaged urban youth. *International review for the sociology of sport*, 44 (2–3), 247–264.

Sparkes, A., 2002. *Telling tales in sport and physical activity: a qualitative journey*. Champaign, IL: Human Kinetics.

Sparkes, A.C. and Smith, B., 2009. Judging the quality of qualitative inquiry: criteriology and relativism in action. *Psychology of sport and exercise*, 10 (5), 491–497.

Sport and Recreation South Africa, 2008. *White paper. Getting the nation to play*. Pretoria: Sport and Recreation South Africa.

Sport for Development and Peace International Working Group, 2008. *Harnessing the power of sport for development and peace: recommendations to government*. Available from: http://www.un.org/wcm/webdav/site/sport/shared/sport/pdfs/SDP%20IWG/Final%20SDP%20IWG%20Report.pdf [Accessed September 30 2011].

Strauss, A. and Corbin, J., 1994. Grounded theory methodology: an overview. *In*: N. Denzin and Y. Lincoln, eds. *Handbook of qualitative research*. London: Sage, 273–285.

Sugden, J., 2006. Teaching and playing sport for conflict resolution and co-existence in Israel. *International review for the sociology of sport*, 41 (2), 221–240.

Tashakkori, A. and Teddlie, C.B., 2010. *Sage handbook of mixed methods in social and behavioral research*. 2nd ed. Thousand Oaks, CA: Sage.

Turcotte, K., 2003. *The nutritional status of children aged 1–7 years in Kayamandi (Western Cape, South Africa) as determined by 24-hour recall and anthropometric measurements*. Montreal: McGill University.

United Nations, 2003. *Sport for development and peace: Towards achieving the millennium development goals*. Report from the United Nations inter-agency task force on sport for development and peace. New York, United Nations.

United Nations, 2005. *International year of sport and physical education*. New York: United Nations.

United Nations, 2006. *Report on the international year of sport and physical education: 2005*. New York: United Nations.

University of Stellenbosch, 2001. *Socio-economic survey that was conducted in the Kaya-mandi residential area of the Stellenbosch municipal area during April to May 2001.* Stellenbosch: University of Stellenbosch, Department of Sociology.

Van Eekeren, F., 2006. Sport and development: challenges in a new arena. *In*: Y. Auweele, C. Malcolm, and B. Meulders, eds. *Sport and development*. Lannoo Campus: Leuven, Belgium, 19–34.

Weed, M., 2009. Research quality consideration for grounded theory research in sport & exercise psychology. *Psychology of sport and exercise*, 10 (5), 502–510.

Willis, O., 2000. Sport and development: the significance of Mathare Youth Sports Association. *Canadian journal of development studies*, 21 (3), 825–849.

Media framing and the representation of marginalised groups: case studies from two major sporting events

Stacy-Lynn Sant, K. Meaghan Carey and Daniel S. Mason

Faculty of Physical Education & Recreation, University of Alberta, Edmonton, AB, Canada

Sports teams and events have emerged as central features in the pro-growth development initiatives undertaken by cities and regions throughout the world. Until very recently this competition for event hosting has been limited to northern and western cities, although there have been several notable exceptions, such as the Mexico City 1968 Summer Olympic Games and Sarajevo 1984 Winter Olympic Games. In the past few years, cities in South Africa and Asia have hosted major sporting events and other major cities in the southern hemisphere will be hosting various world games, including the Olympic Games and FIFA World Cup Final Tournament. Hosts of major sporting events often highlight an array of potential benefits for the city and/or nation. These benefits are often thought of in economic terms, including impacts such as increased employment and tourism (Hall 1992, Getz 1997); however, other benefits include an enhanced city image, new sport facilities, and improved transportation infrastructure. Infrastructure development and regeneration schemes are now strongly linked with major sporting events, as bid proponents and event organisers use these benefits to rationalise the public expenditure and to gain popular support; however, it has been argued that projected gains are often unrealised (Ritchie 1984, Crompton 1995, Mules and Faulkner 1996, MacAloon 2008). Roche (2000) identified that major sporting events combine the interests of political and business elites and the interests of multinational corporations to produce and manage the events.

While major sporting events, such as the Olympic Games and the Common-wealth Games, have been used by their organisers as platforms to promote specific interests, there is also the opportunity for inequalities and injustices faced by marginalised groups to be exposed. In media terms, the reach and span of hosting a major sporting event is unrivalled by any other major event (i.e. G8 Summit, International Exposition). To this point, limited research has been conducted on organised resistance to the hosting of major sporting events (see Dansero *et al.* 2012, Lenskyj 2002, 2008, Luijk and Frisby 2012); this may be due in part to what Lenskyj (2004) identified as the event organisers' ability to suppress opposition and to create the illusion of cohesive resident support. However, in the organisation of major games, there may be evidence of the loss of civil liberties, such as right to protest or assemble in public spaces, a loss of employment or ability to earn a live-lihood and a loss of living space as many homeless and low-income residents may be displaced due to infrastructure development. For example, during the 2010 Commonwealth Games, most street vendors (both food and merchandise) in Delhi were unable to continue their operations due to changes in the food vendor policies and site security concerns (Pandey 2010).

The following discussion emanates from our work examining how cities compete for sports franchises and events and the associated discourses surrounding economic and community development. Primarily, the method to be discussed– frame analysis – evolves from several studies examining news media discourse in cities, exploring the types of arguments and justifications made for why cities invest in sports franchises and hosting of major sporting events (see Schwirian *et al.* 2001, Chalip *et al.* 2003, Scherer and Jackson 2004, Delaney and Eckstein 2008, Sapotichne 2012). Further to these examples, the study of the ways in which the media and sport interact crosses disciplinary boundaries and can be found in literature concerned with the sociology of sport, history of sport, gender studies, cultural studies, urban studies, communication and leisure studies. Much of the writing on sport and the media broadly addresses issues of athlete representation and identity (see Wachs and Dworkin 1997, Wright and Clarke 1999, Harris and Clayton 2002, Birrell and McDonald 2012) and globalisation, as well as aspects of the political economy of the media (see Delgado 2003, Knight *et al.* 2005, Zaharopoulos, 2007, Cho 2009). Our goal here is to add to this body of literature by employing framing analysis (to be outlined below).

While our focus (see Buist and Mason 2010, Mason 2010, Carey *et al.* 2011) has traditionally been on the views of political and business elites and how they have framed the issue of funding in order to influence public opinion as to the merits of supporting these types of investments, within this work, we have also witnessed the issues faced by marginalised other groups (those lacking political and economic power) coming to the forefront of event coverage in the mainstream media. Thus, the examination of frames in the mainstream media allows us to uncover how issues surrounding these groups are framed. Through the use of frames, marginalised groups may present – or have presented for them – a frame package, which promotes a particular definition of the problem or issue, attribution of responsibility and recommendation for corrective action. By analysing frames in the media, we are also able to identify key players/actors in marginalised groups and their interests. Key players are mainly concerned with furthering their interests by directing the perception and frame selection of journalists (Pan and Kosicki 1993). Frames are therefore conveyed to the media by way of interviews, which in turn provides a context to help the audience interpret the issue or problem. This article seeks to provide a template to study frames and understand how the media can, and are, being used in order to further a community development agenda vis-à-vis major sporting infrastructure development projects.

We hope to provide some basic tools for examining discourses surrounding community development and sport events from the perspective of those groups that historically have not benefited locally from these events, such as those displaced from housing razed to build event infrastructure, or those who may see precious public resources redirected to service the hosting of a major sporting event. In doing so, it is our aspiration that more qualitative research will be undertaken to examine how groups traditionally marginalised in the event bidding and hosting process have begun to employ media framing as a strategy to protect and further their interests, or have had their interests highlighted in media coverage of an event.

Following an overview of framing theory, we provide two case studies – the 2010 Commonwealth Games held in Delhi, India, and the 2010 Olympic Winter Games held in Vancouver, Canada – that examine how marginalised groups were represented in the news media in a manner that may have furthered their own objectives. In the study of the Commonwealth Games, the marginalised group is unskilled labourers who were working on Games' infrastructure development sites and in relation in the Olympic Games, the marginalised group is Aboriginal people living in British Columbia, Canada. We conclude with a brief discussion of future research possibilities using framing in this context.

Literature review

Media framing

Framing has its foundations in sociology and psychology; scholarship on framing also draws from communication, psychology, economics, political science, sociology, cognitive linguistics and media studies perspectives (Borah 2011). Framing can be used as a paradigm for both understanding and investigating communication and related behaviour in a wide range of disciplines (Rendahl 1995). Regardless of its specific application, framing provides a means to describe the production and 'power of a communicating text' (Entman 1993, p. 51), and research is conducted within a wide range of paradigmatic perspectives. As a result, various definitions of and types of frames, as well as varying methodological approaches, have emerged. The 'theoretical and methodological pluralism' in framing research 'has led to a fragmented understanding of what framing is and how it works' (D'Angelo and Kuypers 2010, p. 3).

Despite the increasing use of 'framing' as a theoretical framework, the term has also not yet been precisely and consistently defined (Giles and Shaw 2009), however, several definitions have been proposed to explain and refine the term. Goffman (1974) is credited with laying the 'sociological foundations of framing' (Scheufele and Tewksbury 2007, p. 11). Goffman stated that frames help people to organise what they see in everyday life, so that they can make sense of the world around them. He referred to a frame as a 'schemata of interpretation', that is, a framework which renders 'what would otherwise be a meaningless aspect of the scene into something that is meaningful' (p. 21). In a synthesis of the research area, Reese (2007) defined frames in a similar manner by stating that they were 'organising principles that are socially shared and persistent over time, that work symbolically to meaningfully structure the social world' (p. 11).

The research on framing that stems from the sociological tradition refers to 'frames in communication' or 'media frames' (Chong and Druckman 2007). Generally, this research focuses on the 'words, images, phrases, and presentation styles' (Druckman 2001, p. 227) that are used to create news stories and the processes that underlie frames construction. In contrast, framing research that grew out of the psychological tradition has focused on the processes involved in the formation of 'individual frames' or 'audience frames' (Borah 2011) and how news frames are used by receivers to process information and make decisions. Scheufele (1999) emphasised that the distinction between media and individual frames is necessary, as frames are not only used to present information but they are also used by the audience to understand what is presented. He stated that framing is therefore both a *microlevel* and *macrolevel* construct.

An individual frame (or audience frame) can be defined as a schema of interpretations that allows individuals or societies to perceive, organise and make sense of information (Pan and Kosicki 1993). Similarly, Entman (1993) defined individual frames as 'mentally stored clusters of ideas that guide individuals' processing of information' (p. 53). For the purposes of our analysis, we focus on the media frames in newspaper coverage of major sporting events. Framing as a macrolevel construct refers to the way in which journalists and other communicators present an issue so that it may resonate with the audience's underlying schemas. Building on Goffman's work in 1974, Tuchman (1978) was the first researcher to 'recognise the integral role that framing plays in news gathering by media workers and news processing by audiences' (Hallahan 1999, p. 222). Tuchman proposed the following definition for a media frame: 'the news frame organises everyday reality and the news frame is part and parcel of everyday reality' (p. 193). Similarly, Gitlin (1980) defined frames as 'persistent patterns of cognition, interpretation, and presentation, of selection, emphasis, and exclusion' (p. 7). Likewise, Gamson and Modigliani (1987) defined media frames as 'a central organising idea that provides meaning to an unfolding strip of events' (p. 143). To summarise these definitions, the authors (Tuchman, Gitlin and Gamson and Modigliani) saw news frames as a crucial component of the news process as it allows journalists to organise information and present it to audiences.

Entman (1991, 1993) went a step further to explain how the media provide audiences with frames that help them interpret events. In his study of the media coverage of the Korean and Iranian plane disasters in the 1980s, Entman (1991) focused on the 'attributes of the news itself', that is, media frames. He suggested that frames are 'constructed from and embodied in the keywords, metaphors, concepts, symbols, and visual images emphasised in a news narrative' (p. 7). He proposed that newsmakers often repeat certain keywords and visual images that highlight some ideas rather than others, thereby making these ideas more salient in the text. These constructed frames in turn help the 'receiver' to interpret the events, thereby influencing public opinion. Entman (1993) emphasised that framing involved two key elements: selection and salience, which shape his definition:

> To frame is to select some aspects of a perceived reality and make them more salient in a communicating text, in such as way as to promote a particular problem definition, causal interpretation, moral valuation, and/or treatment recommendation for the item described. (1993, p. 52)

Two types of media frames are highlighted in the literature: *issue-specific* and *generic* news frames (de Vreese 2005). Issue-specific frames relate only to particular events or topics; and according to de Vreese, this approach to the study of news frames allows for 'profound specificity' in the investigation of a particular issue (p. 55). An example of a study of issue-specific news frames includes the work of Reese and Buckalew (1995), who analysed local television coverage of the Persian Gulf War.

Generic frames are those that can be identified across varying issues. Research on generic frames focuses on news coverage of election campaigns and linkages of news frames 'to journalistic conventions, norms and news values' (de Vreese 2005, p. 56). Semetko and Valkenburg (2000) examined generic frames that were applicable across different issues. These authors identified five generic news frames: 'conflict', 'attribution of responsibility', 'human interest', 'morality' and 'economic consequences'. Semetko and Valkenburg found that generic frames were related to journalistic conventions. In the context of hosting major sporting events, both issue-specific and generic frames may be present. There may be elements or issues specific to a given case, such as environmental issues associated with the construction of a certain venue or facility, while there may also be issues common to all events, such as the opportunity costs where funds are diverted from other public services to fund the hosting of the event.

According to Chong and Druckman (2007), research on framing in the political science and communication disciplines focuses on how *elites* produce *framing effects*. In their work, the authors identified elites as politicians, media outlets and interest groups. Although there has been a wide array of research on individual frames and their associated framing effects, little work has been done on the actual *creation* of frames in communication. Gamson (1989) stated that 'analysing news as framing incorporates the intent of the sender of the message' (p. 158) and that there are usually multiple senders. He referred to these senders as *frame sponsors* and termed their efforts to frame information as *frame enterprise* (Gamson and Lasch, 1983, Gamson, 1984). In studying the framing of a major sport event, frame sponsors are often the organising committee and business and political leaders from the host city, region or country. Carey, Mason and Misener's (2011) study of the 2016 Olympic Games bidding process found that the key factors associated with the Rio de Janeiro bid (bid committee, government officials) framed the bid in terms of the potential the games had to positively transform the city for its residents and the entire nation. In contrast to the other three bid cities, coverage of the Rio de Janeiro bid focused heavily on the community development aspect of the bid, including the proposed infrastructure, and the perceived social benefits of hosting a major sporting event. Pan and Kosicki (1993) asserted that frame sponsors are concerned with directing the perception and frame selection of journalists. In the Rio de Janeiro Olympic bid, by presenting a positive development discourse, frame sponsors directed media attention away from other topics that may have jeopardised the bid, such as high levels of crime and poverty in the area surrounding the proposed Games sites.

Van Gorp (2007) found that frame sponsors strategically attempt to influence the media to report on an issue in a manner that is consistent with *their* frame, and that is achieved by frame sponsors making prior decisions about how their viewpoints will be presented. Tewksbury *et al.* (2000) refer to these types of frames as *advocate frames*. To illustrate the use of advocate frames, Van Gorp employed the example of press releases assuming that in press releases, the use of a particular frame is quite deliberate as press releases are meant to inform as well as convince the reader. Similarly, Hallahan's (1999) study of framing and public relations suggested that public relations practitioners ensure that the story is framed in a way that is consistent with the source's *preferred framing*. In this case, the public relations practioner's client is considered to be the frame sponsor or source. When considering the case of hosting major sporting events, and building sports infrastructure in cities, proponents typically possess superior financial resources and influence to manage information being supplied to news sources and garner popular support for the event (Paul and Brown 2001).

The most advanced work on the strategic creation of frames comes from scholars in the area of social movements. Their research has focused on how 'framing is used as a tactic by political entrepreneurs to coordinate individuals around particular interpretation of their problems' (Chong and Druckman 2007, p. 118). The way social movement groups utilise frames to mobilise support for their causes can be related to the use of frames by sponsors to influence reporters' perceptions and interpretations of an issue, thereby strategically shaping the news content. Mass media can therefore serve as either conveyers of elite-sponsored frames or as originators of frames in their own right (Gamson and Modigliani 1989). Van Gorp (2007) echoed this view by making an important distinction between framing *by* the media and framing *through* the media. Thus, while proponents of sporting events and related infrastructure have traditionally been able to influence media coverage (Buist and Mason 2010), there are opportunities for other stakeholders, such as community and neighbourhood groups, to influence public opinion and get their messages out to the public through the strategic use of frames.

Scholars from a wide range of academic fields employ framing theory in their research and as such, framing studies are usually conducted using varying paradigmatic assumptions. Simon (2001) identified two main paradigms operating in framing research: 'positivistic' and 'constructivist'. Positivist researchers tend to study individual frames and define them as mental structures that guide individual's information processing (Entman 1993). Researchers in the positivist paradigm 'work mainly in laboratory settings using experimental techniques' to test the results of framing on individuals (Simon p. 78). Studies on framing effects are commonly done by researchers in the areas of psychology and economics. Although D'Angelo (2002) shares Simon's views on the paradigmatic assumptions underlying the study of framing effects, he refers to these assumptions as 'cognitivist' rather than 'positivist'.

According to Simon (2001), research on framing conducted in the constructivist paradigm mainly examines frames present in news programming; and define these frames as organising principles, which create meaning. This constructivist approach to framing is found among scholars in media studies, communications and sociology, and provides the foundation for our own work on framing. In addition to the cognitivist/positivist and constructivist standpoints, D'Angelo (2002) highlighted two other perspectives guiding framing research: 'critical' and 'constructionist'. Researchers working in the critical paradigm examine the 'ideological functions of newswork' (p. 878). These scholars claim that journalists report on issues and events from the perspective of the values of political and economic elites in order to maintain the status quo. Constructionist researchers view frames as a toolkit, which citizens may use to form their opinions about issues and events (Gamson and Modigliani 1989).

In the context of urban competition, sporting events are sought in order to realise a number of different goals, which include both economic and social development goals. Hall (2006) recognised sporting events as a key emerging entrepreneurial endeavour for cities seeking to meet the goal of attracting and retaining mobile capital (c.f. Harvey 1989, Kearns and Philo 1993, Misener and Mason 2009). Business and political elites often consider sporting events as a unique opportunity to secure resources for development and promote their city, which may not have been available to them without the event (Andranovich *et al.* 2001). At the municipal level, there is evidence of cities using the hosting of sporting events as a policy tool to attract new forms of capital to act as a stimulant to local economies (Mason *et al.* 2007), promote tourism (Chalip *et al.* 2003) and reinvent the image of the city (Smith, 2005). For example, Florek, Brietbarth and Conejo (2008) found that by hosting the FIFA World Cup Final Tournament in 2006, Germany was able to improve its image among visiting football fans. This was considered a positive side effect of hosting the event for the German tourism industry, as it was hoped that the improved image would increase tourism-related activities well after the World Cup was staged. Torino and Vancouver – hosts of the 2006 and 2010 Winter Olympic Games, respectively – viewed the Games as an opportunity to increase their visibility in the international media and to improve their image, with the overall goal being to present their regions as tourist destinations (c.f. De Moragas and Botella 1995, Burton 2003, Dansero and Puttilli 2010).

Logan and Molotch (1987) identified that the local media tend to privilege a pro-growth agenda as they benefit from the increased revenues associated with that growth. For this reason, our work falls under the critical approach. In addition, this also underscores why understanding how groups not among the business and political elites must attempt to find a way to represent their concerns and represent their constituents through the media.

Analysis of frames

Frame analysis, also called framing analysis, is a multidisciplinary research method employed by social scientists to investigate how people understand certain events and issues. The majority of studies on framing are based on the positivistic assumption that there is a truth that can be 'found', and that it is directly 'observable'. These studies mainly use (quantitative) content analysis or other forms of quantitative methods. However, some researchers (including ourselves) opt for qualitative analyses of frames, featuring methods such as qualitative content analysis, discourse analysis or modified content analysis (Suddaby and Greenwood 2005).

From a constructionist point of view, Van Gorp (2010) provides one of the most detailed practical guides in the extant literature for conducting a content analysis of framing. He suggests that a frame analysis should combine both an 'inductive framing analysis' and a 'deductively executed content analysis' (p. 85). Four main procedures of analysis make up the inductive phase of Van Gorp's frame analysis: collection of source material; open coding of texts; arranging the codes around 'axes' of meaning; and selective coding. The main product of the first phase is the construction of a *frame matrix*. Each row in the matrix highlights a 'frame package' that appears in the texts and each column represents 'an enumeration of framing and reasoning devices by which the frame manifests itself' (p. 93). Van Gorp also provides useful criteria for evaluating the suitability of a frame.

There has been a rise in the use of qualitative methodology, specifically, rhetorical work in framing (Kuypers 2010). Rhetorical framing analysis is situated in the critical paradigm of framing research and attempts to explore 'how language choices invite us to understand an issue or event' (Kuypers 2010, p. 298). Kuypers (2010) defined rhetoric as: 'the strategic use of communication, oral or written, to achieve specific goals' (p. 288) and stated that those using rhetoric usually think about their goals in advance so that they are able to better plan what to say to achieve the desired effect. He used his study of the War on Terror to illustrate how a rhetorical framing analysis is conducted. This study explored how the news media relayed President Bush's messages about the War on Terror. The author began by inductively identifying *themes* in the president's speeches. He then conducted a textual analysis by looking at the texts for keywords, phrases and labels that indicated how these themes were framed; the process was then repeated for each news article. Kuypers (2010) did not go into detail about the process and procedures for conducting a rhetorical framing analysis, however, he expressed that this type of analysis can allow researchers to move from 'a more descriptive notion of framing research to a fully critical and interpretive endeavour' (p. 308).

Cases

We employ a qualitative analysis of frames to examine two specific cases: 1) the discourse on Aboriginal participation during the bid process for the Vancouver 2010 Winter Olympic Games and 2) the marginalised group of labourers (inclusive of displaced street vendors) involved in the construction of event infrastructure for the 2010 Commonwealth Games in Delhi, India. Data were collected from several newspapers as previous studies have suggested that newspapers are one of the best vehicles for influencing public opinion and interpretation of issues and events (Lowe and Goyder 1983). A description of each marginalised group, along with details of the data collection, analysis and results and discussion will be presented in the following sections.

Case 1: Vancouver 2010 Winter Olympic games

In response to the 1992 United Nations Conference on Environment and Development (UNCED) Action Plan for Sustainable Development, the International Olympic Committee (IOC) adopted its own version of Agenda 21: Sport for Sustainable Development in 1999. One of the objectives of the Olympic Movement's Action Plan was to promote and acknowledge the role of indigenous people through hosting the Olympic Games as they 'often suffer social exclusion' (IOC 1999, p. 42).

Description of the community

In Canada, indigenous people are called Aboriginals and include First Nations, Inuit, and Metis people (Government of Canada 1982). Aboriginals have lived in the territory now called the province of British Columbia long before the arrival of the British. In the late 1700s, the British Crown established treaties with First Nations, which allowed for the acquisition of their traditional lands. As more European settlers arrived in Canada, Aboriginal families and communities were relocated to reserve lands and traditional forms of government were replaced by a federally imposed 'Band Council' system (c.f. Silver *et al.* 2012). With the exception of the Douglas treaties of 1850–1854, agreements that defined the rights and responsibilities of First Nations and the Federal Government were not reached in British Columbia. Aboriginal title to the rest of the land in the province was therefore left unresolved. In the decades after the Douglas treaties, the colonial government took away First Nations' rights to acquire Crown land, reduced the size of reserves and paid no compensation for the loss of these traditional lands and resources. The traditional lands of the Lil'Wat, Musqueam, Squamish and Tsleil-Waututh First Nations, which were proposed as sites for some of the 2010 Olympic events, are also not subject to a comprehensive treaty agreement (Silver *et al.* 2012). According to Wood and Rossiter (2011), most of the land that now constitutes the province of British Columbia has been purchased or appropriated, reallocated or developed by non-Aboriginals. The dispossession of Aboriginal groups has fostered cultural and socio-economic marginalisation of this community in the province (O'Bonsawin 2010), which has added to the tensions between Aboriginal groups and governments in British Columbia. First Nations continue to lobby the provincial and municipal governments to recognise their communal title to the land and their rights to access resources. In the case of the new development projects and land uses, the government 'must guide proponents to consult and compensate Aboriginal interests fairly' (Silver *et al.* 2012, p. 296).

Indigenous inclusion in the Olympics has mainly focused on the use and representation of indigenous culture in ceremonies, symbols and emblems (Forsyth 2003). Historically, the participation of indigenous people has been an afterthought of bid and organising committees. For example, the Calgary Games Organising Committee (OCO'88) developed a Native Participation Programme in response to pressures from local First Nations who were seeking more representation and involvement in the planning of the Games. Since First Nations participation was limited to cultural displays in the Opening and Closing Ceremonies, this programme represented an important step forward, however, it was implemented in 1984, a mere four years prior to hosting the Games (OCO'88 1988).

The prospect of hosting the 2010 Winter Olympic Games was seen as an opportunity for the city of Vancouver, British Columbia (BC), to increase tourism revenue, invest in Canadian sport development and to improve the city's transportation infrastructure. During the domestic bid phase (1997–1998), bid proponents presented a staggering array of building proposals and public works improvements, most notably, an expanded rapid transit system from the international airport to downtown Vancouver and an improved roadway from the downtown Vancouver area to the Resort Municipality of Whistler. At this time, little consideration was given to the benefits or legacies that would flow to local Aboriginal communities. In 1998, the Canadian Olympic Association awarded Vancouver the right to put forward Canada's international bid for the 2010 Winter Olympic Games. There was no participation of Aboriginal people in the domestic bid phase; however, since some of the Games' events were to be held in the traditional territories of four First Nations groups –Squamish, Musqueam, Lil'wat and Tsleil-Waututh – the 2010 Bid Corporation required the approval of these Aboriginal governments in order to move ahead with its international bid. Vancouver won the bid to host the 2010 Games in July of 2003. We employ a framing analysis to answer the following question: how did Aboriginal groups leverage the 2010 Games for community benefits? By analysing frames surrounding this issue, we were able to uncover how the leaders of this group constructed and developed the issue in a manner that promoted their community development agenda.

Data collection

In order to conduct a qualitative frame analysis, articles were obtained from two local print media sources- *The Vancouver Sun* and *The Province* for the period

1997–2003. *The Vancouver Sun* is owned by CanWest Global and *The Province* is owned by one of CanWest Global's subsidiaries. The articles were identified and collected using a search for keywords related to the bid. This search yielded a total of 152 articles– 123 in *The Vancouver Sun* and 29 in *The Province*. A keyword search within those articles returned 16 articles which focused primarily on Aboriginal participation in the bid process. Of the 16 articles, 13 appeared in *The Vancouver Sun* and 3 in *The Province*. The majority of articles appeared in the period 2001–2003, reflecting the absence of Aboriginal involvement in the domestic bid process.

Frame analysis

In the first phase of our frame analysis, each article was coded for several basic characteristics including: newspaper source, date, staff reporter, document type and the section the article appeared in. Since newspaper articles often mention persons who are discussed, quoted or referred to in some way, each article was also coded for the key players/actors. This was done in an attempt to determine the persons who were driving the discourse of Aboriginal participation in the bid process. The second phase of our analysis employed an inductive approach to identify the main themes in the data. The themes that emerged in this first phase of analysis provided a basis for the development of codes to further analyse the data-set. Manual coding of the data yielded eight coding frames related to Aboriginal participation in the international bid phase; these included: participation, cooperation, sport development, partnerships, land transfer, opportunities, economic development, housing, fairness and social programmes. During this phase, reasoning and framing devices were also identified in order to construct the frame package. The themes were then analysed to explore how the issue of Aboriginal participation was framed in the local newspaper media.

Results and discussion

The first frame identified was related to the 'potential benefits' that would flow to the Four Host First Nations as a result of supporting Vancouver's international bid for the 2010 Games. These benefits included jobs, partnerships with legacy organisations, full and meaningful participation in the bid process, housing, money, programmes, infrastructure and land. The second frame that emerged was 'fairness', which included statements used to justify the flow of potential benefits to Aboriginals as a result of supporting the bid. This frame included historical arguments, benefits promised to other organisations and denial of benefits being pay-offs for approval and support.

The media represented Aboriginal participation in the bid process by focusing on the benefits that would flow to the Four Host First Nations rather than those that would flow to other Aboriginal groups in the province. In 1999 (the early stages of the international bid), representatives from the Squamish and Lil'Wat Nations were appointed to the Board of Directors of the Bid Corporation and later in 2002, the Musqueam and Tsleil-Waututh Nations also received representation. Lyle Leo, representative for the Lil'Wat Nation, was quoted as saying 'The benefits can be unlimited ... they are there for the asking, we just have to make it happen' (Bramham 2002, para. 4). Chief Gibby Jacobs of the Squamish Nation also expressed his hope that the 2010 Games would bring opportunities for his people and was quoted as saying 'we are looking forward to the benefits to our communities' (O'Brian 2002, para. 1). Stakeholders sponsoring the frame which focused on potential benefits flowing to the Four Host First Nations included key individuals such as Lyle Leo, Chief Gibby Jacobs, Chief Leah George-Wilson of the Tsleil-Waututh Nation, Chief Allen Stager of the Lil'Wat Nation and Chief Ernest Campbell of the Musqueam Nation.

These key players or sponsors framed their participation and support of the bid in terms of the potential benefits they would receive. For example, Chief Gibby Jacob was quoted as saying:

> From the outset when the idea was put forward to hold the Olympics, we have said if the Games are held on our traditional territory, we want to go along with those who are co-hosting it and we wanted benefits. (Bramham 2003, para. 6)

Chief Allen Stager, referring to the Lil'Wat Nation's support of the bid stated that 'we have to be careful about what we want to get, we don't want to rush things' (Bramham 2002, para. 6). It is important to note that these representatives from the Four Host First Nations were able to draw the media's attention to the concerns of their groups, due in part to the legitimacy conferred to them by virtue of their positions within the Bid Corporation. In this case, the representatives functioned as elites as they were the ones shaping the discourse of Aboriginal participation in the bid process, thus providing an opportunity to further their political agenda.

In order for the Bid Corporation to present a technically sound bid to the IOC, they needed the approval of the Four Host First Nations who owned the land that was being proposed for some of the Nordic events. This group was able to use their approval as a bargaining tool and this was played out in the media. The Four Host First Nations negotiated several benefits with the Bid Corporation and the Governments in BC which included but was not limited to full and meaningful participation in the bid process, a $2.3 million CAD skills training programme, 300 acres of Crown land, 50 moveable houses from the Athletes' Village and money towards a $15 million CAD First Nations cultural centre. Bid opponents referred to the Aboriginal groups' request for benefits as blackmail and threats. Chris Shaw, a spokesman for the No Games Coalition, claimed that 'Putting aside $5–$10 million for these groups, looks like a pay-off'; he added 'it looks like they are buying their acquiescence and active support' (Bramham 2002, para. 8). Another unnamed bid opponent stated that a bid payout in return for Aboriginal support 'looks like a bribe' (Inwood 2002, para. 1). This ties in to the theme of 'fairness' which emerged from the data-set. Key players from the Four Host First Nations were angered by claims that they were blackmailing the Bid Corporation and the provincial and federal governments. They believed that what they were asking for was no different to compensation promised to other stakeholders for loss of revenue and rental of venues during the Olympic events. In 2002, compensation to IntraWest (owner of Whistler Blackcomb) was estimated at $10–$30 million CAD. Aboriginal leaders believed what they were asking for was fair and justified.

The news media also used what Gamson and Modigliani (1989) call 'reasoning devices' to inform the public on how to judge this issue. In the excerpt below, journalist Daphne Bramham attempted to provide the reader with a definition of the problem and uses examples of other groups' negotiations with the Bid Corporation and Governments to appeal to the audiences' sense of morality:

If it sounds like blackmail, it's worth remembering that what the First Nations are asking for – a share in the profits and benefits – is no different than what Intrawest Corp., the owner of Whistler- Blackcomb, will be asking for if Canada gets the games. It's no different than the University of British Columbia or Simon Fraser University striking the best deals they can for the hockey and speed skating arenas proposed to be built on their land … Call it blackmail if you will, but in some circles, it's just considered good business. (Bramham 2002, para. 8)

In this case, there was an issue-specific frame related to the concerns of local indigenous groups being treated unfairly as opposed to other groups who were negotiating benefits. This issue became more salient in local media coverage as it became bound up in a more *generic* frame of justice. Other framing elements used to highlight the issue of Aboriginals' right to share in the benefits of the 2010 Games include historical examples. In presenting this issue, reporters highlighted that it was important to remember that although Whistler was near Squamish Nation territory and on the land of the Lil'Wat Nation, that 'for all its [Whistler] wealth and economic spinoffs, scarcely a single cent has flowed to their communities' (Bramham 2002, para. 11). Depictions of poverty and crime on Aboriginal reserves, lack of access to jobs in the resort area and repetition of keywords were also used to increase salience of the issue and evoke an emotional response from the audience.

The examination of Aboriginal participation in the Olympic bid process provides an example of how the leaders of groups historically marginalised from projects and decision-making acted as frame sponsors and engaged in frame enterprise, which illustrates framing though the media. In fitting with the IOC's Agenda 21, the bid process can be seen as an opportunity for indigenous persons to assert self-determined objectives either through participation or resistance (c.f. Silver *et al.* 2012). The Four Host First Nations, like other stakeholders in the bid process, were able to leverage the 2010 Games for benefits to their communities, and get their messages across through the mainstream media coverage of the bid in Vancouver.

Case 2: Delhi 2010 commonwealth games

In line with the broader pro-growth discourse associated with hosting a major sporting event, the 2010 Commonwealth Games was envisioned by the Indian Government as a coming of age party, a chance to further position India on the global stage as a legitimate economic competitor or at least as an 'equal' to traditional centres of power (to be discussed below). However, instead of highlighting the advancement of the nation, media coverage of the event preparation and organisation focused on organisational crises which displayed the inequalities and issues of corruption, hygiene and government organisation. It was within this context that the plight of local labourers was brought to the forefront in the international media.

The Commonwealth Games is regarded as a second tier major sporting event in comparison to the Olympic Games and the FIFA World Cup Final, as it generally receives more regionalised media attention limited to Commonwealth Countries. The Delhi 2010 Commonwealth Games was an exception, receiving international coverage from most, if not all, major media outlets, including *The New York Times, CNN* and the *BBC*. The struggles faced by event organisers were dissected in the global media, ranging from corruption allegations and terrorism concerns, to health and safety concerns for workers, athletes and visitors. For example, *The New York Times* ran articles with titles such as 'As Games Begin, India Hopes to Save Its

Pride' (2010, October 2) and 'All Is Ready for Big Games in India, Except What Isn't' (2010, September 19). Other international news media sources provided critical coverage: *The Sydney Morning Herald* (Australia) published the headline 'Delhi Games Weaken Emerging Superpower' (2010, September 24) and a *The Telegraph* (UK) article lead with 'Commonwealth Games 2010: athlete housing 'not fit for humans', says Team Scotland' (2010, September 21).

Description of the community

The infrastructure development associated with major sporting events typically privileges specific areas of host cities, along with affluent residents and international tourists. While much discussion in the media typically focuses on these infrastructure projects, little attention is generally given to those behind it – labourers. The role of this marginalised community in major sporting event preparation has been advocated for and studied by civil rights groups and NGOs, such as Human Rights Watch, Centre on Housing Rights and Evictions and Play Fair.

This case study will examine the marginalised group of unskilled, poor workers, such as those working at construction sites for event infrastructure and the street vendors – this collective group will be referred to as labourers. To meet the demand for workers for a development project as significant as hosting the Games, labourers were recruited from rural India and, as reported in the media coverage, workers were not provided with adequate accommodations and would often sleep in tents along the side of the road near the work sites (Busfield 2010). In the exploration of how marginalised groups were portrayed in the media, for this case, we employed a framing analysis to answer the following question: how did the media represent the poor and displaced labourers of the Delhi Games? Through the analysis of frames surrounding the treatment of this group and conditions in which they worked and lived, we were able to explore how framing by the international media exposed the inequalities and injustices faced by the labourers.

Data collection

This case has been adapted from a larger research project, which examined the management of negative media coverage by the 2010 Commonwealth Games Organising Committee and the Indian Government through identifying the construction of frames by the media. The study analysed 475 media articles, as well as 87 photos and 41 videos from news outlets reporting on the planning and organisation of the Games. While the data-set included news articles from Indian sources, it was limited to English publications and those with national or international distribution. Although this study relied on traditional forms of media, we do acknowledge the importance of non-traditional forms, such as blogs, and social media, particularly in relevance to marginalised groups as they often use these forms of media to vocalise their opposition or resistance to political or economic elite agendas. However, our interest here is how the mainstream media portrayed this traditionally marginalised group in its coverage, which typically privileges a pro-event agenda.

Frame analysis

Data analysis began with a deductive coding process using four frames commonly employed by the news media when reporting a crisis: attribution of responsibility, conflict, economic consequences and human interest (Neuman *et al.* 1992, Liu 2010). The second phase of data analysis involved an inductive approach to tease apart themes identified during the deductive phase of coding. It was within the deductive phase that the identification of the Delhi labourers as a marginalised group occurred within the human interest frame; however, the framing of the Delhi labour issue by the media was further explored in the deductive phases, which examined their role in critiquing the event organisers and how the media used this to highlight the inefficiencies of the organisation and social inequalities present in India.

Early in the preparation for the event, the media reported on human rights violations, including working in unhygienic and unsafe conditions, workers not receiving minimum wage or overtime payments (Shelia reviews work 2008), and protests against the displacement of residents (Loudon 2006). In the months leading up to the October 2010 event, the global news media were reporting widely on struggles occurring with event preparations; it was also at this time that the working conditions and displacement of workers were heavily featured by the news media. For example, an Indian newspaper published headlines such as 'Workers at Games sites getting a raw deal' and 'Rampant violation of labour laws at Games sites'. The discussion of the treatment of labourers often employs a powerlessness frame to express the dominance of elite forces over weaker individuals or groups (Neuman *et al.* 1992). The media framed quotes from this group in such a manner to convey the hardships faced by this group and the lack of power they have to change the situation. In discussing the sanitization of the space prior to the stage of the event, an article from the BBC included a quote from a street vendor speaking to the impact of losing his fruit stall:

> What can we do now? We will be forced to turn to crime, we will steal, we will rob people … Or maybe I will poison my kids and then take poison myself and commit suicide. We'll either die ourselves or kill other people. What other option do I have. (Pandey, 2010, para. 6–7)

Another example within the data, which shows the framing of this group as powerless, was an article in *The New York Times* that quoted a labourer who came home from an event construction site to find his home no longer visible from the road due to 10-foot banners that had been erected. In the article he stated that 'They know that we're labourers and we're dirty, and they don't want anyone to see us from the road' (Delhi hides workers 2010, para. 6); later in the article it was reported that the labourer grew 'increasingly angry as he spoke'. Discussion focused on the powerlessness of the labourers against the actions or agenda of the dominant elites, in this case the government that wished to hide elements of the local community they did not want seen by those outside the city. As stated above, in the framing of a major sporting event, the frame sponsor is often the organising committee and political elites from the host region; what is interesting with the case of Delhi is that these traditional frame sponsors were not the ones controlling or shaping the discourse surrounding the event. In this case, it was the news media and interests groups producing the frames. As frame sponsors are concerned with directing perception (Pan and Kosicki 1993), the media elites, from both international and domestic news agencies, appeared to be concerned with framing the story of labourers in Delhi in such a way to incite an emotional response from the audience and even assign blame for the hardships the labourers were facing. By placing a human face or an emotional angle on an event, issue or problem, it influences a moral judgement and the audiences' perception of severity or importance (Cho and Gower 2006).

This offers an example where not only the selection of words conveyed a powerful message, but where images were also used to evoke emotion, and were arguably selected to achieve the desired effect of bringing international attention to the conditions of the poor Indian workers and vendors. Images published through the news media showed protestors clashing with armed police (Lubin 2010), unlicensed street vendors who were being displaced (Pandey 2010), labourers in poor working conditions without proper safety equipment (Borger 2010) and labourers living outside of the main stadium, covering their mouths with rags during disease fumigation (Wade 2010). The *Guardian* published images of child labourers working on Games sites, with a caption claiming some were as young as four years old (see Komireddi 2010). Furthermore, there were several examples identified where 'photo essays' were used in the absence of traditional articles to report the organisation of the Games and the treatment of the labourer group. These 'photo essays' used multiple images with few written words to provide a timeline or explanation of the events that occurred (see Commonwealth Games construction 2010, Lubin 2010).

As noted above, the portrayal of labourers in Delhi in the mainstream media is interesting as it examines a group of highly disadvantaged citizens who were likely without the resources or access to any media platform (such as internet or print media) to shed light on the conditions they faced. In this case, the framing of this issue by the media and by interest groups (both in India and internationally) created an opportunity where the hosting of an international sporting event placed a 'spotlight' on these conditions, forcing the Indian government to examine the treatment of labourers working on Games sites and address the violations that were occurring.

Conclusions and research possibilities

In this paper, we showed how framing analysis can serve as a means through which one can understand how local community groups and interests may be able to convey their needs and interests through the mainstream media, a platform that generally privileges a pro-growth agenda promoted by business and political elites that typically champions the hosting of major sporting events in cities. As we have discussed, there are issue-specific and generic frames that can be found in any case (de Vreese 2005).

One useful point at which future framing research can be undertaken would be to examine an issue, which culminates with a referendum. In doing so, one can examine media coverage and how it might influence public opinion leading up to a vote. This provides a clear point at which various stakeholders will frame their arguments leading up to the decision day. This will also signal the point at which other local groups may actively enter into the debate over the hosting of events. Possible ways to examine this would include how frames evolve over time; as the date of the referendum approaches various parties might change their strategies and/ or reveal their true intentions. For example, Buist and Mason (2010) found that newspaper coverage of a stadium referendum in Cleveland became more supportive of the initiative as the referendum approached, and letters written to the paper that opposed the project were not published in the paper immediately prior to the vote.

Studies that examine how opposing groups attempt to counteract these tactics would provide an important window into how local community groups attempt to overcome the bias in mainstream media coverage that focuses on the positive outcomes of events and overlooks or even downplays other community impacts. In another study of two referenda in Seattle, WA, Sapotichne (2012) found that opponents in the first referendum were successfully able to find a counterargument to proponents who made widespread claims of economic development benefits. This provides an example of how event opponents were able to mobilise and thwart a stadium referendum despite lacking the resources of stadium proponents.

Another potentially fruitful line of inquiry would be to examine how groups have attempted to piggyback on issues in order to further their interests. For example, a local community group might be in need of certain services or considerations and may seize the opportunity to reach these aims by making it an element/condition of the broader sporting event or infrastructure issue. In the brief case of the 2010 Olympic Games provided above, we see how local aboriginal leaders were able to use the debate over their support of the Games to raise awareness of broader issues, such as the poverty facing their people.

Other research opportunities might include using framing analysis, combined with other methods, such as interviews, in order to examine how community interests strategically mobilise their resources in order to reach their goals. As noted by Gamson (1989), there is a need for research that focuses on the intent of the sender of the message. Thus, in the case of local community groups and major sporting events, research could focus first on how these groups seek to represent their interests, and then examine media frames to understand how their messages are made available to audiences. In doing so, we may gain a better understanding of how resistance and/or inclusion may be an outcome for groups who, by virtue of the power of elites who support event hosting, may not be playing on equal footing in this context.

Local community groups often face an uphill battle in their efforts to represent their interests. In the case of hosting large-scale events, the mainstream media – in this case, newspaper coverage – tends to focus on the positive benefits and legacies associated with event hosting. However, as we see in the two cases presented here, local aboriginal groups were able to leverage their involvement in the Olympic Games to garner attention to their needs. In the case of Delhi, the plight of labourers was picked up by journalists and received widespread media coverage. Thus, although the mainstream media remain arbiters of the largely positive discourse associated with major sport event hosting, opportunities may arise where community groups may be able to help their constituents by strategically using such coverage as a platform to draw attention to their causes.

Notes on contributors

Stacy-Lynn Sant is a PhD candidate in the Faculty of Physical Education and Recreation at the University of Alberta. Her research focuses on the legacy of mega-events, prospective hosts' bid strategies and the leveraging of events for long-term tourism benefits.

K. Meaghan Carey is a PhD student in the Faculty of Physical Education and Recreation at the University of Alberta. Her research focuses on sport and leisure amenity provision in small cities, sport events and tourism.

Daniel S. Mason is a professor of Physical Education and Recreation and adjunct with the School of Business at the University of Alberta. His research focuses on sports leagues and franchises, cities, events and infrastructure development.

References

Andranovich, G., Burbank, M.J., and Heying, C.H., 2001. Olympic cities: lessons learned from mega-event politics. *Journal of urban affairs*, 23 (2), 113–131.

Birrell, S. and McDonald, M.G., 2012. Break points narrative interruption in the life of Billie Jean King. *Journal of sport & social issues*, 36 (4), 343–360.

Borah, P., 2011. Conceptual issues in framing theory: a systematic examination of a decade's literature. *Journal of communication*, 61 (2), 246–263.

Borger, J., 2010. Delhi games: commonwealth fears damange to wider reputation. *The Guardian,* 22 Sep. Available from: http://www.guardian.co.uk/sport/2010/sep/22/delhi-games-commonwealth-fears-reputation.

Bramham, D., 2002. First nations stake claim on 2010 Olympics: if the games are held in Vancouver and Whistler, Mount Currie and Squamish natives want a fair share of the economic benefits, *The Vancouver Sun*, 10 June, p. B3.

Bramham, D., 2003. It's only fair that natives benefit from Olympics. *The Vancouver Sun*, 16 Jan, p. B3.

Buist, A.N. and Mason, D.S., 2010. Newspaper framing and stadium subsidization. *American behavioral scientist*, 53 (10), 1492–1510.

Burton, E., 2003. Olympic Games host city marketing: an exploration of expectations and outcomes. *Sport marketing quarterly*, 12 (1), 35–45.

Busfield, S., 2010. Commonwealth Games in crisis – as it happened. *The Guardian*, 23 Sep. Available from: http://www.guardian.co.uk/sport/blog/2010/sep/23/commonwealth-games-live-blog.

Carey, M., Mason, D.S., and Misener, L., 2011. Social responsibility and the competitive bid process for major sporting events. *Journal of sport and social issues*, 35 (3), 246–263.

Chalip, L., Green, C., and Hill, B., 2003. Effects of sport event media on destination image and intention to visit. *Journal of sport management*, 17 (3), 214–234.

Cho, Y., 2009. Unfolding sporting nationalism in South Korean media representations of the 1968, 1984 and 2000 Olympics. *Media, culture & society*, 31 (3), 347–364.

Cho, S.H. and Gower, K.K., 2006. Framing effect on the public's response to crisis: human interest frame and crisis type influencing responsibility and blame. *Public relations review*, 32 (4), 420–422.

Chong, D. and Druckman, J.N., 2007. Framing theory. *Annual review of political science*, 10 (4), 103–126.

Commonwealth Games construction under labour spotlight. 2010. *The Guardian*, 17 Sep. Available from: http://www.guardian.co.uk/world/gallery/2010/feb/02/child-labour-commonwealth-games-india#/?picture=358844735&index=2.

Crompton, J.L., 1995. Economic impact analysis of sports facilities and events: eleven sources of misapplication. *Journal of sport management*, 9, 14–35.

D'Angelo, P., 2002. News framing as a multiparadigmatic research progam: a response to Entman. *Journal of communication*, 52 (4), 870–888.

D'Angelo, P. and Kuypers, J.A., 2010. Introduction. *In*: P. D'Angelo and J.A. Kuypers, eds. *Doing news framing analysis: empirical and theoretical perspectives*. New York, NY: Routledge, 110–134.

Dansero, E. and Puttilli, M., 2010. Mega-event tourism legacies: the case of the Torino 2006 winter Olympic games- a territorialisation approach. *Leisure studies*, 29 (3), 321–341.

Dansero, E., *et al.*, 2012. Olympic Games, conflicts and social movements: the case of Torino, 2006. *In*: B. Hayes and J. Karamichas, eds. *Olympic Games, mega-events and civil societies: globalization, environment, resistance*. Houndmills, Basingstoke: Palgrave Macmillan.

Delaney, K. and Eckstein, R., 2008. Local media coverage of sports stadium initiatives. *Journal of sport & social issues*, 32 (1), 72–93.

Delgado, F., 2003. The fusing of sport and politics media constructions of US versus Iran at France '98. *Journal of sport & social issues*, 27 (3), 293–307.

Delhi hides workers and beggars as Games near. 2010). *The New York Times*, 28 Sep. Available from: http://www.nytimes.com/2010/09/29/sports/29iht-GAMES.html.

De Moragas, M. and Botella, M., 1995. *The keys to success: the social, sporting, economic and communications impact of Barcelona '92.* Barcelona: Centre d'Estudis Olímpics.

de Vreese, C.H., 2005. News framing: theory and typology. *Information design journal and document design*, 13 (1), 51–62.

Druckman, J., 2001. The implications of framing effects for citizen competence. *Political behavior*, 23 (3), 225–256.

Entman, R.M., 1991. Framing US coverage of international news: contrasts in narratives of the KAL and Iran air incidents. *Journal of communication*, 41 (4), 6–25.

Entman, R.M., 1993. Framing: toward clarification of a fractured paradigm. *Journal of communication*, 43 (4), 51–58.

Florek, M., Breitbarth, T., and Conejo, F., 2008. Mega event= mega impact? Travelling fans' experience and perceptions of the 2006 FIFA world cup host nation. *Journal of sport & tourism*, 13 (3), 199–219.

Forsyth, Janice, 2003. Teepees and tomahawks: aboriginal cultural representation at the 1976 Olympic games. *In*: K.B. Wamsley, R.K. Barney, and S.G. Martyn, eds. *The global nexus engaged: past, present, future interdisciplinary Olympic studies. Proceedings of the sixth international symposium for Olympic research.* London: University of Western Ontario International Centre For Olympic Studies.

Gamson, W.A., 1984. *What's news: a game simulation of TV news.* New York, NY: Free Press.

Gamson, W.A., 1989. News as framing: comments on graber. *American behavioural scientist*, 33 (2), 157–166.

Gamson, W.A. and Lasch, K.E., 1983. The political culture of social welfare policy. *In*: S.E. Spiro and E. Yuchtman-Yaar, eds. *Evaluating the welfare state: social and political perspectives.* New York, NY: Academic, 397–415.

Gamson, W.A. and Modigliani, A., 1987. The changing culture of affirmative action. *Research in political sociology*, 3, 137–177.

Gamson, W.A. and Modigliani, A., 1989. Media discourse and public opinion on nuclear power: a constructionist approach. *American journal of sociology*, 95 (1), 1–37.

Getz, D., 1997. *Event management and event tourism.* New York, NY: Cognizant.

Giles, D. and Shaw, R.L., 2009. The psychology of news influence and the development of media framing analysis. *Social and personality psychology compass*, 3 (4), 375–393.

Gitlin, T., 1980. *The whole world is watching: mass media in the making and unmaking of the new left.* Berkeley: University of California Press.

Goffman, E., 1974. *Frame analysis: an essay on the organization of experience.* Cambridge, MA: Harvard University Press.

Government of Canada. 1982. *Constitution Act, 1982.* Available from: http://laws-lois.justice.gc.ca/eng/Const/index.html.

Hall, C.M., 1992. *Hallmark tourist events: impacts, management, and planning.* London: Belhaven Press.

Hall, C.M., 2006. Urban entrepreneurship, corporate interests and sports mega-events: the thin policies of competitiveness within the hardoutcomes of neoliberalism. *Sociological review*, 34, 59–70.

Hallahan, K., 1999. Seven models of framing: implications for public relations. *Journal of public relations research*, 11 (3), 205–242.

Harris, J. and Clayton, B., 2002. Femininity, masculinity, physicality and the English Tabloid Press the case of Anna Kournikova. *International review for the sociology of sport*, 37 (3–4), 397–413.

Harvey, D., 1989. *The condition of post-modernity.* Oxford: Blackwell.

International Olympic Committee, 1999. *Olympic movement's agenda 21: sport for sustainable development.* Lausanne: IOC Sport and Environment Commission.

Inwood, D., 2002. Plan to reward natives for games smacks of payoff, critics charge: But bands say offer worth up to $20 million is chance to share benefits. The Province, 20 Nov, p. A3.

Kearns, G. and Philo, C., 1993. *Selling places: the city as cultural capital, past and present.* Oxford: Pergamon Press.

Knight, G., MacNeill, M., and Donnelly, P., 2005. The disappointment games narratives of Olympic failure in Canada and New Zealand. *International review for the sociology of sport*, 40 (1), 25–51.

Komireddi, K. 2010. It's right to boycott the commonwealth games. *The Guardian*, 28 Sep. Available from: http://www.guardian.co.uk/commentisfree/2010/sep/28/commonwealth-games-boycott-india?INTCMP=SRCH.

Kuypers, J.A., 2010. Framing analysis from a rhetorical perspective. *In*: P. D'Angelo and J.A. Kuypers, eds. *Doing News Framing Analysis: Empirical and Theoretical Persepctives*. New York, NY: Routledge.

Lenskyj, H.J., 2002. *The best Olympics ever? Social impacts of Sydney 2000*. Albany: State University of New York Press.

Lenskyj, H.J., 2004. Making the world safe for global capital: the Sydney 2000 Olympics and beyond. *In*: J. Bale and M. Christensen, eds. *Post-Olympism? Questioning sport in the twenty-first century*. Oxford: Berg.

Lenskyj, H.J., 2008. *Olympic industry resistance: challenging Olympic power and propaganda*. Albany: State University of New York Press.

Liu, B.F., 2010. Distinguishing how elite newspapers and A-list blogs cover crises: insights for managing crises online. *Public relations review*, 36 (1), 28–34.

Logan, J.R. and Molotch, H.L., 1987. *Urban fortunes: the political economy of place*. Berkley, CA: University of California Press.

Loudon, B., 2006. Delhi crackdown sparks fatal riots. *The Australian*, 22 Sep. Available from: http://www.theaustralian.com.au/news/world/delhi-crackdown-sparks-fatal-riots/story-e6frg6so-1111112250745.

Lowe, P. and Goyder, J., 1983. *Environmental groups in British politics*. London: Allen and Unwin.

Lubin, G., 2010. Check out the worst planned international sports event ever. *Business Insider*, 21 Sep. Available from: http://www.businessinsider.com/commonwealth-games-bridge-disaster-2010-9?op=1.

MacAloon, J.J., 2008. "Legacy" as managerial/magical discource in contenporary Olymoic affairs. *The international journal of the history of sport*, 25 (14), 2020–2071.

Mason, D.S., 2010. The stadium game in an uncertain environment: a preliminary look at arena discourse in Edmonton, Canada. *In*: S. Butenko, J. Gil-Lafuente, and P.M. Pardalos, eds. *Optimal Strategies in sports economics and management*. Heidelberg: Springer Berlin, 97–123.

Mason, D.S., Buist, E.A., Edwards, J.E., and Duquette, G.H., 2007. The stadium game in Canadian communities. *International journal of sport finance*, 2 (2), 94–107.

Misener, L. and Mason, D.S., 2009. Fostering community development through sporting events strategies: an examination of urban regime perceptions. *Journal of sport management*, 23, 770–794.

Mules, T. and Faulkner, B., 1996. An economic perspective on major events. *Tourism economics*, 12 (2), 107–117.

Neuman, W.R., Just, M.R., and Crigler, A.N., 1992. *Common knowledge: news and the construction of political meaning*. Chicago, IL: University of Chicago Press.

O'Bonsawin, C.M., 2010. 'No Olympics on stolen native land': contesting Olympic narratives and asserting indigenous rights within the discourse of the 2010 Vancouver games. *Sport in society*, 13 (1), 143–156.

O'Brian, A., 2002. Whistler residents back Olympic bid: most of those attending a special council meeting Monday support bringing the Winter Games to B.C. *The Vancouver Sun*, 22 Oct, p. A2.

OCO 88 (Calgary Olympic Winter Games Organizing Committee) (1988). VX *Olympic Winter Games Official Report*. Available from: http://www.aafla.org/5va/reports_frmst.htm.

Pan, Z. and Kosicki, G.M., 1993. Framing analysis: an approach to news discourse. *Political communication*, 10, 55–75.

Pandey, G., 2010. Delhi street vendors evicted before Commonwealth Games. *BBC News South Africa*, 20 Aug. Avalible from: http://www.bbc.co.uk/news/world-south-asia-10716139.

Paul, D.M. and Brown, C., 2001. Testing the limits of elite influence on public opinion: an examination of sports facility referendums. *Political research quarterly*, 54, 871–888.

Reese, S.D., 2007. The framing project: a bridging model for media research revisited. *Journal of communication*, 57, 148–154.

Reese, S.D. and Buckalew, B., 1995. The militarism of local television: the routine framing of the Persian Gulf War. *Critical studies in mass communication*, 12, 40–61.

Rendahl, S., 1995. Frame analysis: from interpersonal to mass communication. *Paper presented at the Centrral State Communication Association*, Indianapolis, IN.

Ritchie, J.R.B., 1984. Assessing the impact of hallmark events: conceptual and research issues. *Journal of travel research*, 23 (1), 2–11.

Roche, M., 2000. *Mega-events and Modernity: the Olympics, internationalism and superna-tionalism: international sports events and movements in the inter-war period*. New York, NY: Routledge.

Sapotichne, J., 2012. Rhetorical strategy in stadium development politics. *City culture & society*, 3, 169–180.

Scherer, J. and Jackson, S.J., 2004. From corporate welfare to national interest: newspaper analysis of the public subsidization of NHL hockey debate in Canada. *Sociology of sport journal*, 21 (1), 36–60.

Scheufele, D.A., 1999. Framing as a theory of media effects. *Journal of communication*, 49 (1), 103–122.

Scheufele, D.A. and Tewksbury, D., 2007. Framing, agenda setting, and priming: the evolu-tion of three media effects models. *Journal of communication*, 57, 9–20.

Schwirian, K.P., Curry, T.J., and Woldoff, R.A., 2001. Community conflict over arena and stadium funding: Competitive framing, social action, and the socio-spatial perspective. *Sociological focus*, 34 (1), 1–20.

Semetko, H.A. and Valkenburg, P.M., 2000. Framing European politics: a content analysis of press and television news. *Journal of communication*, 50 (2), 93–109.

Shelia reviews work at the three 2010 Games sites. 2008. *The Times of India*, 16 Dec. Avail-able from: http://articles.timesofindia.indiatimes.com/2008-12-16/delhi/27946618_1_duac-pwd-commonwealth-games-village-site.

Silver, J.J., Meletis, Z.A., and Vadi, P., 2012. Complex context: aboriginal participation in hosting the Vancouver 2010 winter Olympic and Paralympics games. *Leisure studies*, 31 (3), 291–308.

Simon, A.F., 2001. A unified method for analysing media framing. *In*: R.P. Hart and D.R. Shaw, eds. *Communications in US elections: new agendas*. Lanham, MD: Rowman & Littlefield, 75–89.

Smith, A., 2005. Reimaging the city: the value of sport initiatives. *Annuals of tourism research*, 32 (1), 217–236.

Suddaby, R. and Greenwood, R., 2005. Rhetorical strategies of legitimacy. *Administrative science quarterly*, 50, 35–67.

Tewksbury, D., Jones, J., Peske, M.W., Raymond, A., and Vig, W., 2000. The interaction of news and advocate frames: manipulating audience perceptions of a local public policy issue. *Journalism and mass communication quarterly*, 77, 804–829.

Tuchman, G., 1978. *Making news: a study in the construction of social reality*. New York, NY: Free Press.

Van Gorp, B., 2007. The constructionist approach to framing: bringing culture back in. *Journal of communication*, 57 (1), 60–78.

Van Gorp, B., 2010. Strategies to take the subjectivity out of framing analysis. *In*: P. D'Angelo and J.A. Kuypers, eds. *Doing news framing analysis: empirical and theo-retical perspectives*. New York: Routledge.

Van Luijk, N. and Frisby, W., 2012. Reframing of protest at the 2010 winter Olympic games. *International journal of sport policy and politics*, 4 (3), 343–359.

Wachs, F.L. and Dworkin, S.L., 1997. There's no such thing as a gay hero sexual identity and media framing of HIV-positive athletes. *Journal of sport & social issues*, 21 (4), 327–347.

Wade, M., 2010. President lands amid more Delhi allegations. *The Sydney Morning Herald*, 19 Aug. Available from http://www.smh.com.au/sport/president-lands-amid-more-delhi-allegations-20100818-12f86.html#ixzz28lab2jza.

Wood, P.B. and Rossiter, D., 2011. Unstable properties: British Columbia, aboriginal title, and the 'new relationship'. *The Canadian geographer*, 55 (4), 407–425.

Wright, J. and Clarke, G., 1999. Sport, the media and the construction of compulsory hetero-sexuality a case study of women's rugby union. *International review for the sociology of sport*, 34 (3), 227–243.

Zaharopoulos, T., 2007. The news framing of the 2004 Olympic games. *Mass communication & society*, 10 (2), 235–249.

'It is fun, fitness and football really': a process evaluation of a football-based health intervention for men

Steve Robertson[a], Steve Zwolinsky[a], Andrew Pringle[b], James McKenna[b], Andrew Daly-Smith[b] and Alan White[a]

[a]Centre for Men's Health, Leeds Metropolitan University, Leeds, UK; [b]Research Institute of Sport, Physical Activity & Leisure, Leeds Metropolitan University, Leeds, UK

Concerns about gender inequalities in longevity, particularly premature male mortality, have prompted a range of innovative approaches to health promotion work dating back to the 1980s. In developing such work, sport, and football in particular, has emerged as a gendered cultural field that has utility for engaging men in community health initiatives. Evaluations of such work have shown that health initiatives using football settings, football interventions or even club branding can have positive impact on various health measures in the short and longer term. However, little work to date has looked at the underlying mechanisms that generate success in such projects. This paper presents secondary analysis of data collected during the evaluation of the Premier League Health (PLH) programme specifically focusing on these underlying mechanisms and how/where gender (masculinities) appears in these processes. We draw on interview data with 16 staff who had been involved in the delivery of the PLH initiative and 58 men who took part. Thematic analysis highlighted two overarching (and underpinning) themes: 'Trust', what processes it was key to and how it was developed and sustained; and 'Change', including what it was facilitated by and what impact it had. The paper adds to our understanding of how active listening, flexibility and sustained engagement are key to community-based sports projects' success. Furthermore, it demonstrates how the physicality and sociability of involvement, rather than any direct focus on 'health', are important in acting as a springboard for facilitating reflection and aiding lifestyle changes for men.

Introduction

Despite increasing interest and action on aspects of men's health since the 1990s, concerns around gender inequalities in longevity persist and the challenge of how best to engage men in public health initiatives continues to be one of the major themes within the men's health arena (Robertson and White 2011). In the UK, since around 2000, specific attention has been given to using sport generally and football specifically, as a means of successfully engaging men in health promoting activity.[1] Research and evaluation of interventions have shown how football and football settings can be effective in providing opportunities to engage men from socio-economically deprived backgrounds who are not currently meeting health lifestyle guidelines (Pringle *et al*. 2011, Hunt *et al*. 2013, Gray *et al*. 2013) and in engaging men with a variety of mental health issues who have found it difficult to attend 'standard' NHS services (Darongkamas *et al*. 2011; Pringle and Sayers 2004). In terms of impact following engagement, Zwolinsky *et al*. (2013) showed that interventions carried out through football clubs were effective in making statistically significant differences to lifestyle factors (physical activity, diet, smoking, and alcohol consumption) toward nationally recommended guidelines and Brady *et al*. (2010) showed sustained improvement in measures of cardiovascular health at 1 year after a 10-week football-based intervention for overweight/obese men. A further study by Darongkamas *et al*. (2011) showed that establishing a football team for male mental health service users improved a range of self-reported psychosocial measures such as 'mood', 'outlook', 'social life' and 'confidence'. Alongside playing, watching football has also been shown to generate similar opportunities for providing a sense of belonging, altering mood and providing a cathartic release of tension for men (Pringle 2004). There is then growing evidence in terms of the opportunity football provides to initially engage men and to subsequently improve proxy indicators for physical health (lifestyle factors) and to benefit mental well-being.[2]

To date, little work has focused on the processes by which such improvements in health and well-being are achieved for men through such initiatives. Within this paper, we explore qualitative data gathered from a large-scale evaluation study to consider the processes at work when top flight English football clubs established health promotion initiatives for men. We pay particular attention to what generated 'success' and to the role of gender (masculinities) within these processes. The paper situates itself in a gender relations framework understanding masculinities as varying 'configurations of practice' that men move within and between in differing social contexts rather than as more static character traits (Connell 1995, Robertson 2007). Furthermore, after Robertson and Williams (2012), we recognise masculinities as both the producer and product of structure and agency; that is, we recognise that whilst men's health (and other) practices are diverse, they are not simply a matter of individual 'choice'. Although social circumstances and structures do not determine action in a simplistic sense, they can and do constrain the choices available; they act to encourage particular configurations of (gendered) practice and restrict others.

Premier League Health programme description

Premier League Health (PLH) was a three-year programme of men's health promotion located in 16 top flight English football clubs. The programme emerged from recognition that (a) men, particularly young men from socio-economically deprived backgrounds, have a high clustering of lifestyle related health risk factors (Fine *et al*. 2004); (b) football stadia are often located in or near socially-deprived localities and have community development programmes; and (c) that previous health promotion work has suggested sport/football interventions may help engage men in health promotion activity (as outlined in the introduction). Bringing these factors together, a collaborative proposal was developed by the English Premier League and Leeds Metropolitan University and submitted to the Football Pools, to explore the feasibility and effectiveness of implementing men's health promotion interventions using the power and branding of top flight football clubs.

PLH specifically targeted men aged between 18 and 35 years from socio-economically deprived communities. In total, the programme engaged 4020 men, with 80% aged between 18 and 44 years, and 71% describing themselves as White British (see Pringle *et al.* 2013 for full demographic details). The processes of recruiting men varied across the 16 projects and included: advertising projects/ interventions on screens at games; local newspaper adverts; recruitment via community groups (e.g. Children's Centres, drug rehabilitation programmes and job centres); and GP referrals. Programme interventions delivered by the clubs were free; many projects laid on transport; and some incentivised participation through use of match day tickets, opportunities to play a game at the club ground, provision of club branded kit and equipment, etc. Interventions varied between clubs, generally reflecting local community needs, and included: educational activities on match days for supporters; weekly physical activity/lifestyle classes; and varied outreach approaches targeted at specific groups of men in local communities. Some interventions were based around match days; some based around the club ground; and others were community-based but club branded and linked. The clubs worked with local community partners in developing the intervention and these partners often contributed time and other resources to support the work. These interventions therefore were not standardised across the programme, though they were delivered by project staff who received shared education and training in health and behavioural change activities and in working with men on health issues. These project staff were a mix of accredited health trainers, coaching staff and allied health professionals; some of whom already worked within the clubs' community programmes and others who were brought in especially to deliver on the PLH work. The initial training consisted of a two-day workshop organised and delivered by sport and men's health specialists at Leeds Metropolitan University but drawing in a range of practitioners and previous men's health project workers to provide a mix of evidence-based and practice-focused sessions. This was followed up a year later with a further two days that focused more on shared PLH learning to date again facilitated by staff from Leeds Metropolitan University. The demographics of men attending the PLH programme and the impact on outcome measures have been reported elsewhere (Pringle *et al.* 2011; Pringle *et al.* 2013; Zwolinsky *et al.* 2013).

Method

For this paper, the existing data-set of PLH interviews was subject to secondary analysis asking the specific research questions: (1) 'What are the underlying processes and features at work within the programme that lead to success' and (2) 'Where and how does gender (masculinities) appear in these processes'. Approval for the evaluation was gained through Leeds Metropolitan University ethics review processes. The data analysed and presented in this paper were collected from interviews with 16 staff responsible for delivering and/or managing the initiatives in their respective clubs and 58 men who had participated in the initiatives.[3] These men had similar demographic profile to the other men engaged in the PLH programme (see previous section) having been recruited to the programme through the same routes. Integrating interviews from these two sources was important in garnering a range of viewpoints to explore the research questions in detail and the process of integration was facilitated by the analytical approach outlined below. The interviews mainly took place during or immediately after a project session and ranged from 15 to 25 min with the men themselves and from 25 to 40 min with those delivering/managing the initiative. The interviews were semi-structured with questions focusing around: reasons for engagement with the initiative; reasons for staying involved; and previous experience of engaging with health services. The interview topic schedule was developed through internal project team discussion guided by previous research in the area and initial conversations with the clubs and with those who would be involved in delivering the work. It included the same topic areas for both the men and for those delivering the initiatives. Interviews were digitally recorded and transcribed verbatim, and participants were given pseudonyms.

All the data were primary-coded in relation to these questions by SR looking at both the semantic and latent content of the data; that is, considering both the surface and deeper meaning within the accounts given (Braun and Clarke 2006). This represents a slightly amended approach to thematic analysis than that outlined by Braun and Clarke (2006) who implicitly suggest that analysis has to be either semantic or latent. We suggest that analysis can (and whenever possible should) incorporate both. This coded data were then collated into potential themes. Two team members, SR and SZ, then met to refine the specifics of each theme and an initial thematic framework was generated. Finally, all team members were invited to consider this framework and to further refine if necessary (no further refining took place). Throughout this process, and into the writing process, the coding, collating and refining of themes occurred with reference to previous conceptual and empirical work in an iterative and dialectical way (see Robertson 2003 for another example of work around men, sport and health that uses this approach to data analysis). In this way, we also challenge the distinction Braun and Clarke (2006) make between inductive vs. theoretical thematic analysis as our process facilitates both with theme generation being broadly inductive but also informed (though not determined) by previous theoretical and conceptual work. In the extracts that follow, participants are identified by use of a pseudonym (but not by club to assist with anonymity and confidentiality) and staff are identified as HT (for health trainer[4]) with clubs being made anonymous by the use of alphabetical lettering.

Results and discussion

Two overarching (and underpinning) themes emerged through the analysis: Trust (including what processes it was key to and how it was developed/sustained) and Change (including what it was facilitated by and what it impacted on). The relationship of these two themes to each other and to sub-themes/codes is shown in Figure 1.

Trust

Trust was the single biggest factor flowing through the interviews of both the staff and the men engaging with the initiatives and was entwined, both implicitly and explicitly, with a range of processes required for making projects successful.

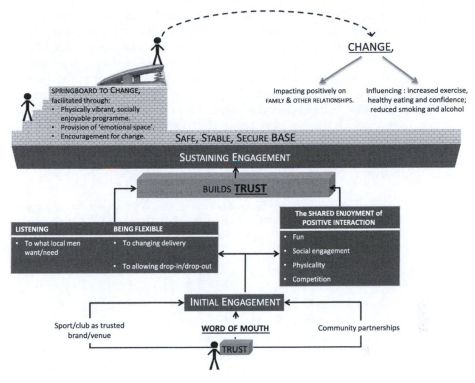

Figure 1.   Relationship of 'trust' and 'change' themes.

Initial engagement

Men, particularly those from socio-economically deprived communities, are frequently described as a 'hard to reach' group in terms of health promotion initiatives (e.g. Brady *et al.* 2010, p. 2966, Hunt *et al.* 2013). Yet, histories of the structural embedding of neglect, abuse, resentment, cultural misunderstanding and mistrust that some men from within such communities may feel in relation to health (and other) professionals can help explain why such men might be hard to reach (Kierans *et al.* 2007). Developing trust was therefore an essential element in helping initial engagement within the PLH projects.

The greatest factor facilitating engagement was word of mouth and the concomitant importance of trusted relationships between friends and members of a community in recognising an initiative as both safe (often presented as 'overcoming fears') and worthwhile (often presented as 'good' or 'enjoyable'):

> I think a lot of guys are apprehensive about going to a project blind that they know nothing about. Getting somebody down to the first session is always the most difficult thing, because guys are unsure about what it is, whereas with word of mouth, if they hear it from a friend … I think it's the whole trust thing, they trust their friend. If they know their friend is at a session they find it easier to go along rather than going down on your own and not really knowing what you're signing up for. [HT, E]

Significant here is how this difficulty in engaging people in a community project is specifically presented by this worker (and others) as a gendered concern impacting particularly on men. Previous research has suggested that men often have a suspicion and mistrust of community initiatives, possibly generated through a general lack of participation in local community activities, and compounded by the discursive construction of (daytime) community spaces as women's domains (Sixsmith and Boneham 2001). Whilst other outreach projects aimed at marginalised communities or groups, and show word of mouth as essential in facilitating engagement (Peck *et al.* 2008, Tumiel-Berhalter *et al.* 2011), it seems that this may have even more resonance for men in developing the trust required to initiate involvement. The implication of this for the projects was that recruitment tended to take longer than anticipated but could increase rapidly once trusted contacts had been firmly established:

> Flyers and referrals initially got some interest and from then on it was more of a case of people attending, telling their friends, people attending. [Once] We got word of mouth, because initially we really struggled for the first six to nine months engaging men, they just weren't coming. We weren't sure really why that was and we looked at the marketing strategy and realised that we were doing all we could do. But I think word of mouth, massive help. [HT, D]

Such accounts from the staff involved in the projects were reinforced in many interviews with the men who said that they had either come because of the influence of a friend or had influenced a friend to attend:

> I: How did you first find out about it?

> Oliver: Well [name] is my mate and I knock around with him and he said to me, 'I want as many people to come as possible' and I asked a few others and they all come down and just really enjoyed it.

Established (trusted) community partnerships – including those with NHS services, Sure Start Centres, local job centres, Urban Care & Neighbourhood (UCAN) centres, etc. – were also very important for projects in facilitating engagement for men and in creating integrated working opportunities:

> I: How did you find out about it?

> Neil: From Sure Start, my kids go to the Sure Start centre I found out through that and I've just been a regular from that.

> More recently we've brought on [a community rehabilitation project]. We're now part of their project, it's their lads that attend our sessions. They are mostly homeless people or ex-convicts, drug addicts, and they do a 12 week rehab program with [community project], where they do lifestyle classes and as part of that program they come and do physical activity tying in with our program. [HT, B]

Given women's generally greater involvement in community projects, and the role they are often attributed in influencing male partners in relation to help-seeking (e.g. Coles *et al.* 2010), their contribution was also recognised. In particular, when women had existing, trusted community contacts, they often acted as intermediaries in introducing male partners to PLH projects:

I: How did you first find out about it?

Ian: My partner was on a course at Sure Start and I went in and I met [worker] and he was like 'we offer this for dads.' He was on about this course starting off and I've been involved ever since really.

As well as word of mouth and community partnerships, sport club branding could also engender trust, or at least a level of familiarity, in the initiative being promoted for many of the men (see also Brady *et al.* 2010, Hunt *et al.* 2013):

I think it [success in engaging] was about how we used the football club and the lads to promote sessions, and how we initially got it out there by promoting and utilising that status [HT, B]

I: Was that one of the main reasons why you came down because it's associated with [club]?

Frank: I've always been a [club] supporter since I was four years old, I've been coming here for 34 years. I absolutely love the club. I mean not any day goes by where I do not wear the colours, this is how passionate they are to me.

It is difficult to tell from data here whether it is the club branding, or sport itself as a (gendered) cultural field, or the football venue as a (gendered) 'safe/familiar' local social space, that generated trusting engagement. It is likely that all three of these plays a part but the balance of influence of each might be different for different men depending on their prior interest and engagement with the club/sport/venue. There were nuances recognised by those leading the PLH projects about what club-related intervention work was appropriate and when it was appropriate. In particular, it was recognised that whilst providing basic information about health (and about the projects) at matches was acceptable, attempting interventions beyond this *on match days* was potentially problematic:

People just want to watch the football at the weekend [HT, A]

They're all passive messages that people can read in their own time. I think that's very important for men. When we had the approaches that were in your face when people have got other things going on, like trying to get in to watch the match, people weren't interested, it wasn't on their agenda. [HT, C]

This echo's previous empirical work (Dunn *et al.* 2010) on engaging men at football games and links to a wider point, which we return to later, about how much 'health' can be directly inserted into football club-based initiatives.

Developing and sustaining trust

Beyond initial engagement, trust has been recognised as a recurring theme of importance in sustained community health work (e.g. South *et al.* 2012) and was clearly vital for men's involvement with PLH and also to the processes of change discussed later. But, how is such trust developed? After making initial engagement, the trust required for sustained involvement seemed to develop through two key processes: active listening and flexibility, and positive social interaction.

Rather than a linear model of projects being designed by health professionals and delivered to (passive) lay male participants, the interventions in PLH developed through processes that proactively learned about men's interests, needs and concerns and responded flexibly to these. This was the case even when initial project plans had been quite fixed but subsequently failed to meet needs that later became apparent. This flexible development often relied on using links with community partners to help more fully understand local men's needs and interests. As an example, the decision to run badminton alongside football was significant in reaching South Asian men who had limited interest in football but who made up a large part of the local community for one club:

I: What would your best advice for another club be?

HT, A: I think the main thing would be to work *with* the community. It's very easy to say we want to set up this, and you might not get high attendance to the session. It would have been easy to centre our project on football but it's not really what the community wanted. So speak to the community, listen to what they want and to their needs.

I came down cos it was Badminton [Chris]

This was reflected at other clubs who adjusted or extended available options in initiatives to meet the expressed needs of the men they were engaging:

I: What kind of things do you do in the sessions?

Wayne: I do boxing and circuit training. I'd like to do football but I've got a cartilage tear in my knee so I can't do football because of the injury

I: Do you like the fact that it isn't just football?

Liam: Yeah you can do training, boxing, and then you can get involved in the half marathons and whatever else if you're interested, so it's dead good like.

For the men, this listening and flexibility often related very much to the practical arrangements of the sessions. The majority of the men felt that sessions being free was important to their being able to attend – though once they were fully involved, some also said they would pay a nominal fee if required. Being local, or accessible via provided transport, was also important, as was the timing of the sessions to fit in around work and other commitments. Listening to these aspects and evolving projects accordingly were important for success across the clubs.

Very significant in terms of sustained engagement was the opportunity to drop into and out of both individual sessions and the initiative itself. Many of the men engaging with PLH had the complex social problems and often chaotic lives associated with socio-economic deprivation (Coote *et al.* 2004) which could make regular, 'on-time' attendance difficult and it was important that this did not create problems:

Chris: I've missed one or two weeks.

I: And what's it like coming back?

Chris: It makes no difference whatsoever. I missed four weeks consecutive but nobody says anything, nobody asks you questions, you just turn up and they're glad to see you.

I: Do you think that's important?

Chris: Course it is, yeah! If people miss for any reason, when they come back it's like the gap doesn't exist, it would be as though they just slept. When they come back you just ask them how they are, there is no script to it, it makes no difference at all.

There have been times where I've not been able to come for weeks. But I know I'm able to just walk back through that door, I know that there is still a happy atmosphere and just go back in and do what I was doing before I left. Obviously there might be new people there but you just get talking. [Dave]

The importance of being able to move into and out of, drop and pick up, social connexions unconditionally and without question has been recognised in previous empirical and conceptual work on men's relationships (Robertson 2007, p.110, Robertson and Monaghan 2012). The ability to engage in a social space specifically without the need for 'personal sharing' has also been shown to be important (Robertson and Monaghan 2012, p. 160) and should not be underestimated in terms of its impact on building trust and making projects 'acceptable' and indeed enjoyable for men.

Linked to this notion of flexibility, ironically, was the importance the men attached to the stability that regular sessions provided. For many men, the projects provided a structure that facilitated the personal discipline important for regulating other areas of their life:

The fact it was once a week, a regular weekly thing, it fits, it's easy and keeps you in a routine. [Noel]

Harry: When I left the detox unit I found out about here and I started ... you know structure, which was really important to me to have a structure, somewhere to go, to take part in things really.

I: Do you think you lost that structure before?

Harry: 100%, at its worst due to my behaviour, my drug taking. You know this kind of structured up part of my week.

This resonates with discipline and control being important aspects of (hegemonic) masculinity practices (Courtenay 2004). In contrast to some work presenting hegemonic masculinity as almost always health damaging (e.g. Peate 2004), we would suggest that for many of the men attending PLH, it was important to (re)develop, to (re)gain control and order rather than viewing such configurations of practice as automatically negative and pejorative aspects of masculinity (Macdonald 2011).

Yet, stability and (re)gaining control was not achieved by regular attendance for short time-limited periods. As seen earlier, the opportunity to drop out of projects for periods of time *but knowing you can return at any point* was very significant in providing a secure, trusted base. This meant that interventions that were of relatively short duration, for example, an 8–12 week intervention to improve physical activity (which was how a lot of the PLH projects were originally envisaged), were quite quickly seen as not meeting the wider needs of many of the men who required something a little more enduring:

> When we did the first 12 week sessions, it didn't feel like we'd done all we needed to do. It was taking four to six weeks to get to know somebody, and get to gain their respect. By the time you'd got to know them it was kind of like 'we're done, see you later.' We were conscious we were losing people from the program, they weren't doing anything, they were just coming, playing football, and then back into their life. So now we have a continuous session and it's very, very personal now and it's very individual. [HT, B]

> The project was supposed to be a 12 week intervention but we learnt very early on as soon people got involved they didn't really want to leave so we very quickly established on-going sessions. So now, they've still got the support there for one another, they're still in an environment with the football club and the staff who've seen their development and hopefully it's established enough that they can do it on their own. [HT, C]

> Originally we were doing a ten week course and then we cut it, then we'd do another ten. But there was a void there, because these guys were enjoying it, so why did we stop it after ten weeks and throw them away? There's no point, so we just left it open. [HT, J]

The importance of longer term, community development projects, rather than short-term interventions, for improving men's health has been noted for some time (Robertson 1995) and is shown here to be a significant mechanism for generating positive outcomes. Yet, the challenges of developing and delivering more sustained approaches to addressing men's health needs within a neoliberal policy framework remain a cause for concern (Williams *et al.* 2009).

In addition to active listening and flexibility, positive social interaction was a central mechanism in men's sustained engagement with PLH projects. The challenges for developing supportive, health-enhancing relationships (social capital) for men in socio-economically deprived locations have been recognised in previous research (Dolan 2007, Sixsmith and Boneham 2001) and sport/football has been identified as a way to help meet these challenges for some men (White and Witty 2009). The PLH projects acted as a gendered cultural field where men felt safe and comfortable in developing peer relationships in a setting that fostered health-enhancing activity:

> It's fun, fitness and football really, just sort of team bonding, get to know other people with similar interests […] The social element is huge. [Frank]

> I did 20 years in the army and I miss exercising with other people, I miss the fun of doing it. I come from a very male environment and I'm looking for a little bit more than just going for a run down the sea front where you're actually on your own all the time. I like to come down, I like to mix in with a different group of people and it's fun! [Johnny]

Previous work has identified the importance of 'vibrant physicality', the embodiment of feeling good, to men's sense of enjoyment, health and well-being

(Monaghan 2001, Robertson 2006) and how social engagement facilitates the maintenance of health-enhancing behaviour (Marcus and Forsyth 2008). This was evident within the PLH projects with many men citing terms like 'enjoyment', 'fun', 'feeling really good' 'got my mojo back' or 'feeling high as a kite' as reasons they continued involvement. However, evidence here, as shown in the quotes above, suggests that this is not only about the enjoyment of individual exercise; rather, understanding notions of 'feeling well' (even 'feeling fit') more fully requires consideration of embodied masculinities developed through enjoyable inter-subjective social encounters.

The sport/football-based nature of the PLH interventions raises the interesting issue of 'competitiveness' as a possible facilitator and barrier to sustained engagement in the projects and this is made more significant by the (often pejorative) role competitiveness is ascribed in the performance of (hegemonic) masculinity. There is no doubt that the competitive nature of a sport-based intervention appealed to some of the men:

> It gets competitive, people are fouled and everything, just general football isn't it. I'm a competitive person, always have been, even though it's just a kick about between friends. I make sure that people know I don't play to lose, I want to get a win obviously. I want to be the best at what I'm doing. [Ian]

> Obviously when you're out there with the football it's a bit competitive and stuff like that but everyone goes home with a smile on their face and enjoys the game. [...] It's always going to be competitive; no one comes to a game of football to lose even if it is with your mates. [Kevin]

The use of the word 'obviously' in both the above accounts implies that there is an expectation that men playing football will, by their very (essentialist) nature, be competitive. However, care needs to be taken in reading this too simplistically. Whilst an element of competition undoubtedly added to the men's sense of enjoyment (being another aspect of what constituted 'vibrant physicality'), the extent of this was tempered by both the men themselves and those running projects to ensure that the balance of the group dynamics, and particularly the friendship and inclusivity seen as such an important part of engagement, was maintained:

> We have banter, good fun. There's no animosity between anybody, even if there is, if somebody's got a bit of grievance, then the guys, they nip it in the bud. Any aggression or anything, we're all together even when we're playing the matches, you just calm down a bit so ... and the encouragement from the lads is dead good, we've all like bonded together. [Liam]

> If it started getting a bit too focused on competition we would lose a lot of what it's all about really, the spirit of this place, it's open to all people of all abilities. [Chris]

> We've tried to build the social element into it, it helps draw people in when they see friendly faces and feel welcome. Rather than focusing on elements of competition we try to make it a friendly atmosphere. [HT, A]

To this extent, our findings partly confirm previous evaluations which found that (older) men recognise the value of passing time together in less competitive ways (Ruxton, 2006). Spandler and McKeown (2012) have suggested that football can simultaneously embody negative aspects of masculinities (in which they include competitiveness) alongside positive aspects such as team spirit, community and solidarity. Our findings confirm this though we would probably go further and also suggest that this binary could be broken in a way that allows even aspects of competitiveness, when contained within a friendly, committed community group of men, to be viewed in a more positive light.

It is clear then that the social aspects of interventions were important to men and this had implications for the structure and form of project delivery if their engagement was to be sustained. As well as getting the shape of projects right in terms of the issues outlined earlier (timing, location, cost, ongoing programme, etc.), the content of sessions had to be well thought through. One aspect in particular, the direct 'health' content of sessions, had to be kept in balance with the men's primary motivation for attending – the 'fitness, fun and football' if trust was to be maintained. Having to negotiate this balance was a common narrative of those delivering the projects but also appeared implicitly in some of the men's accounts:

> We had a big resistance. I got somebody in, it was on men specific cancers, and this lady came and gave a PowerPoint presentation. There were a couple of people in the group who said that I tricked them, that I lured them with football and then give them all health, and if they want to have health talk they would go to the doctors, which is fair enough. [HT, L]

> The health trainer would give them snippets, small talks. Definitely short and sweet because the area we are in is very deprived and they [the men] have a lot of this [health] stuff thrown at them, 'you must do this'. [...] So it's more, 'if you'd like to learn more, come and see me afterwards, see the health trainer' [HT, D]

> It makes it easy for you to come along because it's so relaxed and enjoyable. You start laughing and joking and the barriers come right down. It makes you feel like you're not doing it because you have to but because you want to. *It doesn't even feel like you're learning anything sometimes*, you're just having a laugh. [Eddie, emphasis added]

Evidence here supports previous work that recognises how the structural embedding of health as a 'feminised' concept (Robertson, 2007: 139) can create problems in addressing 'health' directly within health promotion initiatives for men (Coles *et al.* 2010). Recognising this, listening to the men's views, their motivations for attending, and adjusting projects accordingly, was clearly key to building trust, sustaining engagement and thereby facilitating change.

Change

Trust then, developed and sustained through the mechanisms outlined in the previous section, acted as a springboard for change. This change was facilitated through three main mechanisms: the physically vibrant, socially enjoyable aspects of projects; the 'emotional space' for reflection that the projects created; and improved self-efficacy-generating enthusiasm for further change. Each of these is considered below.

The importance of social connections and the associated vibrant physicality acted as a mechanism that helped generate not only a feeling of well-being but also established positive lifestyle changes. At its most basic, the pleasure experienced by engagement in projects generated change almost by default, in a way that seemed like a happy (often implicitly unexpected) by-product to the men:

I: Do you set yourself any targets or goals, like we were talking about weight loss before …

Barry: No I don't really, if it comes it comes, then it's a bonus. I just enjoy what I'm doing at the sessions here so …

I thought it might be loads of hard work but it's enjoyable and it's made me more active. I want to be out more and before I was just sat in my house all the time just piling weight on. [Mark]

I: What do you like about the programme?

Thomas: Have a good laugh with the lads, you get loads of fitness, lose a bit of weight and that, mainly we have a good laugh with the lads.

For some men, the very act of engaging with the initiative, making these social and wider community connections, was a significant change *in and of itself*:

I've never been a confident person. The initial trying to get into the scheme was quite a big step for me, just for meeting new people, I don't really find that easy, and everyone sort of made me feel so welcome, it's a really nice atmosphere. [Barry]

I've got PTSD [Post-Traumatic Stress Disorder], so getting out is not something I'm very good at. So coming here I was nervous at first but then [project facilitators] made me feel dead welcome so I came and stuck it out. And there was no one judging me if I didn't come, if I said "I'm not feeling too good, I'm not coming tonight". It was a dead relaxed atmosphere everyone was having a joke and taking the mick out of each other but it made me feel dead relaxed. Before I came down I was bricking myself, I hadn't been out for months. [Eddie]

Yet even for those men who did not have trouble with initial engagement, the physical activity and social involvement within projects generated positive shifts in how they thought and felt about themselves, increasing confidence and leading to a range of lifestyle changes. As one project facilitator explains:

There is nothing better than feeling good about yourself. If you feel good about yourself and your confidence levels are high, your esteems up, you're capable of things. […] They start doing things they couldn't do at the beginning and start to think 'maybe now I'm in a position to have a go at that'. So we're opening up gateways to all other kinds of things [HT, G]

Confidence and associated self-efficacy and self-esteem (which do not just 'appear' intra-psychically but become embodied through active involvement; Robertson 2006) then formed a basis for further life changes for the men. This changed embodied emotionality not only shifted men's lifestyle practices but also impacted on inter-subjective encounters with others and greater opportunities for community engagement. Some men spoke about increased involvement with their children, either directly through joint involvement with the project or as an indirect (but important) consequence of their involvement:

My son comes here, he's 21, it gives us something to do together, he loves it […] And they do a family programme as well, so I do that with my daughter, she's got Asperger's, it gives her a release of anger when she's on the punchbag. She loves that so, yeah, it's brought me closer with my daughter like. [Garth]

Before I joined I didn't want to do anything. Now I walk to the shops, take the kids to school, do everything I never used to do. [Mark]

Other men spoke about taking the learning from the project to family members but also to work colleagues:

I always talk to the guys at work, like things you get taught. Like breakfast, it's bran flakes or porridge that sustains you, doesn't give you peaks and sugar rushes and you're not hungry and craving the wrong thing. So, yeah, I pass a lot of it [learning] on. [Karl]

It seems then that whilst the 'feminisation of health' means that care has to be taken in addressing health directly within projects (as highlighted earlier), we suggest that, given the right context and motivation, men are not only interested in positive life changes for themselves but are able and willing to act as conduits for facilitating change in their family and others health practices (see also Williams 2007, White *et al.* 2009). The importance of these opportunities for change within the family created by the projects was also recognised by those delivering the interventions:

Like I say, we've got guys with kids, the kids have never been to a football match. They might not support [club] but it [match tickets used as reward/incentive in project] gives them an opportunity to spend more time together. [HT, B]

Overall, and in line with previous research (McElroy *et al.* 2008), the physical and social engagement within the projects impacted on men's sense of identity. This was mainly talked about as increased 'confidence' or 'esteem' but also reflected a generally more positive outlook:

When you start getting fit your frame of mind changes, you've got a brighter outlook [Fred]

This changed sense of self and outlook led to changes in lifestyle practices in terms of self-reported; 'reduced smoking', 'weight loss', 'increased activity' and 'healthier eating'. These changes in lifestyle then often had positive impact on men's wider relationships with family, friends and work colleagues facilitating opportunities for forming new (potentially less harmful) social connexions.

Men's engagement in projects seemed to provide an 'emotional space', creating opportunities for assessing and adjusting their lives:

The work that I do is quite stressful and doing exercise is not only a good way of de-stressing but it also occupies your time. In London a lot of people de-stress by maybe going to the pub or things that are not that healthy. With this, it sounds a bit corny, it obviously helps your body but it helps your mind as well because it puts everything in order. [Wayne]

I: Did the project help you settle down?

Ian: It keeps my mind away from certain things, like I'm not tempted to go out and do stuff [drinking and cannabis]. It's like security if you like. It's nice, it gets you away from whatever else is going on, troubles or whatever.

It's a big motivating factor for me coming along here. [...] It's been part of the parcel that's kept me off heroin and crack for six months. I haven't smoked for six months, my diet's healthier, my whole well-being and outlook, the way I think, is much healthier as well. [Harry]

It seems from these men's accounts that space provided by the projects facilitated change in a way that was not necessarily related to specific, conscious decisions. Rather, in line with Bourdieu's (1979) work, it seems that entering a new cultural 'field' (the project) assisted in keeping some men from other health damaging 'fields' (particularly drink and drug culture) providing the opportunities for the formation of new habits, practices and motivations (associated with the project aims). These become (gradually) embedded and embodied; that is, they become part of the men's new 'habitus', part of their new 'logic of practice' (Bourdieu 1992). As Kenny says 'It's [doing exercise] sort of built into the brain, hardwired into the brain' and as Fred explains 'Talking tonight about smoking is the first time I've mentioned it, it's just not in my head anymore'.

These shifts in men's outlook and material practices, which this 'emotional space' creates, were also observed by those facilitating the projects:

[The men] have learnt how to eat healthily and they've curbed their temper at home, they're more appreciative of other people's issues and just not their own. So it's not just them, there are other things going on in life they need to think about, and to question themselves; 'is it always me that is right?' [HT, G]

A lot of the men have problems at home, drug and alcohol problems, problems with the law and family issues and I think it's just two hours away from that life where they can concentrate on having a bit of a laugh with the lads, getting fit as a bit of a bonus point as well. But it's just two hours away from that hectic life they've got to focus on having a bit of fun. [HT, H]

I think it's giving them space and time to be themselves and develop themselves and get a chance to look at themselves and others and see how they relate. The group they may have been in, or still are in, outside [the project] may have an overriding influence on them. We all know about peer pressure, and maybe they get to see a different way. Little things like that can be massive. [HT, G]

This 'emotional space' then provides opportunities for reflecting on gendered identity. As mentioned earlier, and linked to work by Spandler and McKeown (2012), it seems that, despite the obvious (masculine) gendered links with football, approaches taken within projects could act to mitigate some of the negative masculinities elements and encourage positive aspects of sociability. Earlier quotes from Garth and Mark suggest that men *have* become more involved in family life, and, as suggested below, more able and willing to consider the impact of their behaviour on those around them:

I do worry about am how I'm gonna end up, so this is why changing my health is very important to me. I've got four grandchildren I'd like to see them grow up, and my wife, I'd like to be around a lot longer for her as well [Colin]

This was partly seen to be due to projects working in ways that might shift hegemonic gendered norms and practices:

I: Is the male-centred element of the project important?

A male only approach can make them feel a bit more comfortable about coming in and opening up with other people; it helps break down the masculine stereotypes. [HT, A]

As we were doing the evening sessions I could see some of them stretching, closing their eyes and breathing. I said, 'What's going on with you lot?' And they said, 'We all go to yoga together', I said 'Yeah sure!' 'No, we really do!' And you know, yoga isn't seen as a particularly manly thing and these group of lads were quite depressed and trying to recover from drug addiction, and they all started going to yoga together, I thought it was brilliant! [HT, C]

There is then a great deal of skill involved in developing projects that appeal to men, and that are male focused, whilst at the same time delivering them in ways that act to resist (rather than replicate) damaging configurations of masculinity practices. The 'emotional space' offered within projects that aimed to fully understand and meet men's expressed needs seemed to help maintain this balance. The individual qualities of those delivering the PLH work – such as enthusiasm, commitment and appropriate sensitivity to men's needs, recognised in previous men's health programmes (e.g. White *et al.* 2008) – should not be underestimated in generating the right mood and tone within projects.

Finally, improved self-efficacy was a key mechanism for generating and sustaining change. Noticing small changes in the way they felt or looked often provided motivation for the men to sustain involvement in the project but also facilitated change beyond the project. Observed or felt changes in one area often created momentum for further change in other areas when men recognised their ability to achieve goals and meet challenges:

I've lost weight, got fitness, I'm a lot better at football, cut down on smoking. It's even helped me in my day to day life style; like before I came here I just used to stay in or smoke drugs, play on my PlayStation. Now, I come here I do whatever, I go home see my girlfriend and keep busy round the house, keeps me active every single day. There's not a day goes by that I'm not active. [Dave]

Feeling enabled in this way could also be supported by others; it could be encouraged by those facilitating the sessions, or the other men attending, in both direct and indirect ways:

I've just packed in smoking, smoked for thirty years. It was hard to quit but with the support here … because it's 'fitness, fitness, fitness' and, you know, 'you're doing good why do you wanna go back to that' [smoking] [Liam]

I: Has this helped you stop smoking?

Fred: Without a doubt. It became part of the package if you see what I'm saying. I did this on a Monday, smoking group Tuesday, and I didn't want to come here and say 'Oh, I've started smoking again'. Not that these fellows [other men in project] would have said anything but I didn't wanna let anyone down.

Change then becomes embedded (and embodied) through engagement in socially enjoyable, physical engagement in PLH projects that allow the emotional space (often rarely available to these men) for reflection on self-identity; that is, it allows them to focus on what Giddens (1991) terms the 'reflexive project of the self'. Furthermore, the positive feelings of well-being that this engagement then embodies, through both individual and inter-subjective encounters, provides motivation to maintain and further deepen this reflexive process and the concomitant changes in the men's social practices.

Conclusion

There is no doubt that evaluating complex community-based interventions is a difficult process that is influenced by conflicting agendas as to 'what counts' as evidence and how/where this should be gathered (Coote *et al.* 2004). This paper presents one aspect of a larger evaluation that focuses on understanding how change mechanisms occurred within the PLH programme and the role of gender (masculinities) within these processes. There are of course limitations within such work. The interviews that form the basis of the data presented were conducted with those delivering the projects within the PLH programme – who may well wish to present a positive view of the work they undertook – and with men who had or were taking part – who may have a different view to those who engaged and then rapidly left the projects (or indeed those who never wished to engage).

Nevertheless, there are important lessons that can be learnt from this analysis that help advance our understanding of the practice of promoting health through sport settings/approaches and the role of leisure and pleasure within this. Community outreach approaches delivered through links with football clubs and through utilisation of existing community partnerships can indeed provide a first contact point for men who historically have fallen outside the reach of orthodox statutory service delivery. Establishing and sustaining trust is a key mechanism in the delivery of such work. Men's limited engagement in (day time) community spaces meant that building trust relies heavily on utilising existing networks and relationships (often through 'word-of-mouth') to create a safe, familiar environment for projects to function. Sustaining trust is subsequently achieved through actively listening to what the men want from projects, flexibly adjusting to meet these needs and by recognising and emphasising the physical and social pleasure that comes from engaging with others in the projects. This sociability is an important mediator in maintaining health practices and, for some men, in re-engaging in health promoting (rather than health damaging) social networks.

Such trust takes time and effort to gain and maintain. Most PLH staff found that it crucial to provide ongoing, rather than time-limited, projects for the men that they could come and go from as they dealt with other often chaotic aspects of their life. This longer term approach, delivered in a friendly, non-judgemental environment which often required drawing on existing community links, created a strong and secure base and a springboard for the men that facilitated reflection and aided lifestyle changes. Feeling the benefits of such changes improved feelings of control which subsequently encouraged further involvement and change for the men in ways that felt natural and enjoyable rather than forced.

Further understanding some elements of these underlying mechanisms would benefit from additional work. Whilst those studies discussed in the introduction have highlighted the benefits to health and well-being that can accrue through men's engagement in football (directly or as supporters), or through stadia premises, little empirical research has yet fully considered exactly how this works and for which men. Work here concurs with other work that suggests that while club brand and stadia as familiar settings might be useful for facilitating engagement, care needs to be taken in attempting interventions seen too directly as 'health', particularly work undertaken on match days as some of the PLH initiatives were. More needs to be done to unpack exactly what this means for those developing future interventions in relation to what level of direct reference to 'health' is acceptable and at what point in which interventions. Linked to this, the role of competitiveness in team sports-based interventions warrants further exploration. Whilst many of the men (and those delivering projects) felt that competition was an important element in generating the vibrantly physical enjoyable aspects of the intervention, it was also clear that the extent of this needed to be bounded in order to enable all to participate, enjoy and benefit. Finally, it appears that the positive feelings generated through physical interaction with other men in social spaces that do not require but can facilitate personal sharing and health related discussions, acted almost unconsciously to enable lifestyle change. Whilst we have started a consideration of this within this paper, future work could explore further how such an environment is created and more thoroughly consider how these positive feelings, this embodied emotionality convert to lifestyle change and to greater positive community and social engagement.

Funding

FA Premier League (the commissioners) with funding provided by the Football Pools (the sponsors).

Acknowledgements

The authors gratefully acknowledge the contribution of all those individuals and agencies who partnered PLH, including the Football Pools, the Premier League, the participants and people in the 16 EPL clubs, along with the people in the authors' organisations who supported this work.

Notes

1. This is part of a wider approach to using various aspects of 'what men like' (i.e. links to masculinities) to involve men in health promotion and has also included initiatives that engage men through rugby (Witty and White 2011), in the workplace (Dolan *et al.* 2005) and at pubs, barbers and racing venues (DeVille-Almond 2009).
2. We do not however suggest that utilising football in this way is unproblematic and purely beneficial. Previous research (e.g. Robertson 2003, Spandler and McKeown 2012) also highlights the care that needs to be taken when using sport/football to promote the health of men and we are cognisant of such work.
3. Data were not collected from two of the clubs, one withdrew and one had the main staff member leave and access to participants for interviews could no longer be easily facilitated.

4. Not all these staff were health trainers; this notation is just a simple means of differentiating them from the men attending the initiatives.

Notes on contributors

Steve Robertson is a professor of Men, Gender & Health at Leeds Metropolitan University. His main research interests are around social theories of masculinities and their application to health and illness. He has also worked on: masculinities and disability; the sociology of (male) bodies; men, masculinities and mental well-being; and men's engagement with health services. He is the editor-in-chief of the International Journal of Men's Health.

Steve Zwolinsky is a research officer at the Centre for Men's Health, Leeds Metropolitan University. His primary research interests revolve around understanding the clustering of lifestyle risk factors in men and in understanding gender inequalities in male life expectancy.

Andrew Pringle is a reader in Physical Activity, Exercise and Health at Leeds Metropolitan University. He has over 20 years of experience in teaching, research and practice in 'public health'. He has a particular interest in the role of professional football as a vehicle for health improvement with hard-to-engage groups and has also carried out investigations into the effectiveness of physical activity interventions with adult populations.

James McKenna is a carnegie professor of Physical Activity and Health and the head of the Active Lifestyles research centre at Leeds Metropolitan University. He is currently working on a long-term evaluation of a staged recovery intervention targeted on wounded injured and sick service personnel, based on inclusive sport and adventure education. His main research interest is in exploring the effects of physical activity on mental and physical health across the lifespan.

Andrew Daly-Smith having started as a physical activity and exercise coach for children, Andy joined Leeds Metropolitan University in 2005 and is now a senior lecturer in Physical Activity, Exercise and Health. His primary research interest relates to the effects of exercise on cognition in overweight and obese children though he has also worked on evaluations of playground interventions and healthy lifestyles of children.

Alan White is a professor of Men's Health at Leeds Metropolitan University. He has been developing his research and scholarly activity around men's health for over 17 years. There are three main strands to his work: Gendered Epidemiology (exploring the data relating to men and their health and health service usage); Men and Public Health (how men engage with the health service and how the health service meets the needs of men); and Men's Experience of ill-health. He was the principle investigator on the PLH evaluation and has recently headed up an international team of academics to complete 'The State of Men's Health in Europe' Report for the European Commission.

References

Bourdieu, P., 1979. *Distinction: a social critique of the judgement of taste*. London: Routledge.

Bourdieu, P., 1992. *The logic of practice*. Cambridge: Polity Press.

Brady, A., Perry, C., Murdoch, D., and McKay, G., 2010. Sustained benefits of a health project for middle-aged supporters at Glasgow Celtic and Rangers football clubs. *European heart journal*, 31 (24), 2696–2698.

Braun, V. and Clarke, V., 2006. Using thematic analysis in psychology. *Qualitative research in psychology*, 3 (2), 77–101.

Coles, R., Watkins, F., Swami, V., Jones, S., Woolf, S., and Stanistreet, D., 2010. What men really want: a qualitative investigation of men's health needs from the Halton and St Helens Primary Care Trust men's health promotion project. *British journal of health psychology*, 15 (4), 921–939.

Connell, R.W., 1995. *Masculinities*. Cambridge: Polity Press.

Coote, A., Allen, J., and Woodhead, D., 2004. *Finding out what works: understanding complex community-based initiatives*. London: Kings Fund.

Courtenay, W.H., 2004. Making health manly: social marketing and men's health. *Journal of men's health and gender*, 1 (2), 275–276.

Darongkamas, J., Scott, H., and Taylor, E., 2011. Kick-starting men's mental health: an evaluation of the effect of playing football on mental health service users' well-being. *International journal of mental health promotion*, 13 (3), 14–21.

DeVille-Almond, J., 2009. Getting out there. *Community practitioner*, 82 (4), 18.

Dolan, A., Staples, V., Summer, S., and Hundt, G., 2005. "You ain't going to say I've got a problem down there": workplace-based health promotion with men. *Health education research*, 20 (6), 730–738.

Dolan, A., 2007. 'That's just the cesspool where they dump all the trash': exploring working class men's perceptions and experiences of social capital and health. *Health: an interdisciplinary journal for the study of health, illness and medicine*, 11 (4), 475–495.

Dunn, K., Drust, B., and Richardson, D., 2010. I just want to watch the match! A reflective account of men's health themed match day events at an English Premier League Football club. *Journal of men's health*, 7 (3), 323.

Fine, L., Philogene, S., Gramling, R., Coups, E., and Sinha, S., 2004. Prevalence of multiple chronic disease risk factors 2001 national health interview survey. *American journal of preventive medicine*, 27 (2S), 18–24.

Giddens, A., 1991. *Modernity and self-identity: self and society in the late modern age*. Cambridge: Polity Press.

Gray, C.M., Hunt, K., Mutrie, N., Anderson, A.S., Leishman, J., Dalgamo, L., *et al.*, 2013. Football fans in training: the development and optimization of an intervention delivered through professional sports clubs to help men lose weight, become more active and adopt healthier eating habits. *BMC public health*, 13, 232. Available from: http://www.biomedcentral.com/content/pdf/1471-2458-13-232.pdf.

Hunt, K., McCann, C., Gray, C.M., Mutrie, N., and Wyke, S., 2013. "You've got to walk before you can run": positive evaluations of a walking programme as part of a gender-sensitized, weight-management program delivered to men through professional football clubs. *Health psychology*, 32 (1), 57–65.

Kierans, C., Robertson, S., and Mair, M.D., 2007. Formal health services in informal settings: findings from the Preston men's health project. *Journal of men's health & gender*, 4 (4), 440–447.

Macdonald, J., 2011. Building on the strengths of Australian males. *International journal of men's health*, 10 (1), 82–96.

Marcus, B.H. and Forsyth, L.H., 2008. *Motivating people to become physically active*. 2nd ed. Champaign, IL: Human Kinetics.

McElroy, P., Evans, P., and Pringle, A., 2008. Sick as a parrot or over the moon: an evaluation of the impact of playing regular matches in a football league on mental health service users. *Practice development in health care*, 7 (1), 40–48.

Monaghan, L., 2001. Looking good, feeling good: the embodied pleasure of vibrant physicality. *Sociology of health & illness*, 23 (3), 330–356.

Peate, I., 2004. Men's attitudes towards health and the implications for nursing care. *British journal of nursing*, 13 (9), 540–545.

Peck, L.E., Sharpe, P.A., Burroughs, E.L., and Granner, M.L., 2008. Recruitment strategies and costs for a community-based physical activity program. *Health promotion practice*, 9 (2), 191–198.

Pringle, A., 2004. Can watching football be a component of developing a state of mental health for men? *Journal of the royal society for the promotion of health*, 124 (3), 122–128.

Pringle, A. and Sayers, P., 2004. It's a goal!: basing a community psychiatric nursing service in a local football stadium. *Journal of the royal society for the promotion of health*, 124 (5), 234–238.

Pringle, A., White, A., Zwolinsky, S., Smith, A., Robertson, S., and McKenna, J., 2011. The pre-adoption demographic and health profiles of men participating in a programme of men's health delivered in English Premier League football clubs. *Public health*, 125 (7), 411–416.

Pringle, A., Zwolinsky, S., McKenna, J., Smith, A., Robertson, S., and White, A., 2013. The effect of a national programme of men's health delivered in English Premier League Football Clubs. *Public health*, 127 (1), 18–26.

Robertson, S., 1995. Men's health promotion in the United Kingdom: a hidden problem. *British journal of nursing*, 4 (7), 382–401.

Robertson, S., 2003. "If I let a goal in, I'll get beat up": contradictions in masculinity, sport and health. *Health education research*, 18 (6), 706–716.

Robertson, S., 2006. "I've been like a coiled spring this last week": embodied masculinity and health. *Sociology of health & illness*, 28 (4), 433–456.

Robertson, S., 2007. *Understanding men and health: masculinities, identity and well-being*. Buckingham: Open University Press.

Robertson, S. and Monaghan, L., 2012. Embodied heterosexual masculinities part 2: foregrounding men's health and emotions. *Sociology compass*, 6 (2), 151–165.

Robertson, S. and White, A., 2011. Tackling men's health: a research, policy and practice perspective. *Public health*, 125 (7), 399–400.

Robertson, S. and Williams, R., 2012. The importance of retaining a focus on masculinities in future studies on men and health. *In*: G. Tremblay and F. Bernard, eds. *Future perspectives for intervention, policy and research on men and masculinities: an international forum*. Harriman, TN: Men's Studies Press.

Ruxton, S., 2006. *Working with older men: a review of age concern services*. London: Age Concern Reports.

Sixsmith, J. and Boneham, M., 2001. Men and masculinities: accounts of health and social capital. *In*: C. Swann and A. Morgan, eds. *Social Capital for health: insights from qualitative research*. London: Health Development Agency.

South, J., White, J., and Gamsu, M., 2012. *People-centred public health*. Bristol: The Policy Press, University of Bristol.

Spandler, H. and McKeown, M., 2012. A critical exploration of using football in health and welfare programs: gender, masculinities and social relations. *Journal of sport & social issues*, 36 (4), 387–409.

Tumiel-Berhalter, L.M., Kahn, L., Watkins, R., Goehle, M., and Meyer, C., 2011. The implementation of good for the neighborhood: a participatory community health program model in four minority underserved communities. *Journal of community health*, 36 (4), 669–674.

White, A. and Witty, K., 2009. Men's under-use of health services: finding alternative approaches. *Journal of Men's Health*, 6 (2), 95–97.

White, A., Cash, K., Conrad, P., and Branney, P., 2008. *The Bradford & Airedale health of men initiative: A study of its effectiveness in engaging with men*. Leeds: Leeds Metropolitan University.

White, A.K., South, J., Bagnall, A.-M., Forshaw, M., Spoor, C., Jackson, K., *et al.*, 2009. *An evaluation of the working in partnership programme self care for people initiative*. Leeds: Leeds Metropolitan University.

Williams, R., 2007. Masculinities, fathering and health: the experiences of African-Caribbean and white working class fathers. *Social science & medicine*, 64 (2), 338–349.

Williams, R., Robertson, S., and Hewison, A., 2009. Masculinity, 'men's health' and policy: the contradictions in public health. *Critical public health*, 19 (3), 475–488.

Witty, K. and White, A., 2011. Tackling men's health: implementation of a male health service in a rugby stadium setting. *Community practitioner*, 84 (4), 29–32.

Zwolinsky, S., McKenna, J., Pringle, A., Daly-Smith, A., Robertson, S., and White, A., 2013. Optimizing lifestyles for men regarded as 'hard-to-reach' through top-flight football/soccer clubs. *Health education research*, 28 (3), 405–413.

Qualitative research in sport, exercise and health in the era of neoliberalism, audit and New Public Management: understanding the conditions for the (im)possibilities of a new paradigm dialogue

Andrew C. Sparkes

Research Institute for Sport, Physical Activity and Leisure, Carnegie Faculty, Leeds Metropolitan University, Fairfax Building, Headingly Campus, LS6 3QT, Leeds, England, UK

This article explores a key issue that was left mostly unsaid in a recent special edition of *Qualitative Research in Sport, Exercise and Health* that invited predominantly quantitative researchers to share their views on qualitative research with a view to stimulating dialogue. This key issue is that of power. To explore this unsaid, I offer some reflections on the wider social and political climate that is shaping the lived realities of both quantitative and qualitative researchers. I begin by noting the neoconservative backlash to qualitative research in recent years and the rise of methodological fundamentalism. Next, I consider how the work of all researchers in sport, exercise and health, whatever their paradigmatic persuasions is framed within a climate produced by an audit culture, New Public Management practices, and a neoliberal agenda. From this, I move on to argue that the shared somatic crisis faced by scholars in universities provides an opportunity for a coming together across difference and the possible emergence of a new paradigms dialogue based on a collective response to the powerful forces that shape contemporary academic life.

Introduction

In his seminal paper, Sage (1989) eloquently described the time of the 'paradigm wars' that took place in the early 1980s between various groups of researchers in which the very existence of qualitative work was at issue. One aftermath of this war, Sage suggests, was the freedom for some to inhabit a sunlit plain where proponents of various paradigms busily and harmoniously engaged in what he calls an 'earnest dialogue' (p. 10), with a view to making progress toward workable solutions of educational and social problems. Unfortunately, in recent years the sunshine seems to have faded and the 'war' metaphor has again come back into use. Denzin (2009, p. 14) speaks of 'the new paradigm war'. For him, the conflicts of the 1980s never really ended; it is just that qualitative researchers having earned their place at the table were blindsided and ignored the quiet methodological backlash that had been brewing under their very noses. Likewise, in a special issue of *Qualitative Research in Sport, Exercise & Health* that invited predominantly quantitative researchers to share their views on qualitative research with a view to stimulating dialogue, Smith and Brown (2011) made the following comment in their editorial:

> There is talk again in journals, at conferences, in university corridors and over coffee in cafes of 'paradigm wars'. Whilst we are not drawn to the metaphor of 'war' for it seems to limit possibilities of dialogue, we cannot hide from the fact that something is going on in our scholarly community that *is* aggressive, *is* combative and *is* causing harm. Without wishing to over exaggerate the point, 'wars' are going on across countries and within numerous university departments over funding social scientific qualitative work ... Qualitative researchers are too attacked for publishing their work in journals that, in comparison to the natural sciences, have low impact factors. They are forced out of institutions because their work is critical or grounded in the political. They are verbally shot at in conferences, in tenure review panels and in job interviews for being 'unscientific' ... And lastly, but by no means least, qualitative research done by sociologists or psychologists are bullied out of departments as they no longer fit into the 'new direction' a university suddenly is taking. This 'new direction' is, it might be said, not taken always for intellectual, moral or pedagogical purposes, but instead for reasons tied to money and the concentration of executive power. (Smith and Brown 2011, p. 263–264)

Against this backdrop, it is interesting to note that the quantitative scholars who contributed to the special issue, and who should be loudly applauded for doing do, stuck in the main to methodological issues, problems and possibilities in response to the question asked of them by the guest editors: 'How do (predominantly) quantitative researchers view qualitative research?' This made for interesting and thought-provoking reading. Unfortunately, for me, what none of them addressed, and which Smith and Brown (2011) hinted at in their editorial, was the key issue of *power* in terms of how it operates to shape any possible dialogue between quantitative and qualitative researchers and with what effect.

For me, questions about power are necessary because how qualitative researchers (like myself) go about their work, and how this work is viewed and valued by themselves and others, is firmly located in the domain of politics at the micro level (e.g. faculty), meso level (e.g. university; professional association) and macro level (Government). As Smith and Hodkinson (2005) remind us.

> There is no point in pretending that power and politics, at both the micro level and the macro level, are not a part of the process by which we make judgments about the quality of research. We live in an era of relativism, and there can be no time – and place-independent criteria for judgment – that is, criteria that are 'untainted' by our various opinions, ideologies, emotions, and self-interests. Power and politics are with us and the only issues are how power is used and how the political process is played out. And of course, the answers will not be found in epistemology; instead, they will be found in our reasoning as finite practical and moral beings. (Smith and Hodkinson 2005, p. 930)

In what follows, therefore, I offer some reflections on what I feel was left 'unsaid' about power in the special edition of *QRSEH* by the contributing scholars. To do this, I draw predominantly on studies conducted in North America, the UK and Australia to examine the wider social and political climate that shapes what is said and left unsaid in the lives of both quantitative *and* qualitative researchers. Accordingly, I begin by noting the neoconservative backlash to qualitative research in recent years and the rise of methodological fundamentalism. Next, I consider how *all* researchers in sport, exercise and health, whatever their paradigmatic persuasions are framed within a climate produced by an audit culture, New Public Management (NPM) practices, and a neoliberal agenda. From this, I move on to argue that the current somatic crisis faced by scholars in universities provides an opportunity for a coming together across difference and the possible emergence of a new paradigms dialogue based on a collective response to the powerful forces that shape contemporary academic life.

The neoconservative backlash and the rise of methodological fundamentalism

In the preface to the 3rd edition of the *Sage Handbook of Qualitative Research*, Denzin and Lincoln (2005) reflect back on the first edition of this volume they edited in 1994 and how, since then, qualitative research has undergone quantum leaps. They also speak of how this development has been resisted in the form of neoconservative discourses that fuelled the emergence of a methodological conservatism embedded in the educational initiatives of George W. Bush's presidential administration that promoted narrowly defined governmental regimes of truth. As part of what Lincoln and Canella (2004) call the rise of 'methodological fundamentalism' with its return to a much discredited model of empirical inquiry, the new 'gold standard' for producing knowledge that is 'worthwhile' was based on quantitative, experimental design studies.

In a time of global uncertainty, governments around the world have attempted to regulate scientific inquiry by defining what 'good' science is by using a very narrow set of criteria. Smith and Hodkinson (2005) describe the situation as follows:

> In both the United States and the United Kingdom, there have been moves to governmentally establish, if not *impose*, certain criteria not only to judge the quality of research but also to distinguish what qualifies as research and what does not ... In both countries, the idea has been to set out the kinds of things that researchers *must* do to have a quality study and then restrict research funding to those researchers who follow the rules and the prescribed methods. (Smith and Hodkinson 2005, p. 926. Emphasis added)

As a result, governmental regimes of various political persuasions are *enforcing* evidence or scientifically based biomedical models of research. For Denzin (2009), Lincoln (2010), and Smith and Hodkinson (2005), these regulatory activities as part of a resurgent scientism raise fundamental philosophical, epistemological, political and pedagogical issues for scholarship and freedom of speech in the academy and, in combination, constitute the conservative challenge to qualitative inquiry which is deemed suspect, unscientific and of little value in the social policy arena. Not surprisingly, calls have been made to resist such pressures towards a single gold standard of research and challenge attempts to impose a narrow concept of orthodoxy on the academy.

Just what forms of resistance qualitative researchers can offer and mount in such a demoralising time is a complex issue as evidenced in the multi-agenda approach proposed by Denzin (2010) that incorporates the intellectual, advocacy, operational and ethical as resources for action. It is important, he argues that qualitative researchers take up the challenge of better educating and making clear to different constituencies and stakeholders the *benefits* that their work has in a variety of domains that range from the local to the international.

In making clear the benefits of qualitative research and influencing the views of others about our work, Denzin (2009, 2010) argues that we need to find new strategic and tactical ways to work with one another in the new paradigm dialogue. This means that dialogues need to be formed between advocates of quantitative and qualitative research, and between the various traditions that are contained within them.

> There needs to be a greater openness to alternative paradigms critiques … There needs to be a decline in conflict between alternative paradigms proponents … Paths for fruitful dialogue between and across paradigms need to be explored. This means that there needs to be a greater openness to and celebration of the proliferation, intermingling, and confluence of paradigms and interpretive frameworks. (Denzin 2010, p. 40)

I agree with and loudly applaud the ideals expressed by Denzin. This said, I recognise that qualitative researchers, and those quantitative researchers who support and wish to engage in a new paradigms dialogue (and there are many as evidenced in the special edition of *QRSEH*), will be variously positioned in ways that impact on their ability not only to engage in a dialogue in the first place, but also in terms of the risks (professional and personal) involved for them if they do so. In this regard, it is worth considering some of the changes that have taken place in the academy in recent years as these provide the climate in which Denzin's agenda and call for a new paradigms dialogue has to be accomplished.

The audit culture, NPM and neoliberalism

Burrows (2012) notes that recently something has changed in the UK academy and that 'many academics are exhausted, stressed, overloaded, suffering from insomnia, feeling anxious, experiencing feelings of shame, aggression, hurt, guilt and out-of-placeness. One can observe it all around; a deep, affective, somatic crisis threatens to overwhelm us' (p. 355). The impact of this somatic crisis and how it works in and through the lives of academics in complex ways at the local level has been illustrated in the studies provided by Davies and Petersen (2005a), Davies and Bansel (2010), Gill (2010), Sikes (2006), and Sparkes (2007).

For Burrows (2012), and Bode and Dale (2012), this somatic crisis has arisen in response to broader transformations of university life associated with the following: de-professionalisation; proletarianisation; the dismantling of academic disciplines and department-based academic units; the growing size and authority of management in determining priorities in research and teaching; the quantification and evaluation of academic work along with the increasing dependence on these quantitative measures to define and assess academic productivity and efficiency as well as the reputation of individuals, disciplines and institutions; the emergence of new academic identities; responses to managerialism; and issues of morale to name but a few. Importantly, the net effect of these, as Ball (2003) warns is the production of new kinds of teacher subjects and social identity, 'education reform brings about changes in our "subjective existence and our relations to one another". This is the struggle over the teacher's soul' (p. 217). Similarly, Davies *et al.* (2006, p. 308) point to how neoliberal discourses work on 'academic subjects to transform them, to transform what is thinkable, and to transform the nature of academic work'.

All of the above are directly related to the rise of neoliberalism, what has been called the NPM, and the imposition of an audit culture on complex systems for which it is inappropriate. How each of these operates in a number of countries to shape academic life at the macro and micro levels has been extensively documented and critiqued by others (e.g. Power 1997, Loughlin 2004, Davies 2005, Davies *et al.* 2006, Darbyshire 2008, Lorenz 2012, Shore 2010). Given the availability of these critiques, I will focus on selected aspects of the audit culture to develop our thinking of how the negative aspects of this on both quantitative and qualitative researchers in sport, exercise and health along with other disciplines might instigate a 'coming together' and encourage a new paradigms dialogue in a period of *shared crisis*.

According to MacRury (2007), the key features characterising an audit culture in universities include outcome-based assessment systems for research productivity and for other indices (e.g. student employability, student retention); arduous external assessment systems; and the publication of miscellaneous league tables. For him, these key features 'comprise the bureaucratic architecture through which learning and teaching are managed – a structuring enabled (and assured) by a highly proactive and formalised system of surveillance and recording' (p. 124). Developing this theme, Craig *et al.* (in press) note that a key aspect of an audit culture resides in the bureaucratic oversight of universities and the evocation of a perverse sort of accountancy mind-set of performance management that is obsessed substantially with quantification and with measures of output. For them, an audit culture can be seen in the practice of universities and government departments assessing the merit of scholarly journals by quantified impact factors (IF); and the merit of individual published scholarly papers by citation counts. All of which, according to Davies and Petersen (2005b) constitute the new *performance paradigm* within the academy that, with its 'personal key performance indicators' is at the heart of the implementation of neoliberal self-enterprise technologies.

> These management techniques individualize performance. They require individuals to negotiate annual recognizable accounts of themselves as appropriate subjects, and to stage a performance of themselves as appropriate(d) subjects. The academic accomplishes him or herself, for the moment of that performance at least, *as* a neo-liberal subject. (Davies and Petersen 2005a, p. 81)

Linked to this performance paradigm, Tourish (2011) provides an insightful critique of the University of Queensland's 'Q index' which measures an individual academic's research income, research publication (weighted by reference to journal ranking lists), higher degree completions and research degree supervision loads. The 'Q index' (to two decimal points) is then compared to average scores at university, faculty and school levels, and to all staff within an academic's faculty at the same appointment level. The 'Q index' is open to inspection by managers. Essentially, as Tourish argues, people become a number: 'I am a 9.22, you are a 10.33, she is a 12.34'. He points out that while this is part of the commercialisation of academia, often justified in terms of accountability and the audit society, it is also likely to reduce intrinsic motivation, damage morale and limit the engagement of academics with the disinterested pursuit of knowledge. The focus of performance indexes such as the 'Q index' is a shift towards industrial measurements of productivity that do not involve serious consideration of intellectual quality (see also, Davies and Petersen 2005a, 2005b, Davies and Bansel 2010).

As part of his examination of the relationship between metrics, markets and affect in the contemporary UK academy, Burrows (2012) provides a similarly insightful critique of the 'h-index' and a range of other metrics that include the following: citations; workload models; transparent costing data; research assessments; teaching quality assessments; and commercial university league tables. In terms of citation metrics, the h-index is based on citation numbers and was proposed by Hirsch (2005) as a useful index to characterise the scientific output of a researcher. Numerous articles have been written about the h-index and a large body of research literature queries the construct validity of citation count as an indicator of scholarly impact (e.g. see Egghe 2009, Lindgren 2011). While there are a multitude of methodological objections to the veracity of this metric as a measure of relative academic worth, the key point, as Burrows (2012) emphasises is the way in which this index has been reified.

> It has taken on a life of its own; a number that has become a rhetorical device with which the neoliberal academy has come to enact 'academic value.' The number is used to: inform the short-listing of candidates for new posts; as an academic 'marketing device' on CVs; as a 'bargaining chip' in professorial salary negotiations; as a variable in statistical models designed to predict RAE outcomes; to rank colleagues in REF 'preparedness' exercise; in decisions about institutional restructuring; and to inform decisions about whether or not to accept papers written by particular authors in journals. (Burrows 2012, p. 361–362)

The same can be said of the various metrics that claim to measure the impact that particular academic journals possess. Here, the IF allegedly provides a mathematical basis for making an ever more subtle distinction within a hierarchy of supposed worth. In short, the rhetoric goes, the higher the IF of a journal the better the quality of the research published within it. Thus, by definition, a low IF for a journal means low-quality research. And, logically, no IF would mean that the research published in the journal is not numerically worthy of merit! Indeed, I have heard allegedly 'learned scholars' and senior managers state that, 'If it hasn't got an IF, then it can't be research'. On this flawed logic, as Darbyshire (2008, p. 39) points out, with IFs as the new academic status symbol, 'The day is not far away when publishing in a low or non-IF journal will be perceived as being more indicative of "poor performance" than not publishing at all'.

> Somewhere in a university, at this moment a memorandum is surely being written, 'advising' staff only to publish in journals with an IF of 'X' or above, pointing out that a failure to achieve this level of 'publication excellence' will be deemed to 'demonstrate' a level of performance that is unacceptable and in need of remediation. That such epistemological fundamentalism could even be considered, let alone tolerated will scarcely raise a ripple of concern as the memo will be couched in the soporifically comforting context of being an 'initiative' designed to show the institution's 'commitment' to 'improved quality' and to 'ensuring' that all staff are suitably 'on message' about this. (Darbyshire 2008, p. 38)

Despite the conceptual flaws it contains and the ways in which historically the IF has operated to serve the interests of certain disciplines over others (Smith 2006, Abbasi 2007), it has in the view of Burrows (2012, p. 362) been grossly reified to the extent that 'many academics, academic managers, journal editors, publishers and librarians cannot help but reorient their actions towards it'. For him, the h-index and the IF provide perhaps the most vivid illustration of the co-construction of statistical metrics and social practices within the academy as part of a complex system of 'quantified control' that operate to shape individual subjectivities and the meaning of scholarship.

Similar points are made by Davies (2005), Davies and Bansel (2010), Davies and Petersen (2005a, 2005b), and Shore (2008) in their consideration of the impact of neoliberalism, the audit culture, the politics of accountability and the illiberal governance on the lives of those who work in university settings. For Shore, the new systems of audit are not, as they claim, just neutral or politically innocent practices designed to promote 'transparency' or efficiency (which they do not anyway); rather they are disciplinary technologies or, as Foucault would call them, 'techniques of the self', aimed at instilling new norms of conduct into the workforce as universities have been transformed under neoliberalism and the rise of NPM from the traditional liberal and Enlightenment idea of a place of high learning into the university as a corporate enterprise with vice chancellors as chief executives along with all that this entails.

For Davies and Petersen (2005b, p. 78), 'The new subjects of neo-liberalism ideally transform themselves to become competitive individuals who strive to produce the products desired by government'. In a similar fashion, Shore (2008) suggests that the ideal new corporate academic self is one that is a 'flexible' in nature and one that will internalise the external norms of management, supervising themselves through the exercise of introspection, calculation and judgement, and thereby transforming themselves into governable subjects of managerial control and power. For him, this is not to infer a 'global conspiracy' at work: rather, these processes and outcomes reflect the logic of economic liberalism harnessed to technologies of modern bureaucracy. The net result, however, is a new 'rationality of governance' that converts 'people' into crude calculable units of economic resource.

> Academics are no longer treated as constitutive members of the university but as employees, an individualized proletarian workforce that must be subordinated to the organizational hierarchy of managers, people of whom the 'University' must demand excellence ... Audit has been successfully deployed to support a regime of NMP that places little emphasis on professionalism and a great deal of reliance on overt managerialism ... Audit technologies may have succeeded in producing greater economy, compliance, and productivity in the workforce, but in the process they have also changed the definition of what constitutes legitimate knowledge and best practice ... the managerialist conception of accountability is coercive and authoritarianism; it also reduces professional relations to crude, quantifiable and inspectable templates. (Shore 2008, p. 289–291)

More recently, Gillies (2011) has also drawn on Foucault's notions of 'governmentality' and 'care of the self' to examine how, influenced by fast capitalism or hot capitalism, the metaphors of 'agility' and 'agile' have displaced its lexical neighbour 'flexibility' both in the business world and in educational discourse. For him, while the term 'agility' might seem to hold more positive connotations than 'flexibility', for example, the former implies greater agency than the latter; there are dangers involved. First, just as neoliberal governance shifts much more from society and community to the individual, so Gillies notes, 'agile' workers become much more responsible for their own economic fates. Here, insecurity is 'embodied and any sense of stable employment relies paradoxically on change and the capacity for rapid change' (p. 213). As such, the rhetoric of 'agile leadership' relies on a workforce whose agility comes from fear, insecurity and an absence of ethos.

Gillies (2011) also points out how 'agility' can be linked to the neoliberal concept of the person as an enterprise. Here, the entrepreneurial self is a neoliberal concept of the, deployment of the self as an infinitely flexible product re-shaped to meet market demands … The agile self reconfigures itself in anticipation of market changes, the value of this identification judged in so far as it secures economic survival or success. (p. 214)

According to Gillies, the strategy is for the agile self to embody corporate desires, to become one with it, and to be captured by the discourse. This marks the neoliberal dream in which the worker is the physical and mental embodiment of the enterprise. Not surprisingly, he notes, 'In the neoliberal world where market forces are universalised, it is the agile, marketable self which is treasured and valorised' (p. 215).

Against this backdrop, and based on a study of a department in a research-intensive university in the UK, Holligan (2011, p. 55) proposes that 'contemporary academics are akin to a twenty-first century peasantry in a feudal order where academic freedom to pursue independent research is subject to prescriptive transformations emanating from neo-liberal projects'. Likewise, in her revisiting of Goffmans notion of the 'total institution' and her development of the new concepts of 'Reinventive Institution' (RI) and 'performative regulation', Scott (2010) describes many features that are relevant to the modern university. For her, a RI is a material, discursive or symbolic structure through which voluntary members actively seek to cultivate a new social identity, role or status. This is interpreted positively as a process of reinvention, self-improvement and transformation. It is achieved though not only formal instruction in an institutional rhetoric, but also the mechanisms of performative regulation in the interaction of the inmate, or for us, academic culture.

> RIs ostensibly represent a shift from coercion to voluntarism, as inmates perceive themselves to have made an informed choice to rewrite their identities. However, a subtler form of power operates through performative regulation, whereby actors not only submit to disciplinary regimes but also participate in their production and administration, though techniques of mutual surveillance; their motivations are shaped by seductive discourses and reinforced by inmate cultures … both TIs (total institutions) and RIs involve a mixture of coercion and voluntarism, but the relative balance has been reversed: whereas TI inmates were not simply docile bodies but potential rebels, RI members find their performative autonomy compromised by the discipline of the interaction order. (Scott 2010, p. 26–27)

Craig *et al.* (in press) note the manner in which collegial control based on trust is replaced with bureaucratic control in an audit culture and the adverse outcomes this produces which include the ways in which women academics are specifically disadvantaged. They go on to argue that an audit culture of the kind they critique induces a psychosis in modern public universities which, they allege, is well represented by the metaphor THE UNIVERSITY WITH AN AUDIT CULTURE IS PSYCHOTIC. Speaking of the symptoms of the psychotic university they comment.

> That is, an institution in conflict with important constituents (scholars, students and the community-at-large) and with its peer institutions. A psychotic university would likely conceive an audit culture as a mechanism for coping with anxiety and the sullying of its reputation – thereby possibly reflecting a *paranoid-schizoid* position. Such a position arises from the university 'splitting' an 'object' (its reputation for research) into a good category (which is idealised) and a bad category (which is despised). However, an audit culture provides a defence mechanism for the university: it keeps

the good and the bad separated and controlled. It helps avoid anxiety situations by retreating into bureaucratic quantitative processes 'out of touch with any emotional life' ... the university reality is reduced to the pursuit of measurable, auditable data that signify so-called excellence .... There is a functional disconnect between the creative rhythm of thinking which is the essence of university life for the academic (or rather, should be in some wistful idyllic sense) and the inapt reality of the university audit culture, which induces the psychotic university. (Craig *et al*. in press, pp. 22–24)

Finally, in relation to various forms of psychosis, Ryan (2012) speaks of academics as *zombies*, given their responses to and apparent helplessness in the face of overwhelming change. For her, the main sources of zombiefication are similar to those already identified above, and involve governance, audit, workload and an acquiescent leadership.

Academic as 'peasants' in universities with the characteristics of both a feudal system and a RI displaying various psychotic symptoms, including that of zombiefication, caused by the pernicious effects of an audit culture and neoliberal agenda, suggest that a crisis exists in the academy. How this crisis is experienced and its affects distributed are likely to be influenced by gender, age, social class, ethnicity, (dis)ability, sexuality and religion, along with type of institution and academic discipline to name but a few variables. For example, studies in various countries have shown how women scholars, despite the discourse suggesting a widening of opportunities, are disadvantaged in specific ways within neoliberal and audit cultures (e.g. Deem and Reed 2007, Pritchard 2011, Klocker and Drozdzewski 2012).

As another example, with regard to discipline, is available with the rapid turn of research intensive universities in the UK towards science, technology, engineering and mathematics (STEM) subjects. This is accomplished at the direct expense of other subjects (e.g. the arts, humanities and social sciences) due to the priority they are given with regard to funding at a national level and recruitment at the faculty level. Those working in STEM subjects are transparently advantaged over their non-STEM colleagues in any clash of interests. For some, this situation provides an opportunity to express their deeply held paradigmatic prejudices while at same time enhancing their career and promotion prospects.

This is not to apportion 'blame' to such individuals, or those in non-STEM subjects, and indeed the many qualitative researchers, for their complicitous silence. In the first instance, as Barney (2010) acknowledges, engaging in political judgement and action is not normal. Rather, he suggests, politics is a 'pathological event that a reasonable person would normally avoid is she had the choice. Politics happens to us, it is not something we normally choose to do' (p. 383). This is because engaging in politics – responding to the exposure of power, joining questions about justice and the good of judgement and action – is not necessarily joyful, festive or fun. Rather, for most, it is onerous work that is disruptive, antagonistic, risky and dangerous. Hence, most academics choose to remain what Barney call 'ordinary cowards' in the face of enforced neoliberal changes in the academy.

In such circumstances, as Anderson (2008) notes, *individual withdrawal* is the most common form of resistance and also an effective means of protecting values and identity. While they might be angered by managerial strategies, actions and discourse, academics generally refuse to engage with them, preferring to complain to trusted colleagues, or refusing or avoiding participation in managerial directives. Most often, they minimise their involvement, complying with the letter, but not the spirit, of particular requirements.

Furthermore, the core notions of audit seem 'reasonable' which make them very difficult for academics to contest. That is, who could legitimately stand opposed to 'transparency', or 'quality', or 'excellence', or 'accountability' as 'good things' per se? To suggest their absence or lack, Darbyshire (2008) argues, would mean that people are 'unaccountable', wishing to be opaque, not striving for excellence and quality, and therefore irresponsible and culpable. For him, such descriptive detritus holds us in a 'semantic snare which makes Alice in Wonderland look like a model of pellucidity' (p. 36). Indeed, for Loughlin (2004), the goal of 'the quality revolution' in management theory was always to produce a language to facilitate the control of working populations by making meaningful opposition to the policy decisions of senior management within organisations strictly impossible. For him,

> The success of the revolution depended upon management claiming 'ownership' of the vocabulary necessary to articulate legitimate objections to or concerns about the nature and direction of organisational change. Quality was stipulatively defined in terms of the mechanisms guaranteeing managerial control of working practices, rendering dissent absurd by definition. (p. 717)

Linked to this, as Shore (2008) argues, the new regime of governmentality engendered by audit and new managerialism is designed to work through our capacities as moral agents and professionals. Here, the values that most academics subscribe to, which include self-discipline and a desire to produce quality research, become instrumental in eliciting compliance and governing conduct. Furthermore, as Shore points out, the university environment has become so steeped in managerial principles and practices that it is difficult to find the Archimedian point outside of the system that enables us to critique it. Again, this makes the audit culture difficult to contest.

Lorenz (2012) makes a similar point in seeking to explain why humanities academics, trained in critique, seem so powerless to argue effectively against changes which they see as damaging to the quality of higher education. For him, this is partly because the NPM employs a discourse that 'parasitizes the everyday meanings of their concepts – efficiency, accountability, transparency, and (preferably excellent) quality – and simultaneously perverts all their original meanings' (p. 599). Lorenz argues that the NPM discourse is a 'bullshit' discourse that, similar to the types of managerialism found in former Communist states is not concerned with truth or lies, but with advancing agendas. The 'hermetic self-referential nature' of such 'bullshit' he believes has 'proved to be completely resistant to criticism for over thirty years' (p. 601).

While Lorenz's (2012) designation of managerial discourse as 'bullshit' may be satisfying, pleasing and even affirming, in expressing the anger that many academics feel about policy – and decision-making in higher education, Bode and Dale (2012) warn that affiliating with this critique has negative consequences.

> Calling managerial discourse 'bullshit' on the one hand minimises the impact of the transformation of universities over the last three decades ('that's just bullshit'); on the other, it offers no effective way of analysing or contesting these transformations. If those who use bullshit to justify changes do not care whether they are lying or telling the truth, there is no more to say ... Arguably, part of the appeal of Lorenz's essay lies in its fit with what has been called the 'archaic hyperindividualism of our prevailing academic ethos', in that designating managerial discourse as 'bullshit' provides a reason to continue to avoid collective action. (Bode and Dale 2012, p. 1–2)

Another reason that the audit culture is not challenged according to Lorenz (2012, p. 608) is that the NPM, much like state Communism, 'is totalitarian because it leaves no room for criticism, which it always sees as subversion'. Thus, managerial definitions of quality and efficiency, construct a particular version of autonomy which appear to them are self-evidently good. Therefore, those who do not desire these managerial constructs of autonomy or openly challenge them (which is part of their academic freedom to do so) are defined, at best, as absurd or, at worst, as 'trouble' that needs to be brought back 'into line', 'on task' or 'on message' via greater managerial control and forms of persuasion that do not exclude intimidation and bullying to achieve the required compliance.

As Ryan (2102) notes, if academics fail to cooperate and comply voluntarily, then managers resort to more authoritarian measures to gain compliance. She notes with interest how, with the rise of NPM, increased financial pressures, and an increasing number of academics at the bottom of the power ladder (the casuals, the probationers, the post-doctoral and contract academics) that reports of bullying and harassment are increasing in the academy. This view is supported by the findings of a survey of 14,000 higher education staff, carried out in 2012 by the University and College Union in the UK which found that harassment, friction and bullying are too often the hallmarks of working relationships in Britain's universities. Indeed, at one in three of the institutions represented in the survey, more than 10% of respondents said they were 'always' and/or 'often' subject to bullying at work.

Beyond such negative tactics, as Shore (2008) argues, the competitive forces encouraged by the new managerial systems are highly seductive in recruiting the behaviour of all academics through their systems of reward and punishment.

> Some academics clearly benefit from the new regimes of audit as they disrupt old hierarchies and provide new avenues for rapid promotion, at least for the more research-active or managerially-inclined staff. Most academics know that faith in audit (like faith in 'the market') is not borne out by its actual effectiveness in doing what it claims, but the structures, careers and interests that have been forged as a result of these audit systems have created a powerful disincentive for individuals to rock the boat publicly. (Shore, 2008, p. 291–292)

Shore (2008) goes on to make the point that the complicity of academics stems from the fact that the system can only be contested collectively. As he argues,

> there are huge costs and penalties if individuals, or individual institutions, try to challenge or opt out of the auditing process. Indeed, the audit process has made it far too costly for individuals and institutions, to even admit shortcomings or problems. (p. 293)

Against this, it needs to be recognised that there are many academics working in STEM subjects who are far from happy with the climate in universities as described above. Indeed, these academics have been vocal opponents of the audit culture and the neoliberal agenda, and have fought vigorously to save non-STEM subject areas being closed in their universities. They, like Roy (2003), recognise 'that once you see it, you can't unsee it. And once you've seen it, keeping quiet, saying nothing becomes as political an act as speaking out. There's no innocence. Either way, you're accountable' (p. 7).

The current crisis as an opportunity for dialogue across difference

The current crisis in the academy for both academics *and* managers is immediate – it is real and it is harsh. Speaking of the force of oppressive languages inside and outside of the academy Davies (2005) notes that 'oppressive state language – that is, currently, the language of neoliberal government – is more violent than its bland, rather absurd surface might lead us to believe. It's at work here, busily containing what we can do, what we can understand' (p. 6). For her, this language in which the auditor is king, acts to destroy social responsibility and critique, and invites a mindless, consumer-orientated individualism to flourish and kills off conscience.

> It co-opts research to its own agendas, it silences those who ask questions, it whips up small-minded moralism that rewards the attack of each small powerless person on the other, and it shuts down creativity. It draws on and exacerbates a fear of difference and rewards rampant, consumerist, competitive individualism. It makes emotion, humour, poetry, song, a passion for a life of the intellect unthinkable. (Davies 2005, p. 7)

The politics of erasure are already in action. As Smith and Brown (2011), and Sparkes (2007) point out, people in the domain of sport, exercise, health and physical education are being harmed. Against an Australian background that includes the proposed mass sacking of academics at two of their most privileged universities, Bode and Dale (2012) argue that the transformation of higher education has reached a new and critical stage. Accordingly, 'dismissing arguments for change as "bullshit" and turning back to research and teaching is insufficient, even irresponsible' (p. 2).

In their analysis of a 58-page document that outlines the case for sacking 41 academic staff in the Faculty of Humanities and Social Sciences at la Trobe University in Australia, Bode and Dale (2012) reveal the type of university, staff and student that the document imagines and brings into being; the contradictory way it argues for these changes and this new structure; and the implications of this rhetoric for our understanding of higher education. Importantly, their analysis treats managerial discourse not as intractable or dismissable 'bullshit', but as a powerful though *highly unstable* system of meaning. For sure, this discourse *does* pervert into their opposites concepts such as efficiency, quality, transparency, accountability and flexibility. And this capacity *does* render this discourse difficult to critique. However, as Bode and Dale emphasise:

> But difficulty is not impossibility; and indeed, the multiple tensions underpinning this discourse … between leading and following, change and stability, expertise as positive and negative – produce an instability that can be identified and put under pressure. Doing so is a necessary first step in clearing away the bullshit that surrounds the transformation of higher education in Australia, and imagining an alternative system. However, it is only a first step. And if 'bullshit' is not impervious to critique, as Lorenz argues, we need to look elsewhere to understand why we have arrived at this current state. This second step may prove even more difficult because, while academics are trained to critique the discourse of others – in this case, university managers and government policy-makers – we are perhaps not so adept at analysing our own assumptions, investments and biases in our workplaces, as opposed to our scholarship. (Bode and Dale 2012, p. 12)

In some ways, therefore, the current crisis presents a moment of opportunity for scholars from all disciplines and subject areas to initiate the first and second steps proposed by Bode and Dale (2012). In so doing, there is the potential for the 'coming together' described by Denzin (2010) as a form of collective resistance to the various forces that are shaping their professional and personal landscapes in unacceptable ways. Ryan (2102) recognises this possibility for collective resistance whereby academics 'voice' their frustrations and concerns by speaking out to broader and more powerful audiences. For her, the public and the media, given their growing distrust of politicians and major corporations, are currently more willing than before to listen with a sympathetic ear in relation to key issues, such as, the deterioration of higher education.

> Such concern provides an important audience for our voice, if we can use it. Collective action through industrial disputation over pay claims have rarely met with public sympathy; however, the public might feel better disposed if industrial action were centred on our health, on issues of occupational health and safety arising from workload and issues around ensuring a sustainable higher education system. Unhealthy zombies are not good for business, so government and university managements might just be open to hearing about cures. (Ryan, 2012, p. 9)

Importantly, as part of this collective response that *will* require radical changes at the level of policy and the setting of priorities and processes, Bode and Dale (2012) argue that rather than academic and senior managers allowing the system to place them at opposite sides,

> from which academics attribute all problems to the 'managerial barbarians' at the gate, the mangers attribute all problems to self-centred and irresponsible attitudes of academics – we need to see ourselves as working towards the same goal – after deciding what that goal should be. (p. 13)

This is an important issue. It needs to be recognised that many managers are hostile to the neoliberal agenda and the audit culture in terms of the ways in which it shapes their working lives, and frames their interactions will staff and students on a daily basis. They too can be critical of the ideologies that inform NPM practices and wish to challenge them but feel disempowered to do so. As such, managers are not immune to the somatic crisis described by Burrows (2012). This shared crisis, even though it might be experienced in different ways, offers a potential point of contact across difference that might lead to alternative forms of dialogue emerging between academics and managers in universities.

In addition to this strategy, the common ground that would bring academics together in a collective response is that of *social justice*. As Denzin (2010) says, 'We all want social justice. Most of us want to influence social policy. All of us – positivists, postpositivists, poststructuralists, posthumanists, feminists, queer theorists, social workers, nurses, sociologists, educators, and anthropologists – share this common commitment' (p. 42). Here, lest we forget, it is important to recognise the historical contribution that many 'positivist' and quantitative scholars have made and continue to make with their large-scale surveys and other methods with regard to illustrating and combating social inequalities and injustices in a variety of fields, such as, education and health. In view of this, perhaps now more than ever there is a need for quantitative and qualitative researchers to work together within a social justice framework that challenges the neoliberal agenda and its consequences. As part of this common commitment, Parker (2011) suggests, we need to rethink the 'longer term implications [of managerialism and an audit culture] for the development of humanity's fundamental stock of knowledge, and its critique of culture, philosophy, ethics, history and the civil society' (p. 448).

This coming together would also involve collaborative efforts to develop different ways of thinking about accountability. Ways that, according to Shore and Wright (1999), involve restoring trust and autonomy and use 'qualitative, multiple, and local measures, and is based on public dialogue' (p. 571). Likewise, Craig *et al.* (in press) argue that we need to think about accountability in ways that 'embrace more responsible features of a modified collegial control; and that we need to supplement brute financial accountability with compassion, multiplicity, social welfare, social responsibility, equity, and trust' (p. 29). They go on to suggest that we should also develop performance indicators that possess pedagogical depth and contest the view that an audit culture leads axiomatically to an economic efficiency that is in the best interests of students and society.

Craig *et al.* (in press) further argue that we should collectively expose the pedagogical implications of narrow business assumptions and interests and resist the physical, intellectual and spiritual colonisation of universities by business interests and auditing paraphernalia. For them, in doing so, and in performing our essential role as university faculty members, we might still have a chance of being by nature disturbers of the peace which will assist our students to think *critically* about beliefs and institutions that structure their thoughts and, ultimately, their behaviours. In making their claim that we should reconsider, and possibly reclaim, the true purposes of a university, Craig and his colleagues draw upon a comment made by the poet John Masefield, in a 1946 address at the University of Sheffield, in which he describes the university as follows.

> A place where those who hate ignorance may strive to know, where those who perceive truth may strive to make others see; where seekers and learners alike, banded together in the search for knowledge, will honour thought in all its finer ways, will welcome thinkers in distress or in exile, will uphold ever the dignity of thought and learning and will exact standards in these things.

For Craig *et al.* (in press), Masefield's words express an enduring set of values that are difficult to reconcile with the market-focused imperatives of NPM currently guiding what they regard as a *perverse* audit culture in modern public universities. They also feel that his words offer a useful insight to a better future than that likely to emerge from the continuous extension of managerial oversight in the pursuit of narrow, market-orientated goals. To this, I would add the sentiments expressed by Martin Niemoller (1892–1984) in his poem, *First they came ...*

> First they came for the communists and I didn't speak out because I wasn't a communist.

> Then they came for the trade unionists and I didn't speak out because I wasn't a trade unionist.

> Then they came for the Jews and I didn't speak out because I wasn't a Jew.

> Then they came for me and there was no one left to speak out for me.

In the current common crisis within the academy, coupled with the conservative backlash against qualitative research, the words of Niemoller's poem should resonate with all scholars. Regardless of subject area, discipline, tradition or paradigm, we need to ask ourselves the question: 'When they come for me – who will speak out for me?' We also need to remember how we are *all* vulnerable in the current political climate and subject to the vagaries of 'managed' change. As Darbyshire (2008) warns us.

> If new discretionary government funding were suddenly made available for universities whose academic staff were prepared to dye their hair pink, there is little doubt that university 'quality management systems' and 'commitments' would be 'strategically realigned', so quickly that the massed mops of academia would soon resemble a Barbie doll convention supporting breast cancer awareness. (Darbyshire, 2008, p. 38)

With this question and warning in mind, and given the current climate as described above, researchers in the domains of sport, exercise and health have some serious thinking to do with regard to their collective future. Of course, this assumes that a collective future is desired by all. This may not be the case. As Bairner (2012) notes, the overwhelming majority of us work in university departments which, with various titles, centre on what are collectively described as the 'sport and exercise sciences'. He points out that dominant amongst the latter are psychology and, in particular, physiology which is also seen by governments and funding bodies as worthy of investment, especially if the main focus of attention is health related.

It is quite feasible, therefore, that those involved in these subjects choose to consolidate their power and resources by either actively or passively allowing other areas within their faculties, such as the sociology of sport, the philosophy of sport, the history of sport, sport pedagogy, physical education and anything associated with qualitative inquiry or the 'soft' social sciences to be culled by management as financial and political 'priorities' change. This is not just a possibility it is already happening and some sub-disciplines have recognised the threat they are under. For example, reflecting on the sub-discipline of the sociology of sport, Silk, Bush and Andrews (2010, p. 106) state that its very existence 'is imperilled perhaps more than ever at the present time'.

Likewise, Bairner (2012) focuses on a number of challenges that currently face the sociology of sport in a climate that favours the natural sciences over the social sciences and humanities. For him, it is vital that the sociology of sport be defended against what he calls 'the tyranny of the natural sciences' (p. 102). This defence, he suggests, needs to be active and involve strategies for gaining greater acceptance from mainstream sociology, acknowledging shortcomings within sport sociology itself, and being much more creative and vital both theoretically and methodologically. Bairner concludes, 'almost anything that helps us to break away from talking among ourselves and allows us to enter into dialogue not only with mainstream sociologists but even with natural scientists is to be encouraged' (p. 115).

Suggestions as to how research communities in sociology, education, sport, exercise and health might begin to confront the dislocating, divisive individualisms of neoliberalism, address its knowledge hierarchies and perhaps engage anew with enduring issues of social justice are offered by Evans (2012). Drawing on ideas from complexity literature, he explores the merits, possibilities and difficulties of making intradisciplinary and transdisciplinary 'border crossings' of an ideational kind as a means to advance thinking in our subjects and disciplines while aiding the course of social justice both in and outside of educational institutions.

For Evans (2012), the idea of 'concept studies' is fundamental to the idea of ideational border crossings as it has the capacity to not only help

> disrupt thinking about the way in which knowledge/s are produced via 'relations within' research communities and the social structures that sustain them, but also reconfigure the ways in which we think about engagements with the knowledge/s (and key concepts) of those others with whom we 'relate to'. (p. 9)

Evans, notes how for Davis and Samara (2010) the power of 'concept studies' is 'hinged to the deliberate attention given to the diversity it seeks'. They continue, 'the diversity in any complex learning system is in essence the source of its intelligence' (p. 858), because 'at this juncture, somehow dissenting voices and the jagged edges of contrasting opinions leads to collective products that are more useful and more insightful than the lowest-common denominator solutions that seem to spark little disagreement (and consequently, limited engagement)' (p. 859). Importantly, as Evans emphasises, such an approach does not necessarily lead to reductionism or seek the appeasement of those whose perspectives we deeply dislike, or produce insipid research.

> It is simply to acknowledge that 'border crossings', if approached in a principled manner involving sharing ideas, concepts and practices between researchers, researched and others with vested interests in the outcomes and implications of what we say and do, is now more than ever what is needed if we are to better address persistent hierarchies, inequalities and power relations, and to better understand the role and importance of research communities in both shaping and contesting these things. None of this need involve relinquishing commitments to our parent disciplines or the perspectives of those many 'great thinkers' who properly define, inform and fire our trade. (Evans 2012, p. 11)

Concept analysis, therefore, does not mean that researchers of various persuasions dissolve or ignore the tensions and differences between them. Rather, this kind of analysis enables them to embrace these differences and tensions positively and creatively while engaging with each other in ways that can retain strong subject-specific attachments and allegiances while simultaneously searching for heightened and shared understandings on ideational common ground.

This said, Evans (2012) recognises the risks involved in terms of the psycho-socio-political pitfalls of border crossings. For him, such crossings, even if only of the ideational kind, 'if divorced from considerations of power, vested interest, control and the cosmologies that sustain communities, are destined at best to disappoint, at worst to damage the very people they seek to serve' (p. 10). As such he sensibly concludes as follows: 'Border crossings in the current context then, may understandably seem at best risky, at worst foolhardy, and will not be for the faint hearted. Those of an ideational kind may be modest but worthy best endeavours in such inclement times' (p. 13).

Given the prevailing power and dominance of neoliberalism, the audit culture and the NPM both within and beyond the academy then perhaps all we can really offer at the moment are our 'best endeavours' depending on how we are positioned in the field. For those who are able to this might mean engaging in aspects of the advocacy and operational agendas described earlier by Denzin (2010). For some this might not be possible and the best they can do right now is to make connections and border crossings with staff in their own and other faculties at their university who might provide lines of support to maintain and develop the practices of qualitative inquiry in all its forms. For others, given their circumstances, the only form of resistance open to them might be the individual withdrawal as described by Anderson (2008). This is not to be underestimated as a form of resistance (and survival) because as Ryan (2012) notes, although individual, it is sufficient to prevent managerialism from becoming embedded as it is framed by an understanding of academic culture and values that attempt to limit the process of colonisation implicit in the managerial project.

Regardless of our positioning, it would seem sensible should we think there are things worth defending, that at the very least we gain an understanding of the relations of power within which we now find ourselves enmeshed and which now shape our present in the ways that I have tried to describe above. As part of this engagement, as Davies (2005) notes, a necessary first step in refusing these new conditions of our existence

> is to be aware of the discourses through which we are spoken and speak ourselves into existence. We must find the lines of fault in and fracture those discourses. And then, in those spaces of fracture, speak new discourses, new subject positions into existence. (p. 1)

For her, along with Davies and Petersen (2005b), and Davies *et al.* (2006), it is imperative that we understand neoliberal discourses and practices, how they work, and their effects in, on and through ourselves and others so that their normalising and naturalising features can be interrupted and read as just one of many discourses though which action can be shaped. Then, its effects can be assessed and weighed against the effects of other discourses. For these scholars, this opens up the possibility of us not being that which we perform, allowing us to counter some of the mechanisms through which resistance is forestalled, which in turn, can initiate the process of decomposing the neoliberal subjects we have become.

In everyday life, Davies (2005) suggests we might need to become better at recognising ourselves and each other in the act of 'taking up the terms through which dominance and oppression take place' (p. 7). We might also, she argues, need to become better at catching ourselves 'mouthing the comfortable clichés and platitudes that together we use to shape the same world that we shake our heads at with sorrow and resignation' (p. 7). Similarly, on a daily basis according to Darbyshire (2008), as a form of articulate and informed dissent, we should not accept without comment the vapid, cliché-ridden 'Qualipak' that crosses our desks so regularly. Loughlin (2004) agrees and suggests that it is imperative that we ask of those in positions of power and influence: *what do you mean?* That is, we must hold *them* accountable.

> What is it that justifies the uses they make of terminology and the conclusions they draw? We must insist upon a serious and well thought out answer. We should challenge the use of consumerist language at meetings and in policy documents – make a point of *not* playing the game, of not reciting the rhetoric on queue. To those who disagree, we must present the arguments, and challenge them clearly to explain theirs. (Loughlin 2004, p. 723)

Importantly, given that the critique I have mounted above is based predominantly on literature emanating from the USA, Canada, the UK and Australia, there is a need for comparative data to ascertain if scholars in other countries are facing similar conditions and experiencing a somatic crisis or variations of it. If so, it is important to know how the intertwined processes involved in an audit culture, NPM practices and a neoliberal agenda work themselves out in different contexts, and how scholars engage with them (or not) in various ways that contest, challenge and resist their oppressive aspects. Such comparisons have the potential to offer new ways of looking at our own situation as well as perhaps providing different strategies for generating fruitful and meaningful dialogue between academics, managers and other stakeholders associated with the academy.

In closing, it remains that the situation as it stands is complex. Unfortunately, there is no one simple response and no singular cure to the problems that prevail. This said, rather than succumb, sink into deep despair and become docile bodies, I think we should look for signs of hope. For example, I find seeds of hope in the special edition of *QRSEH* where the contributors displayed their willingness to engage in a dialogue across difference. I also find hope when I read comments like the following made by Horn (2011) who is a quantitative researcher.

> I have become resigned to believe that quantitative and qualitative scholars do tread two different roads. However, once we (or at least some of us) realise that we are generally headed in the same direction (knowledge generation and dispersal) and that there is great value in each of our approaches, then we and our students can benefit significantly from each other's work. But, it is important, particularly in our work with students, that we do not deliberately try to discredit the work carried on by those on the 'other road' just so that we can justify our own methodological approach and thus our own survival in a climate of economic meltdown. (Horn 2011, p. 299)

There *are* allies out there and there *are* alliances to be formed to support those engaging in qualitative forms of inquiry and they need to be used well. As Loughlin (2004) notes, 'The more we can engage in serious intellectual dialogue, across both national and professional boarders, the better. Academics who want to resist further attacks on their integrity and professionalism will find allies both within and outside academia' (p. 723). Furthermore, there are still institutions, like my own, that support (for the moment at least) a diversity of approaches to research and those of us lucky enough to work in them need to find ways to support and sustain colleagues working in less favourable environments. If we all give our 'best endeavours' then I would go along with Denzin (2010), in his belief that this fruitful dialogue is not only a possibility, 'it is a requirement if a democratic community is to flourish in the academy and within the qualitative research community. Strong academic departments encourage paradigm diversity' (p. 42). My hope is that the observations and suggestions I have provided in this article will act as a stimulus for this dialogue to take place with greater urgency by researchers in sport, exercise and health.

Acknowledgements

I would like to thank the two anonymous reviewers and the following for their reactions to and comments on earlier drafts of this article: David Aldous, Alan Bairner, David Brown, David Carless, Phillip Darbyshire, Bronwyn Davies, Kitrina Douglas, Michael Erben, John Evans, Anne Flintoff, Brendan Gough, Chris Hughes, Michael Loughlin, Steve Robertson, Karl Spracklen and Dennis Tourish. The confusions, contradictions and errors that remain are entirely my own.

Notes on contributor

Andrew C. Sparkes is currently with the Research Institute for Sport, Physical Activity and Leisure and a member of the Carnegie Faculty at Leeds Metropolitan University. His research interests revolve around how people experience their embodied selves in different contexts over time. He has published widely on this topic and on methodological issues in general. His most recent book is *Qualitative research in sport, exercise and health: from process to product*.

References

Abbasi, K., 2007. Why journals can live without impact factor and cluster bombs. *Journal of the royal society of medicine*, 100 (3), 113–1113.

Anderson, G., 2008. Mapping academic resistance in the managerial university. *Organization*, 15 (2), 251–270.

Bairner, A., 2012. For a sociology of sport. *Sociology of sport journal*, 29 (1), 102–117.

Ball, S., 2003. The teacher's soul and the terrors of performativity. *Journal of education policy volume*, 18 (2), 215–218.

Barney, D., 2010. Miserable priests and ordinary cowards: on being a professor. T.O.P.I.A. *Canadian journal of cultural studies*, 23–24 (Fall), 381–387.

Bode, K. and Dale, L., 2012. 'Bullshit'? An Australian perspective; or, what can organisational change impact statement tell us about higher education in Australia? *Australian humanities review*, 53 (November), 1–19.

Burrows, R., 2012. Living with the h-index? Metric assemblages in the contemporary academy. *The sociological review*, 60 (2), 355–372.

Craig, R., Amernic, J., and Tourish, D., in press. Perverse audit culture and accountability of the modern public university. *Financial accountability and management*.

Darbyshire, P., 2008. 'Never mind the quality, feel the width': the nonsense of 'quality', 'excellence', and 'audit' in education, health and research. *Collegian*, 15 (1), 35–41.

Davies, B., 2005. The (im)possibility of intellectual work in neoliberal regimes. *Discourse: studies in the cultural politics of education*, 26 (1), 1–14.

Davies, B. and Bansel, P., 2010. Governmentality and academic work: shaping the hearts and minds of academic workers. *Journal of curriculum theorizing*, 26 (3), 5–20.

Davies, B., Gottsche, M., and Bansel, P., 2006. The rise and fall of the neoliberal university. *European journal of education*, 41 (2), 305–319.

Davies, B. and Petersen, E., 2005a. Intellectual workers (un)doing neoliberal discourse. *International journal of critical psychology*, 13 (1), 32–54.

Davies, B. and Petersen, E., 2005b. Neoliberal discourse in the academy: the forestalling of collective resistance. *Learning and teaching in the social sciences*, 2 (1), 77–98.

Davis, B. and Samura, D., 2010. "If things were simple....": Complexity in action. *Journal of Evaluation in Clinical Practice*, 16, 856–860.

Deem, R. and Reed, M., 2007. *Knowledge, higher education and the new mangerialism: the changing management of UK universities*. Oxford: Oxford University Press.

Denzin, N., 2009. *Qualitative inquiry under fire*. Walnut Creek, CA: Left Coast press.

Denzin, N., 2010. *The qualitative manifesto: a call to arms*. Walnut Creek, CA: Left Coast Press.

Denzin, N. and Lincoln, Y., 2005. Introduction: the discipline and practice o qualitative research. *In*: N. Denzin and Y. Lincoln, eds. *The sage handbook of qualitative research*. 3rd ed. London: Sage, ix–xix.

Egghe, L., 2009. The Hirsch-index and related impact measures. *Annual review of information science and technology*, 44 (1), 65–115.

Evans, J., 2012. Ideational border crossings: rethinking the politics of knowledge within and across disciplines. *Discourse: studies in the cultural politics of education*. DOI: 10.1080/01596306.2012.739466.

Gill, R., 2010. 'Breaking the silence': the hidden injuries of the neo-liberal academy. *In*: R. Flood and R. Gill, eds. *Secrecy and silence in the research process: feminist reflections*. London: Routledge, 228–244.

Gillies, D., 2011. Agile bodies: a new perspective on neoliberal governance. *Journal of education policy*, 26 (2), 207–223.

Hirsch, J., 2005. An index to quantify an individual's scientific research output. *Proceedings of the national academy of sciences*, 102 (46), 16569–16572.

Holligan, C., 2011. Feudalism and academia: UK academics' accounts of research culture. *International journal of qualitative studies in education*, 24 (1), 55–75.

Horn, T., 2011. Multiple pathways to knowledge generation: qualitative and quantitative research approaches in sport and exercise psychology. *Qualitative research in sport, exercise and health*, 3 (3), 291–304.

Klocker, N. and Drozdzewski, D., 2012. Career progress relative to opportunity: how many papers is a baby worth?. *Environment & planning*, 44 (4), 1271–1277.

Lincoln, Y., 2010. "What a long, strange trip it's been ...": twenty-five years of qualitative and new paradigm research. *Qualitative inquiry*, 16 (1), 3–9.

Lincoln, Y. and Canella, G., 2004. Dangerous discourses: methodological conservatism and government regimes of truth. *Qualitative Inquiry*, 10 (1), 5–14.

Lindgren, L., 2011. 'If Robert Merton said it, it must be true': a citation analysis in the field of performance measurement. *Evaluation*, 17 (1), 7–19.

Lorenz, C., 2012. If you're so smart, why are you under surveillance? Universities, neoliberalism, and new public management. *Critical inquiry*, 38 (Spring), 599–629.

Loughlin, M., 2004. Quality, control and complicity: the effortless conquest of the academy by bureaucrats. *International journal of humanities*, 2 (1), 717–724.

MacRury, I., 2007. Institutional creativity and pathologies of potential space: the modern university. *Psychodynamic practice*, 13 (2), 119–140.

Parker, L., 2011. University corporization: driving redefinition. *Critical Perspectives in Accounting*, 22 (4), 434–450.

Power, M., 1997. *The audit society*. Oxford: Oxford University Press.

Pritchard, R., 2011. *Neoliberal developments in higher education: the United Kingdom and Germany*. Oxford: Peter Lang.

Roy, A., 2003. *War talk*. Cambridge: South End Press.

Ryan, S., 2012. Academic zombies: a failure of resistance or a means of survival? *Australian Universities Review*, 54 (2), 3–11.

Sage, N., 1989. The paradigm wars and their aftermath: a 'historical' sketch of research and teaching since 1989. *Educational researcher*, 18 (1), 4–10.

Scott, S., 2010. Revisiting the total institution: performative regulation in the reinventive institution. *Sociology*, 44 (2), 213–231.

Shore, C., 2008. Audit culture and illiberal governance: universities and the politics of accountability. *Anthropological theory*, 8 (3), 278–298.

Shore, C., 2010. Beyond the multiversity: neoliberalism and the rise of the schizophrenic university. *Social anthropology*, 18 (1), 278–298.

Shore, C. and Wright, S., 1999. Audit culture and anthropology: neoliberalism in British higher education. *Journal of the Royal Anthropological Institute*, 7 (4), 759–763.

Sikes, P., 2006. Working in a 'new university': in the shadow of the research assessment exercise? *Studies in higher education*, 31 (5), 555–568.

Silk, M., Bush, A., and Andrews, D., 2010. Contingent intellectual amateurism, or, the problem with evidence-based research. *Journal of sport and social issues*, 34 (1), 105–128.

Smith, R., 2006. Commentary: the power of the unrelenting impact factor – Is it a force for good or harm? *International journal of epidemiology*, 35 (5), 1129–1130.

Smith, B. and Brown, D., 2011. Editorial. *Qualitative research in sport, exercise and health*, 3 (3), 263–265.

Smith, J. and Hodkinson, P., 2005. Relativism, criteria and politics. *In*: N. Denzin and Y. Lincoln, eds. *Handbook of qualitative research*. 3rd ed. London: Sage, 915–932.

Sparkes, A., 2007. Embodiment, academics, and the audit culture: a story seeking consideration. *Qualitative research*, 7 (4), 519–548.

Tourish, D., 2011. Leading questions: journal rankings, academic freedom and performativity: what is, or should be, the future of *Leadership*? *Leadership*, 7 (3), 367–381.

University and College Union, 2012. Occupational stress survey: the relationship stressors in HE. Available from: www.ucu.org.u.

Pathways for community research in sport and physical activity: criteria for consideration

Robert J. Schinke, Brett Smith and Kerry R. McGannon

School of Human Kinetics, Laurentian University, Ben Avery Building, 935 Ramsey Lake Road, Sudbury, Ontario P3E2C6, Canada

This paper focuses on how researchers might approach judging community scholarship and what criteria might be used to evaluate this work. It is suggested that rather than adopting a criteriologist approach that proposes pre-established, permanent and universal criteria, a relativist approach is more suitable for making fair and informed judgments about the quality of research. This approach proposes that criteria should be viewed as lists of characterising traits that are open to reinterpretation as times, conditions and purposes change. Informed by a relativist approach to validity, a list of criteria to evaluate community scholarship coupled with recommendations for application is offered for consideration.

As shown in this special issue of *Qualitative Research in Sport, Exercise and Health* (QRSEH), there is no single or 'right' way to do community research, nor a simple answer as to what constitutes a community within whom one conducts such research. There are multiple interpretive projects for which a range of methodological approaches can be adopted. Depending on the methodological approach chosen, different strategies to collect, analyse, theorise and represent data might also be harnessed. While it is important to recognise the differences between scholarship that exist under the umbrella of 'community research', it is also important to acknowledge that because we all make judgments, and research needs to be held to high standards, an 'anything goes' mentality when it comes to making assessments about the quality of an inquiry is rejected. The foregoing however begs the question, 'what criteria *might* we use to help guide the process of doing community research and make assessments about the quality of an inquiry, that is, the product?' 'And how *might* we distinguish the good from the bad?'

In what follows we offer a *list* of criteria as *characterising traits* (Smith 1993, Smith and Deemer 2000) for potentially guiding the process of doing community research and making judgments about the quality of such research. Acting as *starting points*, we hope that this list might help both authors and reviewers who engage with community research to make fair, informed and disciplined decisions about what might count as high quality community-based work. Before offering a list, however, we must begin by clearing some ground and establishing some points. The list of criteria that we draw upon within this commentary is derived from the literature (e.g. Frisby *et al.* 2005, Wallerstein and Duran 2006, Forsyth and Heine 2010). Since there is no such thing as objective criteria or theory-free knowledge – individual researchers cannot step outside their own social, cultural and historical standpoints (Smith and Deemer 2000, Rolfe 2006) – the criteria offered are also based on phronesis (Flyvbjerg 2001). Phronesis refers to the practical wisdom gained through experience. For example, the list offered herein is partly based on our experiences of doing community research and critically reflecting on what went well and not so well (Schinke *et al.* 2009, Blodgett *et al.* 2011). Further, the list of criteria was developed through the engagement itself of editing this special issue. Witnessing criteria as it was applied in actual inquiries by numerous authors and reviewers of papers, coupled with regular and ongoing dialogue between ourselves as editors about what makes "good" piece of community qualitative research, provided us with additional experience that helped challenge, add to, and modify our own ideas and assumptions about criteria.

Of course, the criteria we offer here should *not* be considered a fixed recipe or standardised template for use on all occasions. To consider criteria in such ways would mean adopting a *criteriologist* approach (Sparkes and Smith 2009, 2013). Such an approach is informed by a set of assumptions that might loosely be described as post-positivist, neorealist or foundational in nature (Smith and Deemer 2000, Smith and Hodkinson 2009, Sparkes and Smith 2009, 2013). Further, a criteriologist approach assumes that the criteria for judging qualitative research needs to be, and can be, *pre-established*, *static*, *permanent* and *universal*. Among the various problems that go with this approach is that in a world of multiple mind-dependent realities there can be no pre-established, static, permanent and universal criteria to appeal to on all occasions in order to sort out trustworthy interpretations from untrustworthy ones (Smith and Deemer 2000, Smith and Hodkinson 2009). Another problem with a criteriological approach is that if our research community wants innovative, interesting and useful research that continues to push the boundaries and add to the knowledge base, then it is neither possible nor desirable to mandate pre-established, static, permanent and universal criteria to judge all qualitative research. This is because when specific predetermined criteria are called upon to judge all qualitative research, there is, as Sparkes and Smith (2009, 2013) point out, the problem of producing a closed system of judgment that can only operate within a very narrow range of what constitutes legitimate research. When this happens, they note, criteria are wittingly or unwittingly used in exclusionary manner. Such an exclusionary practice means that new fields and forms of inquiry are, by definition, excluded or policed from the very start (Garrett and Hodkinson 1998). There is also the danger that innovation is stifled, difference is suppressed, imagination is dampened and potentially useful research is rejected before it has even been engaged with (Sparkes and Smith 2009).

Rather than adopting a criteriological approach, it would seem sensible then to adopt a way of thinking about, and working with, criteria to help guide and judge community research that opens up pathways or lines of inquiry that encourage openness and innovation. One way that has come to prominence in recent years within qualitative research is a *relativist* approach. Relativists adhere to the view proposed by Smith (1993, 2009) where criteria are seen as *characterising traits* that have, at best, mild implications as a prescription for inquirer behaviour and does not necessarily refer to something that is held to be foundational or fixed in stone. Here, researchers might discuss the characterising traits of a particular qualitative approach to inquiry and simply note that these criteria are the way(s) researchers seem to be conducting their particular kind of inquiries at the moment. The difference with this characterising trait approach from the criteriological approach is that, as Sparkes and Smith (2009, 2013) point out, those holding a relativistic position are willing to describe what one *might* do, but are not prepared to mandate what one *must* do across all contexts and on all occasions prior to any piece of research being conducted.

For Smith (1993), and Smith and Deemer (2000), once criteria come to be seen as characterising traits or values that influence our judgments, then any particular traits or values will always be subject to constant reinterpretation as times and conditions change. Criteria from this perspective have a *list* like quality. In saying this, we do not wish to imply that the more criteria achieved on any given list the better the quality of the study. Matching ten criteria from a list does not necessarily make the study twice as good as a study that 'only' matches five criteria (Sparkes and Smith 2009). On this issue, Smith and Deemer offer the following warning:

> The use of the term *list* should not be taken to mean that we are referring to something like an enclosed and precisely specified or specifiable shopping or laundry list. Put differently, to talk of a list in this sense is not at all to talk about, for example, an accumulation of 20 items, scaled 1–5, where everyone's presentation proposal is then numerically scored with a cut off point for acceptance. Obviously, to think of a list in these terms is to miss the entire point. (Smith and Deemer 2000, p. 888)

In contrast, Smith and Deemer (2000), and Smith and Hodkinson (2005) see any list of characteristics as always open-ended, and ever subject to constant reinterpretation so that items can be added to the list or taken away. They emphasise that the items on the list cannot be derived from a distillation of some abstract epistemology, but rather derive from practical experience and the standpoint we adopt on any given issue. Therefore, the criteria used to judge a piece of research can change depending upon experiences, the context and the purposes. This is because a characteristic of research we thought important at one time and in one place may take on diminished and further importance at another time and place.

Against the above backdrop, in what follows we offer a list of criteria that, operating as characterising traits, might be useful on certain occasions for guiding community research and judging the quality of it. After each criterion is described, in a text box we also briefly highlight recommendations in terms of the possible application of each criterion.

A list of characterising traits for judging community research: criteria for consideration

Community driven research

The research has at heart *communities* who *themselves direct* research by identifying a research topic, research questions and methods. An effective community research project is built *from* the interests and living conditions of community members, not *out of* the researcher's interests and conditions. Members see a gap in their community, such as the inability to retain youth in sport programming, high rates of obesity or another community concern, and they wish to better their health and their living conditions through their local knowledge. Community members then claim to tell what counts: what is singled out for attention; what is taken seriously; what requires action, preceded by what kind of preparation and calculation. Thus, in community research participants are not placed beneath academics or at the margins of their scholarship but instead exercise power over the research process and products.

Nearly 10 years ago, Robert began working with the Wikwemikong Unceded Indian Reserve. During their first research project, Robert proposed a topic pertaining to his own interests – culture appropriate motivational practices for sport scientists working with Canadian Aboriginal elite athletes. During the latter part of the project, the community members invited Robert to lunch and proposed a project more meaningful in their community – youth engagement in physical activity on the reserve. Communities are always best versed in the research questions most relevant in their living conditions. Community proposed research tends to pave the way for more relevant research questions and culturally safe methodologies.

Localising research practices/methods

The research methods and practices favour local behaviours, emotions, beliefs and so on. Because organic community scholarship also reveals a unique richness of local practices, the research methods, analysis and data representations should align with this unique richness. Academic scholars might find that the richness in community research is not only derived from the topic matter. It also emerges out from why the idea is being proposed and thereafter, how the community feels the scholarship should be approached.

Research by Blodgett, Schinke, Smith, Peltier, and Pheasant (2011) conducted on Aboriginal reserves in Canada did not readily lend itself to "formal" interviews and categorical representation of themes in stilted data matrices. Instead, in-line with the world view and local practices of the community, talking circles and storytelling were used to gather meaningful "data". This was equally local and featured community led data analyses on the reserve's lands along with several community co-authored vignettes, each revealing of a teaching. A useful way to engage with a community is to ask for community guides to help reveal local practices in terms of methodology and the reasons for chosen practices. Upon understanding these nuances, centralise them and also the community scholars best versed in leading the approach(es).

Decentralised university academics

Following from the above need for the centralisation of community scholars in development, interpretation and dissemination of research is the necessity for scholars from academic settings to decentralise themselves. Decentralisation means that academics "step back" and become supporters and facilitators in the community projects, providing general skills and resources (e.g. external funding).

They relinquish a typical investigative role and are willing to graciously support the community members in their rightful place as the experts of their own experiences and customs.

Within our experiences as academic scholars and project leaders it is often a challenge to step back and support community members forward to centre stage. The repositioning of academic and community scholars enables a redistribution of power, one that will contribute to building community capacity. One of our authors has come to learn of a community that was at one time open to leading its own research. An earlier project team worked with this community, slowly stepping away as the community developed and employed its own self-governed programming. More recently, the community has become involved with several research teams in various projects. Within some of these, there has been a regression to academics leading the scholarship with mainstream research practices. Even communities that move forward and gain capacity can regress. Hence, it is important for scholars to move beyond supporting community development through research to mechanisms where communities are comfortable screening future research in terms of how such work might contribute to their future capacity. Conversely, if academics retain the leadership role throughout projects and direct them, they remain central and the community members become or remain on the periphery.

Prolonged engagement and consultation

Certain practicalities exist for academics in terms of research timelines (e.g. granting agencies requiring project completing within a finite time period, ethics clearance, data collection, analysis and writing). Contrasted with researcher time-lines, communities often expect academic scholars to forge relationships over time in the community, garner trust and learn local practices before methodologies are conceptualised. Consultation further provides the necessary richness evident in good community scholarship. Yet, work that engages the full project team requires considerable time and patience to encourage unpredictability and deeper organic scholarship. Once these relationships are developed, time must also be apportioned to complete the project in its academic sense and afterward, the sorts of longer term commitments that communities might expect.

When Robert first met with the Chief and Council of Wikwemikong Unceded Indian Reserve to seek support for an early research project, he was asked by the elders how long he intended to commit to the community? As he pondered the question, he felt the elders in the room watching him very carefully, almost reluctantly. The expectation was that he not parachute into the community, utilise its resources and then depart once the data were analysed. To the Chief, Robert responded by asking how long the community wished for him to be involved. A useful suggestion when discussing length of commitment is to clarify the community's expectations before making assumptions and finalising the partnership agreement. The community's timeline will likely extend beyond the duration of most funded research grants. Hence, academics need to ponder whether they are able and willing to allocate the time and energy expected from the community, and then discuss any commitment concerns at the beginning of the project.

Community capacity building

With a focus on community partnerships and a centring of local skills and knowledge, openings are further created for local contributors to the project to gain in capacities. Capacity building may entail different areas of growth for community stakeholders/community, such as focusing research question(s), applying for community funding from granting agencies, showing how to develop research ethics applications and how to initiate and follow through on their research project. Ultimately, capacity building is about creating a legacy through community research projects and community – academic research partnerships. When undertaking research projects with cultural minority and marginalised communities, capacity building is especially important so as to contribute to social justice.

There are opportunities in every community research project for community members to develop their research – practice links and capacities. Recognising community members' knowledge of the context, their localised research traditions, and also augmenting additional research skills are three possible means we have attempted to help build capacity. We also propose that sound community research projects serve as openings for a community's membership to develop themselves as scholars, not only in relation to the immediate project, but also for the community's longer term research agenda(s). One facilitative strategy to create openings is for academic researchers to become intuitive and highly sensitive to moments where community scholars signal interest in stepping forward into leadership roles. We have noticed that early on, community members are sometimes reluctant to share their experiences without prompting, almost as if they are sitting on their hands and holding back their words, though intuition has often created openings for better discussions in the short-term and more confident community contributors over the long term. We propose that each encounter and every discussion is an opportunity for capacity building, with the articulation of process enriching the methodology, as well as the community.

Project deliverables

Completing research projects, publishing and engaging in newer ideas are accomplishments that should be lauded and are important 'realities' that academics must produce. However, when engaging with academic researchers, communities may also choose to participate in the research process to develop useful solutions for their communities. Deliverables need to centralise the views, language, customs and skills of the community's resources. This approach not only reveals local voices and furthers capacity; it also opens up a more likely possibility that the research will be useful long after the university scholars have turned it over as property to the community.

Several years ago, a few colleagues from Laurentian University co-developed a leadership manual for Aboriginal youth who reside on one Indian reserve. The manual was developed as a form of workbook with applied exercises developed from local Aboriginal talking circles. During one memorable project team meeting, one of the community members began to consider where to work with the youth in terms of programme delivery. Stephen Ritchie, an adventure leadership faculty member, proposed that the teachings could be offered at the end of each day's journeying during a 10-day canoe expedition as the youth and staff were immersed in travel down a historical fur trading route (Ritchie *et al.* 2010). Canoes and water, a culturally infused deliverable, are locally regarded Aboriginal symbols for rebirth and personal journeying.

Project sustainability

When community-based research projects materialise into deliverables, the question becomes how useful are these emergent applications? When the research is community centering, deliverables become much more useful when derived from the lens of local participants. Usability leads to sustainability, suggesting that community research led by academic scholars and/or mainly in the scholars' interests is less likely to leave a long-term positive impact on a community. When the positive remnants of a project continue long after the academic scholars have left the locale, it can be said that the community project was a successful one. While all forms of community research are not full blown participatory action research, scholars might judge their involvement with communities by whether parts of the research project have positive influences long after the academic scholar(s) have stepped away from the project, leaving it in the hands of the community.

> The day previous to the finalising of this manuscript, Robert sat in his research lab and met with a community co-researcher who returned to university after many years away, and is presently in the process of completing her graduate degree. This community co-researcher has been asked by her community to engage in a form of programme evaluation. She is expected to interview the youth who underwent the first two years of community leadership training. The programme continues and is presently in its sixth year of delivery, and also of interest, the community researcher is meeting with the youth to engage in talking circles that match with the reserve's customs and traditions (talking circles are somewhat akin to focus groups, though with a circular structure of people going around the circle taking turns to either talk about or not talk about the topic, until nothing more is said by its members). What we have found is that sustainability extends beyond programming to how the community and its members engage and re-engage in research long after a previous project is completed and integrated in some form or other.

Coda

In proposing this list of characterising traits and specific examples above, we should emphasise and reiterate that these are not the *only* criteria that can be used for passing judgement on community research. Rather, these are suggestions for guiding and judging community research that can be added to, modified, and subtracted from depending on purpose and context. With that said, we invite readers to not only use their own judgement in applying these criteria to community research. We also encourage the development of other criteria that may emerge from one's engagement with community research in the future. As part of this development, and in keeping with the idea of criteria as characterising traits that are developed in a list-like fashion according to the purposes of any given study, it is important to regularly dialogue and reflect about what makes good qualitative research within each context and how these match with other possibilities utilised in other contexts. We hope that this paper plays a part in this process and, rather than operating as an ending to a special issue, is an opening for more qualitative community research and dialogue.

Notes on contributors

Robert J. Schinke is a full professor in the School of Human Kinetics at Laurentian University and also the Canadian Research Chair in Multicultural Sport and Physical

Activity. Working at the intersection of cultural sport psychology and community-based methodologies, his research is funded by the Social Sciences and Humanities Research Council of Canada, the Canadian Foundation for Innovation, the Indigenous Health Research Development Programme and the Coaching Association of Canada. He is the associate editor for the Journal of Sport and Social Issues, and an editorial board member for the Journal of Clinical Sport Psychology and Qualitative Research in Sport, Exercise and Health. He is also the President Elect of the Association for the Advancement of Applied Sport Psychology and a member of the International Society of Sport Psychology Managing Council.

Brett Smith leads the psycho-social health and well-being strand within the Peter Harrison Centre for Disability Sport at Loughborough University, UK. Working at the intersection of psychology and sociology, and supported by over £4 million in external funding, his research has focused on two themes: disability, health and physical activity and the development of qualitative methods and narrative theory. He serves on seven editorial boards, including Sociology of Sport Journal. He is also an associate editor of Psychology of Sport and Exercise and Editor-in-Chief of Qualitative Research in Sport, Exercise, and Health.

Kerry R. McGannon is a leader in work that "bridges" sport and exercise psychology and cultural studies to understand physical activity promotion and participation. Her work uses interpretive qualitative methodologies (e.g. discourse analysis, narrative) to explore the social construction of gender in sport and exercise and to study of the media as a cultural site that constructs self and identity within the context of health promotion. Her peer reviewed scholarship includes empirical studies and theoretically driven contributions in prominent international sport science journals and scholarly books pertaining to sport and exercise psychology and/or cultural sport psychology. She is presently in the final stages of co-editing with Robert J. Schinke, the book The Psychology of Sub-culture in Sport: A Critical Perspective (Psychology Press). In addition to serving on the editorial boards of *Psychology of Sport and Exercise*, *Qualitative Research in Sport, Exercise and Health* and *Athletic Insight*, she is also on the advisory board for *Qualitative Research in Sport, Exercise and Health* and the section editor of Qualitative Methodologies, Critical and Cultural Approaches for *Athletic Insight*. She also serves as the Chair of the Cultural Diversity Committee for the Association for Applied Sport Psychology.

References

Blodgett, A.T., Schinke, R.J., Smith, B., Peltier, D., and Corbiere, R., 2011. In indigenous words: the use of vignettes as a narrative strategy for capturing aboriginal community members' research reflections. *Qualitative inquiry*, 17 (6), 522–533.

Flyvbjerg, B., 2001. *Making social science matter: why social inquiry fails and how it can succeed again*. Cambridge: Cambridge University Press.

Forsyth, J. and Heine, M., 2010. Indigenous research and decolonizing methodologies. *In*: T. V. Ryba, R.J. Schinke, and G. Tenenbaum, eds. *The cultural turn in sport psychology*. Mongantown, WV: Fitness Information Technology, 181–202.

Frisby, W., Reid, C.J., Millar, S., and Hoeber, L., 2005. Putting "participatory" into participatory forms of action research. *Journal of sport management*, 19 (4), 367–386.

Garrett, D. and Hodkinson, P., 1998. Can there be criteria for selecting research criteria? A hermeneutical analysis of an enescapable dilemma. *Qualitative inquiry*, 4 (4), 515–539.

Ritchie, S.D., Wabano, M.J., Young, N., Schinke, R.J., Peltier, D., Battochio, R.C., *et al.*, 2010. Developing a culturally relevant outdoor leadership training program for Aboriginal youth. *Journal of experiential education*, 32 (3), 300–304.

Rolfe, G., 2006. Validity, trustworthiness and rigour: quality and the idea of qualitative research. *Journal of advanced nursing*, 53 (3), 304–310.

Schinke, R.J., Peltier, D., Hanrahan, S.J., Eys, M.A., Yungblut, H., Ritchie, S., *et al.*, 2009. The progressive move toward indigenous strategies among a Canadian multicultural research team [Special Issue]. *International journal of sport and exercise psychology*, 7 (3), 309–322.

Smith, J., 1993. *After the demise of empiricism: the problem of judging social and educational inquiry.* Norwood, NJ: Ablex.

Smith, J., 2009. Judging research quality: from certainty to contingency. *Qualitative research in sport and exercise*, 1 (2), 91–100.

Smith, J. and Deemer, D., 2000. The problem of criteria in the age of relativism. *In*: N.K. Denzin and Y.S. Lincoln, eds. *Handbook of qualitative research.* 2nd ed. London: Sage, 877–896.

Smith, J. and Hodkinson, P., 2005. Relativism, criteria and politics. *In*: N.K. Denzin and Y. S. Lincoln, eds. *Handbook of qualitative research.* 3rd ed. London: Sage, 915–932.

Smith, J. and Hodkinson, P., 2009. Challenging neorealism: a response to Hammersley. *Qualitative Inquiry*, 15 (1), 30–39.

Sparkes, A.C. and Smith, B., 2009. Judging the quality of qualitative inquiry: criteriology and relativism in action. *Psychology of sport and exercise*, 10 (5), 491–497. doi: doi.org/10.1016/j.psychsport.2009.02.006.

Sparkes, A.C. and Smith, B., 2013. *Qualitative research in sport, exercise & health sciences. From process to product.* London: Routledge.

Wallerstein, N.B. and Duran, B., 2006. Using community-based participatory research to address health disparities. *Health promotion practice*, 7 (3), 312–323.

Index